An Age of Extremes

A HISTORY OF US

Oxford University Press

OXFORD
A HISTORY OF
US

BOOK EIGHT

An Age of Extremes

Joy Hakim

Oxford University Press
New York

Oxford University Press

Oxford   New York

Athens   Auckland   Bangkok   Bombay
Calcutta   Cape Town   Dar es Salaam   Delhi
Florence   Hong Kong   Istanbul   Karachi
Kuala Lumpur   Madras   Madrid   Melbourne
Mexico City   Nairobi   Paris   Singapore
Taipei   Tokyo   Toronto

and associated companies in
Berlin   Ibadan

Designer: Mervyn E. Clay
Maps copyright © 1994 by Wendy Frost and Elspeth Leacock
Produced by American Historical Publications

Published by Oxford University Press, Inc.
200 Madison Avenue, New York, New York 10016
Oxford is a registered trademark of Oxford University Press

Library of Congress Cataloging-in-Publication Data
Hakim, Joy.
An age of extremes / Joy Hakim.
p.   cm.—(A history of US: bk. 8)
Includes bibliographical references and index.
ISBN 0-19-507759-8 (lib. ed.)—ISBN 0-19-507765-2 (series, lib. ed.)
ISBN 0-19-507760-1 (paperback ed.)—ISBN 0-19-507766-0 (series, paperback ed.)
ISBN 0-19-509513-8 (trade hardcover ed.)—ISBN 0-19-509484-0 (series, trade hardcover ed.)
1. United States—History—1865–1921—Juvenile literature.
2. United States—Economic conditions—1865–1918—Juvenile literature. 3. United States—Social conditions—1865–1918—
Juvenile literature. [1. United States—History—1865–1921.] I. Title. II. Series: Hakim, Joy. History of US; 8.
E178.3.H22 1994 vol. 8
[E661]
973.8—dc20   93-26250
CIP
AC

1 3 5 7 9 8 6 4 2
Printed in the United States of America
on acid-free paper

The poem on the facing page is "The Road Not Taken" from *Mountain Interval* by Robert Frost. Available in Edward Connery Lathem, ed., *The Poetry of Robert Frost*. Copyright
© 1969 by Henry Holt & Co. The poem on page 53 is "Historical Reflections" by John Hollander. Reprinted with permission of Atheneum, an imprint of Macmillan Publishing
Company, from *Jiggery-Pokery: A Compendium of Double Dactyls* by Anthony Hecht and John Hollander. Copyright © 1966 by Anthony Hecht and John Hollander. Reprinted by
permission of Atheneum. The excerpt on page 174 is from *The Happy Warrior* by John Dos Passos. Reprinted by permission of Elizabeth H. Dos Passos.

Two roads diverged in a yellow wood,
And sorry I could not travel both
And be one traveler, long I stood
And looked down one as far as I could
To where it bent in the undergrowth;

Then took the other, as just as fair,
And having perhaps the better claim,
Because it was grassy and wanted wear;
Though as for that the passing there
Had worn them really about the same,

And both that morning equally lay
In leaves no step had trodden black,
Oh, I kept the first for another day!
Yet knowing how way leads on to way,
I doubted if I should ever come back.

I shall be telling this with a sigh
Somewhere ages and ages hence:
Two roads diverged in a wood, and I—
I took the one less traveled by,
And that has made all the difference.

—ROBERT FROST,
"THE ROAD NOT TAKEN," 1915

It was the advent of the bicycle that created the present enormous vogue for athletics amongst women....The great bicycle craze of the Nineties...put the world awheel. Bicycles were at first constructed for skirted females. Then some intrepid women revived the bloomer, which had caused so much laughter and indignation way back in the Fifties....It took only a few months for the fad to make a conquest of the entire population.

—HENRY COLLINS BROWN, *IN THE GOLDEN NINETIES*

In life, as in a football game, the principle to follow is: Hit the line hard.

—THEODORE ROOSEVELT

Within twenty or thirty years fortunes rivaling those of the great landlords of older civilizations were accumulated, and they became a new force in American society.

—THOMAS C. COCHRAN, *BUSINESS IN AMERICAN LIFE: A HISTORY*

Work and play, live on hay, You'll get pie in the sky when you die.

—JOE HILL, INDUSTRIAL WORKERS OF THE WORLD

The one absolutely certain way of bringing this nation to ruin and preventing all possibility of its continuing to be a nation could be to permit it to become a tangle of squabbling nationalities.

—THEODORE ROOSEVELT

Contents

Theodore Roosevelt

Previous page, top left: boys playing stickball in a backstreet slum; top right: Frances Willard, feminist and temperance crusader, learning to ride a bicycle; bottom: a cartoon comparing the stature of late 19th-century presidents (from right to left, McKinley, Cleveland, and Harrison) unfavorably with some great predecessors (left to right, Washington, Lincoln, and Grant).

PREFACE
An Age of Extremes

How do you think this messenger boy feels about his life at the turn of the century? He doesn't have to go to school, he smokes, and he probably works long hours.

This book is about the United States during the last decades of the 19th century and the first of the 20th. Men who had fought in the Civil War were now in their sixties or seventies. They didn't know another war was coming.

It was a confident time: people thought life was good and would get even better. A few, like Mark Twain, were concerned. He said there was too much attention to money and gold and glitter. He called this turn of the century a "Gilded Age."

Some historians say it was an "age of extremes." Why? Well, read on; you'll see why.

It was a time in America when there was

- great individual wealth,
- terrible poverty,
- much hope,
- vast immigration,
- new factory jobs, and
- new, BIG businesses called *corporations*.

It was a time when

- railroads controlled much of America's wealth,
- lumbermen cut down enormous forests,
- the Indian wars ended (badly for the Indians),
- the cattle drives were finished,
- some cowboys became circus stars,
- evil Jim Crow settled across all of the South,
- business tycoons acted like emperors,

The Gilded Age brought change for middle-class people as well as rich and poor. City folk who had Sundays off could buy a train or trolley ticket and go to the country or to the beach. Vacations became part of the lives of ordinary people for the first time.

Many poor immigrants worked at home, and their children often had to help. The photographer who took this picture was documenting child labor. Of this scene he wrote: "Picking nut meats with dirty baby in lap. Neighbors helping. One girl is cracking nuts with her teeth, not an uncommon sight."

The story continues on page 12.

• people filled the land until there was no more frontier, and these things were invented or developed:

- electric lights
- horseless carriages
- telephones
- flying machines
- moving pictures
- skyscrapers
- record players
- baseball and football leagues
- bicycles
- typewriters

And more, too.

It was a time when most Americans still lived on farms, although cities were booming. It was the time when Mark Twain wrote *Huckleberry Finn*; when James Whistler painted a famous picture of his mother; when the beautiful Brooklyn Bridge was built, the Panama Canal was dug, and we fought wars with Spain and the Philippine Islanders.

It was a time when women and people of color demanded to be treated as full citizens—and hardly anyone paid attention. When thousands of children worked from sunup to sundown—and a few people began to pay attention.

It was a time when "progressives" and "populists" and "reformers" and "business tycoons" and "working people" all had strong opinions about

A Nation of Practical Idealists

Benjamin Franklin

Here is a good word for you to learn: *pragmatic* (prag-MAT-ick). It means practical-minded. Pragmatic people don't worry much about theories. They just see what works and stick with that.

We Americans are known as pragmatic people. We inherited that trait from a Founding Father. Can you guess who?

Well, it was Benjamin Franklin. He was a pragmatist. Ben looked at the world and used his practical mind to try to make it a better place. The first half of his life he worked hard at his business—printing—and became successful and wealthy. Then he retired, at 40, and devoted the rest of his life to science and invention and his country. He made himself useful.

Nineteenth-century America was filled with pragmatic businesspeople. Something new had appeared since Franklin's time: big business and corporations. It was railroads that helped change things. Before railroads crossed the country, American business was found mostly in small workshops and foundries. A big factory or a big farm makes sense only if your products can reach far markets. With railroads, they could.

Some of the men who built the railroads became immensely wealthy. Cornelius Vanderbilt, who died in 1877, was the richest of them all. Like Benjamin Franklin, he got things done. But there was a big difference between Vanderbilt and Franklin.

Cornelius Vanderbilt was *unscrupulous* (un-SCROO-pew-luss), which means he was a business pirate. He didn't care about playing by the rules. Every time he could, he put his competition out of business. The *New York Times* called him a "robber baron." But he was smart, no question about that. He started out with one boat and soon had a fleet. Then he saw the future of trains and became king of the railroads (although there was plenty of competition on the tracks). He earned most of his money by getting favors from the government. The taxpayers ended up making Vanderbilt very rich. Unfortunately, he set a precedent for some in American business. But not for all.

Ben Franklin had been a successful businessman who was also a responsible citizen. He devoted much of his time to helping other people and his nation, too. He was *altruistic* (al-tru-ISS-tick—it means unselfishly concerned for others) as well as pragmatic.

So were George Washington and Thomas Jefferson and Alexander Hamilton. It was their example that most Americans could point to with pride. Those leaders had been practical and responsible, pragmatic and idealistic. Their example meant that every time someone got greedy and mean-spirited, a voice from the past spoke out. It was a national conscience. It said things like:

Early to bed and early to rise, makes a man healthy, wealthy and wise.

or *A penny saved is a penny earned.*

or, *There never was a good knife made of bad steel.*

Well, you know how a conscience is. Sometimes you try not to hear it. In the 19th century there were businessmen who closed their ears. They were greedy. They abused their workers. They robbed the nation. They influenced presidents and congress. They were not altruistic. They set a bad example.

But not all of the 19th century's wealthy businesspeople were robber barons. A few did hear Franklin's voice: you'll meet some of them in this book.

Cornelius Vanderbilt

Completed in 1883, the Brooklyn Bridge seemed to sum up the times. It brought out genius and heroism in some people, and corruption and greed in others. But it benefited everybody.

how to make life better in America.

It was a time when a lot of people enjoyed themselves. They had more leisure than ever before. Some threw grand parties. Some played those new games, baseball and football. Some joined unions. Some joined social or church groups. Some got involved in politics.

It was a time of prosperity and poverty; of corruption and idealism; and, for almost everyone, a time of faith in the future. In other words, it was a very interesting time.

These children of the Vanderbilt family, like the immigrants on page 10, lived in New York City at the start of this century. Do you see why this was called an age of extremes?

1 Carnegie

Andrew Carnegie (left), in 1851, aged 16, and brother Thomas, dressed for the photographer. Andrew worked in the office of a Pittsburgh cotton factory.

Andrew Carnegie was born in a stone cottage in Dunfermline, Scotland, in 1835. His father was a weaver who worked at a hand loom. But when the Industrial Revolution came to Scotland, Andrew's father could find no work. Power looms produced cloth faster and cheaper than artisans (handworkers) could. Many weavers lost their jobs. They were angry at the government and the business leaders. But there was nothing they could do about it. Poor workers weren't even allowed to vote.

In the little town of Dunfermline workers were determined to gain the right to vote and to strike. Andrew Carnegie's dad was

*To the West, to the West, to
  the land of the free,
Where the mighty Missouri
  rolls down to the sea;
Where a man is a man if he's
  willing to toil,
And the humblest may gather
  the fruits of the soil;
Where children are blessings,
  and he who hath most
Has aid for his fortune and
  riches to boast,
Where the young may exult
  and the aged may rest,
Away, far away, to the land of
  the West.*

—SONG ANDREW CARNEGIE'S PARENTS
SANG TO HIM WHEN HE WAS A BOY

Like the heroes of popular boys' books of the time, Andrew Carnegie's life went from rags to riches. Born in a weaver's cottage (left), when he came back to Scotland from America he bought Skibo Castle (right).

Some children—like Andrew Carnegie—found a life outside the cotton mill windows. For others the factory was the only world they knew.

"The millionaires...are the bees that make the most honey, and contribute most to the hive even after they have gorged themselves," said Carnegie.

one of those who spoke out for workers' rights. You might call him an *idealist*. He wanted to make the world better.

Andrew's mother was a *realist*. She was the practical one. She worried about putting food on the table for her family. When there was no money she stitched shoes and sold groceries. She was the one who sold the family's few belongings and decided that they should "flit" out of Scotland and head for America.

Andrew Carnegie had those two sides to him: his mother's side made him sensible and willing to work hard; his father's side made him want to improve the world. There was another important influence on Carnegie. It was his uncle George. George Lauder loved poetry, and he read the words of Robert Burns and William Shakespeare to his nephew. When Carnegie got to be rich—very, very rich—he could still recite Shakespeare. He had great writers and thinkers as friends, and Carnegie could talk with them in ways his fellow millionaires would never have understood.

But while he was getting rich he didn't seem to worry much about the working people who were laboring for him. He forgot his father's troubles. What he did do was work hard himself, use his imagination and intelligence, and take every chance that came his way.

His first job, in Allegheny, Pennsylvania, was as a bobbin boy in a textile factory. He worked from six in the morning until six at night and was paid $1.20 a day. He was 12 years old. A year later he heard that a messenger boy was needed at the new telegraph office in Pittsburgh. He got the job and set out to be the best messenger boy in town. Soon he knew all the streets and buildings by heart. He watched the telegraph operators and taught himself Morse code. (Messages were sent on wires with that code.) Then he learned to decipher the code from the clicking sound of the telegraph, without needing the tape printer. No one else in Pittsburgh could do that!

One day Andy found a check for $500 on the street. He turned it over to those who could find the owner. A newspaper, the *Pittsburgh Gazette*, wrote a story about him; it called him "an honest little fellow."

And that impressed Thomas A. Scott, who was soon to become a leading railroad man. He hired Carnegie as an assistant—at $35 a month. Andy was now 17 and in a place where opportunity would find him. When it did, he was ready to grab it. He learned about *capital*—which is money—and how to use it to get businesses started. He learned to put money to work. He invested in railroads, railroad sleeping cars, bridges, and oil derricks; by the time he was 33, he was rich.

Then he wrote himself a note. So far it was his mother's side he had followed. At 33 he remembered his father's idealism. He wrote that he would work for money for two more years; then he would work to help others. "No idol is more debasing than the worship of money," wrote Carnegie.

Two years later he must have forgotten that note—or maybe the lure of money was too strong. He kept working hard and getting richer and richer. He entered the iron business, but soon realized that steel was the metal of the future. Carnegie became king of America's steel industry and soon American steel dominated the world. The Carnegie steel company was very profitable: it used the best, most efficient machinery and kept wages very low. Carnegie's

Thomas Anshutz's painting of *The Ironworkers' Noontime.* Pittsburgh, below, became a byword for industrial pollution in Andrew Carnegie's lifetime.

How Do You Make Steel?

For thousands of years, men and women used iron as their most important and useful metal. Long, long ago, someone may have built a fire on top of some iron ore. The heat of the fire, the ore, and the sands of the earth may have combined to form a lump of metal.

The Iron Age is said to have begun in Asia Minor (now Turkey), about 1100 B.C.E., when metalsmiths began hammering tools and weapons of iron. What a marvel it was to have nails, swords, and cutting tools of iron! Ironworking skills spread across Europe, Asia, and Africa. They came to the Americas with Columbus.

Iron is strong but heavy. It breaks under pressure. Moisture makes it rust.

Pure iron is an *element*. But the common metal we call iron is an *alloy*. An alloy is a mixture. Iron is a mixture of two or more elements: iron, carbon, and others such as manganese and sulfur.

Steel is also an alloy. It is iron with a very small amount of carbon (the amount varies). Steel is strong, stronger than iron. It resists rust, and it bends rather than breaks. It is lighter than iron. Imagine what you can do with a metal like that! (Think of all the things in your world made of steel. Then think again. Almost everything you use is made by steel machines.)

Steel had been used in ancient days. When the railroad age began in the 1830s, the railroad builders wanted to use steel for rails and engines. But there was a problem. It was very expensive to make steel. You had to take the unwanted elements out of the iron. That meant a slow process of heating and separating. You began with a huge quantity of iron and were left with a small bit of steel. You can understand why the first railroads were made of iron.

William Kelly's parents had come to America

A Bessemer-process steelworks in 1886. In the egg-shaped converters, the molten iron is white hot. Compressed air is blown up through the converter until the impurities are oxidized—combined with oxygen to form waste, called slag, which is light and easily separated.

from Ireland. When William was a boy he worked as an apprentice in an iron forge. Then he opened his own small business making iron kettles near Louisville, Kentucky. Like everyone else in the iron business, he thought about steel. If only he could find a way to make it inexpensively.

One day Kelly was in a hurry. He was trying to cool off a bucket of hot, liquid iron. He blew cool air from a bellows onto the iron. Fumes from the iron came back into his face. He passed out. Kelly knew that iron workers sometimes died from similar fumes. He found out that the fumes were *carbon monoxide*. That poisonous gas is produced when carbon is heated with oxygen.

Kelly began thinking about those fumes. He knew the air from the bellows contained oxygen, but where was the carbon coming from? Could it be that blowing oxygen on hot iron removed carbon? He decided to find out. This time he built a bellows and a chimney to vent the fumes. For a half hour he blew cool air on iron. He had steel.

No one believed him when he told them what he had done. He was called "Crazy Kelly." For the next few years he worked to perfect his process. He had discovered that blowing air on molten iron turned it white hot; that cold air was actually heating the iron and removing the carbon. Cool air heating something? Everyone thought Kelly had lost his mind, especially when he wanted to build a steel mill. His father-in-law sent him to a doctor. But the doctor understood science and became one of Kelly's strongest supporters.

In the meantime, Henry Bessemer, in England, was working on a similar idea. He took out an American patent. When Kelly heard of Bessemer's patent he claimed he had been first, and, finally, the U.S. Patent Office agreed with him. Today the method is usually called the "Bessemer process," although William Kelly probably developed it five years before Bessemer.

That new method meant that steel could be made at reasonable cost. Steel rails soon replaced rigid iron ones. Builders had a new tool: a strong, versatile metal. Steel became the foundation for America's astounding industrial growth.

workers—men who were like his dad and uncle— were paid very little. Life for their families was awful. The writer Hamlin Garland visited a steel town and wrote this:

> *The streets were horrible; the buildings poor; the side-walks sunken and full of holes....Everywhere the yellow mud of the streets lay kneaded into sticky masses through which groups of pale, lean men slouched in faded garments.*

When salaries were cut at Carnegie's Homestead steel mill, in Pennsylvania, the workers went on strike. Carnegie's manager, Henry Clay Frick, refused to talk to the

At Carnegie's Homestead steel mill, striking men try to attack the Pinkerton detectives, who have been captured and are being escorted by union men carrying rifles.

Andrew Carnegie provided the money for one of the world's finest concert halls: Carnegie Hall in New York. Here is an old joke about it:

A young woman stops an older man on a New York street and says, "Excuse me, sir, how do I get to Carnegie Hall?"

He replies, "Practice, practice, practice!"

Henry Clay Frick's house, on New York's Fifth Avenue, is now a museum, and a splendid one. It is filled with art treasures that Frick bought from all over the world.

Henry Clay Frick

strikers; instead he sent in Pinkerton detectives. (Pinkerton was the name of a company that supplied armed guards. They were called detectives, but they were just men with guns.) Twenty strikers were killed. So were four detectives. Andrew Carnegie was vacationing in Scotland. Had he forgotten his origins?

If you saw the way he lived you would say so. He owned a castle in Scotland (see page 13) and houses in America that seemed like palaces. He lived like a prince while many who worked for him lived like paupers.

Then the most successful banker in America, J. Pierpont Morgan, offered to buy Carnegie out. It was 1901, nine years after the Homestead strike, and Carnegie was 66. It was an opportunity that might never come again. The sale would make him one of the richest men in the world.

At first he hesitated. Perhaps he didn't know what he would do with himself if he was no longer running a business empire. Then he may have remembered the note he wrote when he was 33. Or maybe he remembered his father's ideals. He sold his business interests and began a new career. It was the business of giving away his money. When you're as rich as Andrew Carnegie, that is a big job. Especially if you want to do it well, which he did.

He wrote that "the man who dies thus rich, dies disgraced." He said that millionaires had a duty to distribute their wealth while they were still alive. He didn't want to die disgraced, and he didn't. He began by building libraries in towns all across the country—3,000 of them, costing nearly $60 million. He gave money to colleges and schools and artists and writers and to an institute to promote peace and to another to improve teaching and to another that was to attempt to make the world better. He gave away almost all of his riches.

Not long before he died he turned to his private secretary and asked, "How much did you say I have given away, Poynton?" "Three hundred and twenty-four million, six hundred and fifty-seven thousand, three hundred and ninety-nine dollars," came the answer. "Good heavens!" said Carnegie. "Where did I ever get all that money?"

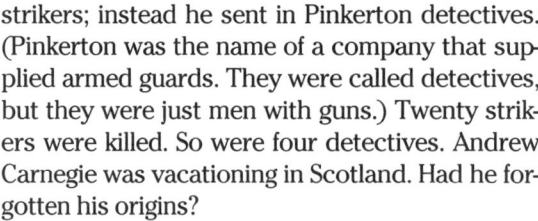

This rather worshipful British cartoon portrayed Carnegie as the kilted benefactor of his country of birth, celebrating his gift of money to provide free university education for deserving Scottish scholars.

2 A Bookkeeper Named Rockefeller

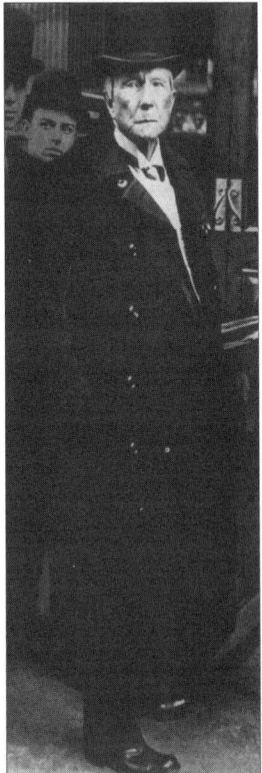

"Mad about money," a friend of Rockefeller said of him, "though sane in everything else."

In 1858, a small-time prospector named Edwin Drake sank a hole 70 feet into the ground near Titusville, Pennsylvania. Black slime soon filled the hole. That slime was oil. When the news got out, people raced for the hills and gullies of western Pennsylvania. Before long that state was a wild and hurly-burly place—something like California in the gold rush a decade earlier. Trees came down and derricks went up. Oil wells caught fire and black, smelly fumes filled the air. Railroads pushed in, towns sprouted like dandelions—and disappeared just as fast. Pithole, Pennsylvania (which was well named), had a hotel that cost $65,000. When the prospectors left, the hotel sold for $50.

One day a quiet, unflappable young bookkeeper was sent to this disorganized area to see what was going on. "Is the oil business worth investing in?" His employers had sent him to find out. "No," he told them, and then went on to invest in it himself and to become one of the most successful businessmen the world has ever known. His name was John Davison Rockefeller.

Rockefeller's Scotch-Baptist mother had raised him to be orderly,

As early as 1865, the year this photograph was taken of Pioneer Run in Pennsylvania's Oil Creek district, the U.S. exported 30 million gallons of crude oil and oil products.

19

Rockefeller's crushing of competition made Standard Oil—with its tentacles in every kind of business—the most hated company in America. Rockefeller bought oil direct from the wells; made his own barrels; and built his own wagons, like this kerosene van (kerosene was the most important oil product before gasoline).

hardworking, and exact. Once, he and his brothers went skating on a frozen river. They were not supposed to do that, but they saved the life of a boy who fell through the ice. When their mother heard what they had done, she praised them for their courage and then whipped them for their disobedience.

The boys were encouraged to work. John raised turkeys and saved $50. When a neighbor asked to borrow the $50 he lent the money—and charged $3.50 interest. It was a lesson he never forgot: money could be made to earn money. That is what capitalism is all about. Some say John D. Rockefeller was the greatest capitalist who ever lived. Others say he almost destroyed capitalism for everyone else in America.

One thing is certain. He soon brought order to that disorderly oil business. But not by being a prospector. He could see that the money to be made was in oil refining. In 1863—he was 24—he and a partner bought a small refinery. With his efficient methods, it quickly grew large. Rockefeller began buying his competitors.

If you have oil to sell, there are two costs that are important: the cost of the oil and the cost of transportation (you need to get the oil to buyers). Because there were competing railroads, and because he had quite a bit of oil to ship, Rockefeller made the railroads give him special prices to ship his oil. Actually, what he did was to pay the full price like everyone else. Then he got the railroads to give him back half of what he had paid. He did that secretly. It was called a *rebate*, or *kickback*, and it wasn't fair. It meant he could charge less for oil than his competitors did. Soon he put most of them out of business. Within 10 years he controlled the nation's oil industry.

The oil business was very lucra-

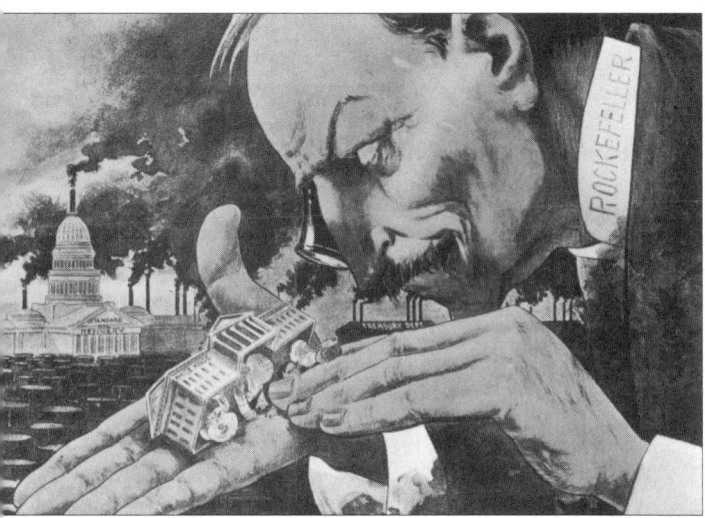

For a while, it seemed as if a man like Rockefeller, who controlled a whole industry, had the government in his pocket. This cartoon's title was "What a Funny Little Government!"

tive, which means there were big profits to be made. Rockefeller's company, Standard Oil, became spectacularly rich. What seems amazing to us today is that all of this happened *before* the internal combustion engine. The internal combustion engine powers automobiles and the other machines that made oil so important in the 20th century. The oil that brought hundreds of millions of dollars to Rockefeller was used mostly to light kerosene lamps (in those days before electric light).

The more you read about John D. Rockefeller, or history in general, the more you will see how hard it is to make judgments—good and bad have a way of getting mixed together. You can decide for yourself what to think of him.

In the 19th century, many people thought Rockefeller was one of the great villains of all time. His bookkeeper's mind seemed interested only in money and profits, not in people. When he put others out of business it didn't bother him at all, as long as it made profits for Standard Oil. That company was called "the greatest, wisest and meanest monopoly known to history." Rockefeller soon had vast interests in many businesses, not just oil, and the less he paid his workers the more efficient the businesses seemed.

Spindletop— A Great Black Gusher

Everyone knew there was oil in Texas. When oil had seeped to the ground's surface, Indians used it to heal wounds. Members of the Spanish explorer Hernando DeSoto's expedition, back in 1542, had found Texas asphalt (a thick, pastelike form of petroleum) useful for repairing their ships. In the early 19th century, several pioneers drilled and found oil.

By the 1880s and '90s, Texans had tapped many small oil wells and brought in drilling machinery, storage tanks, and pipelines. It was the beginning of an oil industry. Then Patillo Higgins and Anthony F. Lucas drilled a test well at a place called Spindletop, near Beaumont. Early in the morning of January 10, 1901, they heard a roaring sound. The drill pipe lifted straight out of the earth, like a rocket. Then came the oil, surging up 160 feet high. It took 10 days just to get the stuff under control. The oil men were soon filling as many as 100,000 barrels a day at Spindletop. The Texas oil boom had begun.

This *Chicago Tribune* cartoon reacted favorably to all the money that Rockefeller gave away—not surprisingly, since one of the institutions he founded was the University of Chicago. But some people thought it wrong to accept money that they felt had been gained by hurting other businesses and workers.

When some miners tried to form unions, he shut the mines and actually let workers starve rather than pay fair wages. His strikebreaking troops shot and killed workers and their families in mining towns in Colorado. Rockefeller claimed he didn't know what was going on—but he did. After the turn of the century, laws were passed that helped prevent unfair business practices, but, until that happened, tycoons like Rockefeller sometimes behaved as if they were kings. John D. Rockefeller had a quiet, dignified manner, but his company acted like a big, tough bully—beating up anyone who tried to fight it.

But, as I said, making judgments is difficult. Because it was so well organized and managed, Standard Oil helped make American business grow into world leadership. And it made life better for most people by bringing products to the market at a low price.

There were two sides to Rockefeller, and they were both beside his bed. That was where he kept his safe—filled with money. But on top of the safe was his Bible. The Bible, and his mother's teachings, made him generous. He gave away vast sums of money to help others. He didn't have to do that. Many of the business barons of his day kept all they earned for themselves. Rockefeller and Carnegie were different. Each took the intelligence and efficiency that had made him rich and used it to distribute enormous sums of money. Rockefeller lived until 1937; he was 98 when he died. For the last 40 years of his life he spent much of his time giving away his money. While Carnegie gave away 90 percent of his fortune, Rockefeller, always orderly and precise, gave away exactly half of his. Still, it was an immense half (half a billion dollars), and it created the University of Chicago, the Rockefeller Institute for Medical Research, and a foundation just to give money to worthwhile causes.

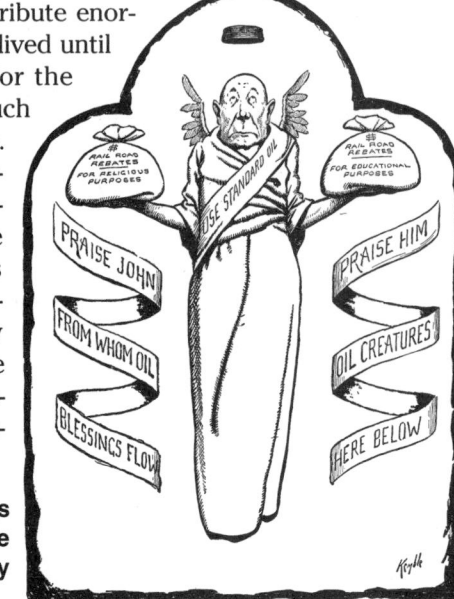

"Praise John from whom oil blessings flow, praise him oil creatures here below." A joky design for a memorial by the University of Chicago to its founder.

3 Mr. Storyteller

A scary, important-seeming creation of L. Frank Baum's who turned out to be only a ventriloquist from Omaha. If you don't know who he is, you'll find out by the end of this chapter.

Lyman Frank Baum wasn't like most other people. And he certainly didn't fit into the Gilded Age. He had no talent for making money. Ask your parents and friends if they know who Frank Baum is and they may shrug their shoulders and say no. But they know his words. You probably do too.

Baum's dad was a tough oil man who fought giant Standard Oil in the days of the Pennsylvania oil rush, and survived with only minor wounds.

Frank was different. He was a gentle boy, often sick, who had to stay home from school and couldn't play ball games with the other boys. He spent a lot of time daydreaming. Once he saw a scarecrow as big as a man, and for a long time he had real dreams—nightmares—about that scarecrow. Frank Baum loved to act and write plays and tell stories, but everyone told him that a young man needed to be sensible and serious if he was to succeed in the world.

His parents sent him to military school; they hoped to make him serious. He did poorly there, got

"To please a child," said Frank Baum (shown here telling stories to several children), "is a sweet and lovely thing that warms one's heart."

23

Perhaps one reason L. Frank Baum liked to make up exciting stories about children was his own strict upbringing. His mother would not even let her children play baseball on Sunday.

sick, and came home. Later he told stories about an army full of generals and officers and one poor soldier who was expected to do all the fighting. In Frank Baum's stories no one liked to fight. A general he told about said, sensibly, "Fighting is unkind and liable to be injurious to others."

Baum grew up and went to work and tried to be serious. He started out in the oil business selling Baum's Casterine—machine grease—but he wasn't much of a salesman. About this time he fell in love. Frank was tall, handsome, and slim, and Maud Gage was pretty and bold. They made a fine couple, and soon married and had children. But they didn't have any money, so Maud suggested they move to South Dakota, where gold had been discovered. Anyone who opened a store in a gold-rush town was sure to be successful. So that's what they did. They called the store Baum's Bazaar.

It might have been a success, but Frank couldn't bear to take money from people who were poor. Besides, what he really liked to do was tell stories to children. And that's what he kept doing, instead of minding the business. It failed.

Then he started a newspaper. He wrote one story for his paper about a town where people rode in horseless carriages and flying machines and slept under electric blankets. Of course, that was all daydreaming nonsense—this was the 19th century, and there were no horseless carriages for sale, and certainly no flying machines. Electric blankets—that was really absurd. Then he wrote a story that poked fun at another newspaper editor. That kind of writing is called *satire*.

Well, the other newspaper editor didn't think it funny at all. Baum was challenged to a duel. Remember, these were the days of the Wild West, when people shot out their differences. But not gentle Frank Baum. He strode out the door of his office with a revolver on his belt—like the actor he longed to be—and then left town. He didn't want to hurt anyone.

You might not find it surprising that his newspaper failed. By this time the Baums had four boys and still no money. They moved from prairie South Dakota to bustling Chicago. There Frank became a newspaper reporter. But the pay—$18.62 a week—was so low he had to give up that job to sell dishes. He wasn't much good at that. It was a very discouraging time for the Baums. About the only thing that seemed to make Frank happy was sitting around telling stories to his four boys.

He told stories about people he made up, but his characters all became real in his mind. They were his friends, and he talked to them and they talked back. Once, when someone asked him how he figured out an adventure, he said his characters did what they wanted to do. One of his character-friends was the old scarecrow who had scared him when he was a boy. Now the scarecrow was a kindly soul.

One day Maud's mother got exasperated with her son-in-law. "Go out and get your stories published!" she said. He did. He published two books of Mother and Father Goose stories. Children liked them.

But the stories his boys liked best were about an emerald city, a tin woodman, a cowardly lion, and that scarecrow. There was a determined little girl in the story—a bold girl—and her name was Dorothy. She lived on the prairie, in Kansas, where she once ran from a cyclone and landed in a magic land. One day, when Frank Baum was telling the story, one of his children asked, "What was the name of the magic land?" Frank needed a name for that land, and quickly, so he looked up, and there was his filing cabinet with the letters O–Z. *The land of Oz*, he said, and so it was named.

He wrote out those stories of Oz and got a friend to draw pictures, and they sent them to a publisher. The publisher sent them back. The stories were too silly; no one would read them, Baum was told. He sent them to another publisher, and another, and another. What a failure he seemed —even his stories were rejected. Then a publisher said he

Raggedy Ann Makes Her Debut

John Gruelle's original Raggedy Ann

Marcella Gruelle was very sick. Her father found an old rag doll in the attic, and it helped cheer her up. Marcella named the doll Raggedy Ann and asked her dad to make up stories about the doll. John Gruelle did. But nothing could help Marcella. She died holding Raggedy Ann in her arms. Marcella's sad father wanted to do something to remember his daughter, so he wrote out the stories that she had loved and had them published. They were so popular that he ended up writing 25 of them. Since then, Marcella's doll and her stories have pleased children all over the world.

The illustrations for the first *Oz* book (right, Dorothy and the Cowardly Lion) were by W. W. Denslow, a tough, jolly newspaper artist "like a walrus." He and Baum made good partners. *Oz* in Russian (top) and Japanese (left).

The ventriloquist from Omaha was—the wonderful Wizard of Oz.

would publish the stories if Baum paid the cost of printing. And so he did. He borrowed the money to do it. The book was published on August 1, 1900. You know what happened after that. *The Wonderful Wizard of Oz* became one of the most popular books ever written. It was turned into a play and a movie. Baum wrote more *Oz* books, and more again. And no matter how many he wrote, the boys and girls who read the *Oz* books wanted still more. They were translated into Russian and Chinese and most of the world's languages, so children all over the globe could read and love them. Almost 100 years later, they are still loved.

Perhaps one reason the *Oz* stories are so popular is that all the characters are as gentle as Baum himself. Well, almost all the characters—there is the Wicked Witch. But even the Wizard isn't mean. Remember when he said, "No one has the right to kill any living creature, however evil they may be, or to hurt them, or make them unhappy."

L. Frank Baum believed that. His friends said he never was unkind to anyone.

4 Powerful Pierpont

J. P. Morgan despised reporters—and he didn't like photographers getting shots of his famously red, bulbous nose.

There are so many myths about John Pierpont Morgan that we need to get a few things straight. He was not the richest man in America. (People just thought he was.) Rockefeller and Carnegie were richer. And he was not the most powerful man in America. There were two or three men who were equally powerful.

But he was very rich and very powerful, and vain and arrogant, too. Which means he was very sure of himself.

He was a bit like a regal lion who lords it over the whole jungle. The jungle where he was king was the world of business and finance. Morgan was a banker —a money man—and he had the ability to take a confused situation and make it orderly. In the years after the Civil War, the American world of business was very disorderly. J. Pierpont Morgan helped make it efficient.

Once, when the United States Treasury seemed on the edge of collapse—it didn't have enough gold in reserve to meet its bills—J. P. Morgan loaned the nation $62 million.

Another time, the country was facing a financial crisis that might have led to a depression (for more about this, see Chapter 10). People were

Wall Street, 1907, jammed with panicked investors who had lost confidence in their banks. Morgan raised millions in loans to save the situation.

Morgan's eyes reminded the photographer Edward Steichen of the headlights of an express train. A young financial reporter, Lincoln Steffens, said: "His eyes glared, his great red nose seemed to flash and darken."

J. Pierpont Morgan was a bull-necked irascible man with small black magpie's eyes and a growth on his nose; he let his partners work themselves to death over the detailed routine of banking, and sat in his back office smoking cigars; when there was something to be decided he said Yes or No and just turned his back and went back to his solitaire.

—JOHN DOS PASSOS,
The House of Morgan

pulling their money out of the banks and the stock market. A leading trust company was about to collapse. If that happened, people would panic. Morgan called the country's leading financiers to a meeting in his own marble library building. He asked them to lend money to save the trust. Then he locked the library's doors. He sat and played solitaire while the bankers paced and argued.

Morgan had one of the world's great private art collections. Some magnificent art treasures hung on the library's walls. A Gutenberg Bible and Thoreau's manuscripts sat on the shelves. Do you think the bankers enjoyed his treasures that night? No one knows the answer to that question, but we do know that at five in the morning, when the financiers agreed to do as he wished, Morgan unlocked the doors and let them out. The country was saved from financial disaster.

Few people dared disagree with J. P. Morgan. He was dignified and very imposing. Besides that, he had integrity. Everyone knew that if Morgan gave his word, you could rely on it. A famous photograph shows him sitting in a chair, a hand gripping the arm rest, eyes electric with energy. "Meeting his blazing dark eyes," said the photographer, "was like confronting the headlights of an express train bearing down on you."

When the trustees of Harvard Medical School needed money to expand their school, they went to several rich men. Rockefeller, with his careful, methodical mind, told them it would take him six months to study their plans. Morgan listened to the Harvard representatives, looked at his watch—he was busy that day—pointed to their plans, and said, "I will build that, and that, and that. Good morning, gentlemen." And he led them to the door.

J. P. Morgan was not like Andrew Carnegie. He did not start as a poor boy and work his way to riches. He started at the top. His father was an international banker. The first Morgans arrived in Massachusetts in 1636. Miles Morgan, an early ancestor, moved from rigid Puritan Boston to more tolerant Connecticut and there acquired land, prominence, and fame as an Indian fighter. By the time the 19th century came around, the family was wealthy, and snobbish about it, too.

Young Pierpont usually got his way. He was smart, with a talent for mathematics and languages. Once, when he disagreed with the answer in his arithmetic book, he claimed he was right and the book wrong. Turned out he was right. He had caught the book in a misprint.

His mind was very orderly. He got a weekly allowance and he kept a record of every penny he spent. When he grew up he did the same thing.

He was sent to schools in the United States and Switzerland and Germany and became a well-educated man, interested in art and music. He was an imposing man, vain about his clothes and his looks. He lived in enormous homes—he had seven of them—and he also owned a yacht and his own railroad cars. Morgan had one problem: a huge, bulblike nose that was often red as a strawberry. It was bad enough to be considered a medical problem—though no doctor was able to help. In that famous photograph of him, sitting in the chair with his blazing eyes, the photographer fixed the negative to shade the well-known nose.

By the beginning years of the new century, the House of Morgan (the name of J. P.'s bank) could be found in almost every important field of American business. It controlled railroads, shipping, the manufacture of agricultural tools, telephones, telegraphs, electrical power, insurance, and city transportation. Remember, it was J. Pierpont Morgan who bought Andrew Carnegie's steel company; then he bought huge metal ore reserves from John D. Rockefeller and founded the U.S. Steel Corporation. It was the nation's first billion-dollar corporation.

An American president, looking at the country's business situation, said, "The great monopoly in this country is the money monopoly."

The president wasn't talking about a board game—although you do a lot of buying and selling when you play Monopoly.

Read the next chapter and you'll find out how a real monopoly works.

Top, Morgan's scribbled guarantee of $30 million to New York City, which was almost bankrupted in the 1907 panic. Right, a typical view of Morgan as all-powerful banker. People thought him the Rockefeller of the financial world.

5 MONOPOLY—Not Always a Game

Rutherford Hayes (shown here with his wife, Lucy, not long after their marriage) said: "Shall the will of monopolies take the place of government by the people?"

Have you a yen for money? In what nations would you find these coins?
forint
franc
kopek
lira
mark
peseta
peso
pound
riyal
rupee
yen
yuan

The Civil War made some people very rich. Military supplies—guns, food, clothing, railroads—were needed, and quickly. Suddenly, there were new needs, new industries, and new fortunes. After the war, American inventiveness led to more new ideas and industries that continued to create riches.

Some of those industries grew very big. They became *monopolies*. That means the whole industry was owned by one company. Some businessmen, like Morgan and Rockefeller, formed business arrangements called *trusts*. The trusts were a form of monopoly. The public suffered.

To understand what a business monopoly is, imagine you are selling soft drinks at a school fair. The day is very hot and everyone is thirsty. You expect to make a lot of money. You plan to sell soda for $1 a glass (your cost is 25 cents a glass).

What you don't expect is to have competition. But, just as you're getting started, you notice another soft-drink stand. Your competitor is charging 75 cents a glass. Of course you have to lower your price or no one will buy from you.

Then, when sales are going well, another competitor appears. She is selling drinks for 50 cents each. You're annoyed, but there is nothing you can do but lower your price. You still make a fine profit, and people get drinks at a fair price.

Competition makes capitalism work well for the consumer. When there is competition it is called "free enterprise" or a "market economy." The people who are thirsty are much better off if businesses are competing. You, the business person, would like less competition. So you make plans to gain a monopoly in the field. You go to the two other soft-drink sellers and buy their stands. If they sell out, you can charge the public anything you want.

Suppose you start with three soft-drink stands and then buy a soft-drink bottling company and then another, and another, until you own the whole industry. Then suppose you buy up the trucking companies that ship your beverages, and then all the sugar producers and the companies that make all the other ingredients needed in soft drinks. You have become king of the soft-drink world. What power you now wield! You can charge people *five* dollars a glass—or anything you want—and everyone has to pay: you have no competition.

That kind of thing happened in the 19th century. Rockefeller's Standard Oil trust was a huge monopoly. It owned more than 90 percent of America's oil industry, as well as pipelines, tankers, and related industries.

There are some benefits in a monopoly. If it is well run,

The system of corporate life and corporate power, as applied to industrial development, is yet in its infancy....It is a new power, for which our language contains no name. We know what aristocracy, autocracy, democracy are; but we have no word to express government by moneyed corporations....It remains to be seen what the next phase in this process of gradual development will be. History never quite repeats itself, and...the old familiar enemies may even now confront us, though arrayed in such modern garb that no suspicion is excited.

—Charles F. Adams and Henry Adams, 1871

The popular view of "King Monopoly," exacting tribute from every worker and businessman in the land and clad in a long cape made from taxes on every conceivable commodity.

Economix

Why is it that everyone's eyes begin to close when you say *economics*, and open wide when you say *money*? I haven't figured that out, but—stay awake—here are some economic terms that will help you understand how nations earn money. Economists say that there are three basic ways that a nation can organize its system of doing business. These are: as a *market* economy; as a *command* economy; or as a *traditional* economy.

In a market economy the customer (*consumer*) determines what will be produced when he or she spends money. If people in the *marketplace* (stores, offices, catalogues, etc.) ask for green shoes and purple surfboards, someone will soon be making them. The United States is said to have a market economy.

A command economy is organized by the government. The government decides what will be produced and who will do the producing. *Communism* and *socialism* are command systems. There is a big difference between them, however. Most communist states have been dictatorial. The ordinary citizen has no say in the decision process. But many socialist states are democratic. If the decision-makers aren't doing a good job, the voters can vote them out. The former Soviet Union, which was communist, had a command economy; socialist Sweden has a (chiefly) command economy.

In a traditional economy people usually do the same work their parents did. If your dad is a government leader, you will be trained for a leadership role. If he is a shoemaker, that's probably what you'll do. In most traditional economies, women work at home. Many Asian and African nations have traditional economic systems.

Now that I've described these systems, I have to tell you that no country is simply market, command, or traditional. There's a fourth system—it is called *hybrid*, which means a mixture. That's what most economies actually are—a little of this and that. It's just that some are more of one than another. France is an example of a true hybrid: its economy is both socialistic and market-driven. See what you can find out about our economic system. How much of a hybrid are we?

"Government of the monopolists, by the monopolists, and for the monopolists." This was a fairly accurate view of the Senate in the 1880s.

a monopoly can be very efficient. But usually it is the consumer who suffers when there is no competition.

Americans decided they didn't want monopolies or trusts. A trust is a legal arrangement that allows many different companies to be owned and run by the same people. It is a form of monopoly. The big 19th-century trusts put all their competitors out of business. They were organized in a way that put them mostly beyond government control.

Now you may be saying, "No one *has* to sell out to a monopoly." But that isn't

In the image (labels on the octopus monster): TRUST, THE TRACTION MONSTER, PULL, SUBWAY FRANCHISE, MONOPOLY, WIRE TRUST, BANKING TRUSTS, GAS MONOPOLIES, ELECTRICITY, SUBWAY FRANCHISES

quite true. The monopolies grew so large that they could use unfair business methods. Suppose you are running your soft-drink stand and a big, rich competitor comes and sells drinks for 15 cents. Remember, the drinks cost you 25 cents. You can't stay in business long with that kind of competition. The big monopolies did that kind of thing to put competitors out of business. They could afford to lose money for a while because they were so wealthy.

In 1887, former president Rutherford B. Hayes asked, "Shall the will of monopolies take the place of government by the people?" The answer the American people gave was *no*.

Americans care about individual rights. That has given us strong anti-monopoly feelings; it also makes us want as few laws as possible.

So regulating business in a capitalist country is not easy. Most businesspeople want as little regulation as possible. But the public needs to be protected from unfair business practices. In the 19th century, big business in America got out of control. Politicians were often corrupted by business influences. (What does that mean? How might they be corrupted?)

It was clear that rules and regulations were needed. The American

This famous and scary cartoon portrayed the monopoly octopus and its stranglehold on the cities through control of oil, steel, subways, telephone wires, electricity, gas, coal—and political influence.

33

Let's Talk Business

WHAT IS A PARTNERSHIP?

Suppose you are a shoemaker, and you make shoes in a small shop by yourself. Then you join with another shoemaker. Now you have a *partnership*. You share the work, the ideas, the profits, and the problems. There are real advantages. It's an easy way to go into business. You can start a partnership with a handshake. Then, if you are sick or you want to take a vacation, your partner can keep the business going. But the arrangement does have a problem. Suppose you've been fooled. Your partner is a bum. He charges things to the business. The business soon has big debts and you don't know about it. Now creditors arrive wanting to be paid back for those debts. Your partner has skipped town. You are stuck with all his debts because you were partners (even though you had nothing to do with those debts).

WHAT IS A CORPORATION?

A corporation is a form of business that evolved from the *stock companies* of the past. The London Company, which sent John Smith and others to Jamestown, was a stock company. In the 19th century, corporations became big and sophisticated.

You are a shoemaker, but you're tired of making shoes one foot at a time. You want to open a factory, use the latest machinery, and make thousands of pairs of shoes each week. There is a problem: renting factory space, buying machinery, and paying salaries will cost a lot of money. You don't have it. What do you do? You decide to form a corporation. Now you can sell stock to *stockholders*. Each stockholder then owns a share in your shoe factory; but the modern corporation gives them a big advantage over a regular partnership or an old-fashioned stock company. It gives them *limited liability*. That means the stockholders are not responsible (liable) for the debts of the corporation. The corporation holds a business charter (from the government) that recognizes it as a separate being with its own rights and responsibilities—apart from its owners or members. Legally, the corporation is almost like a person itself.

WHAT IS A TARIFF?

A tariff is a tax on foreign goods brought into a country. That tax makes the foreign goods more expensive. That means that goods made at home have a better chance of selling. So tariffs help local industry and hurt foreign ones. What do tariffs do to prices? How do they affect the consumer? In the Gilded Age, the Republican Party supported high tariffs, the Democrats low ones.

people demanded reforms. In 1890, Congress passed the Sherman Antitrust Act. Senator John Sherman, who sponsored the law, was a brother of General William Tecumseh Sherman. The Sherman Antitrust Act was intended to make business responsible to the public. It said that trusts and monopolies that restrained free competition were illegal. At first no one—not the president, Congress, or the courts—would enforce the law. Nobody wanted to offend the powerful businessmen. But that changed. The presidents, congresses, and the courts made the law effective.

An anti-Cleveland cartoon. Cleveland wanted to cut tariffs; Republicans said cheap European goods would drown American ones.

6 Builders and Dreamers

John Roebling made America's first wire rope—and he used that invention to build something far bigger, and destined to be world famous.

Nineteenth-century Americans thought they lived in the most splendid era in all of history. You can understand why: all those new cities and inventions were mighty exciting. Even the traffic jams in Chicago and New York didn't seem too bad when you considered the things you could do and see in those great cities. Americans seemed to be doing things bigger and better than had ever been done before. Some men and women started thinking about building buildings taller than any built before.

But there was no point in building a really tall building, because people were only willing to walk up four or maybe five flights of stairs. So that was as high as most buildings went until a Vermonter, Elisha Graves Otis, designed a safe elevator. Then, as they say, the sky was the limit. You could build tall buildings and people could ride up inside as high as the building went.

In 1880, if you lived in the elegant Dakota apartment house in New York City, you could drive home in your carriage, back into the elevator, unhitch the horses, and you and your carriage would be lifted to your apartment door.

Early elevators were often thought to be death-traps; but Elisha Otis's was designed to stop falling if the cable failed. He demonstrated this dramatically at an exposition by having someone cut the cable as he rode in the elevator.

Frederick Law Olmsted

The Dakota got its name because when it was first built its location—at the corner of Central Park and West 72nd Street—was so far north of the rest of the city that it might as well have been in the Dakotas. It is still around, and still elegant. One of its 20th-century tenants was Beatle John Lennon. He was killed in the building's entranceway.

From your apartment at the Dakota you could look out your windows at beautiful new Central Park. America's first great city park was a marvel of the time. Most people, when they think of architecture, think of buildings. But land can be transformed by a designer as a sculptor transforms clay or an architect steel and stone. Frederick Law Olmsted, a great landscape architect, did just that with the scruffy land near the Dakota. He had lakes dug and hills built. He made formal areas with fountains, playgrounds, and concert shells. He created rugged and wild areas. Notice that word *created*. If you visit Central Park today you may think nature made

Two great Gilded Age creations in New York City: the Dakota apartment building (right) seen from Central Park.

those rugged areas. Nature had a lot of help from Frederick Olmsted.

His ancestors had come to America on one of the early Puritan ships; they had been willing to leave their home in England to have freedom to practice their religion. Olmsted loved democracy and America's founding ideas. He believed that democratic cities should have large parks for recreation and for quiet walking, open to all people. He thought a public park should be as handsome as a king's park. It took 20 years and 3,800 men to build Central Park, but when it was finished, New York had a park for the people that was lovelier than any king's park.

And now that there were elevators, tall buildings seemed just the thing for America's new cities. But, if you think about it, you will realize there is a problem in building something very tall. The higher a building goes, the more it weighs.

So, if you wanted to build a tall building, you had to build its walls with stone or brick or something very strong to hold the weight. Tall buildings needed very thick bottom walls. When the first 16-story building was built in Chicago, the walls at its base were 15 feet thick. (Picture two six-foot men and a three-foot child lying down toes to head and you can see what 15 feet is like.)

Now this was an era of innovation. America was becoming the world's leading steel producer, so maybe it isn't surprising that some American architects came up with the idea of using steel as a *frame* for a building.

As you know, steel is very strong. A steel frame could hold all the weight of a tall building. The walls didn't have to hold any weight at all. Think about that. What did it mean?

It meant that thick walls weren't needed to support the building. Walls became just a covering, like skin.

They told us that the modern high buildings had been invented in Chicago and not in New York. That is interesting. It is interesting that it should have been done where there was plenty of land to build on and not in New York where it is narrow and so must be high of necessity. Choice is always more pleasing than necessity. —GERTRUDE STEIN

New York's first skyscraper was called the Flatiron Building. You can see why. It's there, still the same, at Fifth Avenue and 23rd Street.

The architect was free to use almost anything—even decorated metal, or glass—as the skin of a building. Luckily, when this new idea came on the scene, America produced an architect who was a genius. He was able to take that technology and combine it with artistry. His name was Louis Sullivan.

Louis Sullivan has been called the inventor of the skyscraper. That is not quite true. Sullivan didn't invent tall buildings; what he did was build them beautifully. Sullivan loved nature and poetry. Like Frederick Olmsted, he, too, was imbued with democratic ideas. Sullivan tried to express his ideas in his architecture. And he did it. His buildings are graceful and decorated with designs, shadows, and reflections.

To *imbue* (im-BEW) means to penetrate to the core, usually with a feeling or an idea.

Sullivan believed that the individual—each of us—is very important. It was an idea he got from reading the words of people like Thomas Jefferson, Ralph Waldo Emerson, and Henry David Thoreau. Louis Sullivan built tall buildings that are comfortable and human in scale. They are American buildings, not copies of European palaces.

One day, a young Wisconsin-born architect named Frank Lloyd Wright came to work for Louis Sullivan. Frank Lloyd Wright became even more famous than his teacher.

A *mentor* is an adviser, who gives a younger person the benefit of his or her knowledge and experience.

Many people consider Wright one of the world's greatest architects. Like his mentor, Wright was concerned with that American idea of individual worth. His buildings were meant to make life more enjoyable for all who used them. They often seem a part of the landscape; that's because the architect thought a lot about the natural environment and the ways that people have always lived.

Frank Lloyd Wright

One of Wright's homes is built over a brook; another was inspired by an Indian pueblo. Some are called *prairie houses*. How would you design a prairie house? What about the nature of the city—how would you design a city building? A New York City museum that Frank Lloyd Wright designed (the Guggenheim Museum) looks like a big, round, concrete tub. People take an elevator to the top of the tub and walk down a curving ramp to the bottom, looking at paintings as they go. (Do you think that is appropriate?)

Until Louis Sullivan led the way, high buildings lacked unity. They were built up in layers. All were fighting height instead of gracefully and honestly accepting it.... [Sullivan] first perceived the high building as a harmonious unit—its height triumphant.
—FRANK LLOYD WRIGHT

Other things, besides buildings, needed to be built in America. Rivers needed to be crossed.

But some rivers seemed too wide for any bridge. A rickety wooden bridge had made it across the Mississippi by hopping to an island in mid-river. Mostly, though, if you wanted to cross that broad river, you had to wait for the ferry or find a boat. Then James Eads designed three great steel arches and sank them into the Mississippi. They became the base for a bridge that crossed the mighty river near St. Louis. Steel had never been used for a big bridge before. No one knew if it would work. Sixteen men died building that bridge. After a tornado hit—and the bridge survived—it was called an engineering marvel. When it was finished, in 1874, you could take a train from the East Coast to the West and never worry about getting your feet wet.

Steel is not only strong, it is flexible. A German immigrant, John Augustus Roebling, thought about that one day when he saw some worn-out rope. He twisted thin steel wires together and made strong steel roping. That opened up all kinds of new ways to build things. Roebling came up with one of the best new ideas. He decided that a bridge could be *suspended*—which means "hung"—from steel wires at-

James Eads was a good engineer—during the Civil War he built ironclad salvage ships—but his design for these steel cantilevers over the Mississippi was the first bridge he had ever done. It worked.

Another immigrant (from Britain) and manufacturer of steel cable, Andrew Hallidie, used wire ropes in his own invention: the cable car (for more about this, see Book 7 of *A History of US*).

Washington A. Roebling

Emily Warren Roebling

tached to concrete and stone towers. Roebling designed the world's first modern suspension bridges. Actually, his bridges were similar in idea to the rope footbridges the Indians built in Central America 1,000 years ago. Except that Roebling built bridges strong enough to support railroad trains and cross mighty rivers. But when he suggested a bridge across New York's East River between Brooklyn and Manhattan, most people thought he had lost his mind.

It would be the longest and highest bridge ever built anywhere in the world. It would have to withstand powerful winds and ocean tides. Experts said it was impossible. The stone towers needed to anchor the steel rope could not be placed on land; the distance from shore to shore was too great. The towers would have to be built in the river. No one was quite sure how that could be done. New construction methods would have to be developed.

Well, it was done. It was called the Brooklyn Bridge, and it took 14 years to build. It demanded

The story continues on page 42

When the bridge's towers were complete, Master Mechanic Farrington (far right) made the first crossing in a bosun's chair watched by 10,000 people. While the cables were being made, the public could walk out on the footbridge (top). Two workers were killed when a cable snapped (right).

40

When the bridge finally opened on May 24, 1883, the fireworks—14 tons of them—lasted an entire hour.

Again the traffic lights that skim thy swift
Unfractioned idiom, immaculate sigh
* of stars,*
Beading thy path—condense eternity:
And we have seen night lifted in
* thine arms.*

Under thy shadow by the piers I waited;
Only in darkness is thy shadow clear.
The City's fiery parcels all undone,
Already snow submerges an iron year...

O Sleepless as the river under thee,
Vaulting the sea, the prairies' dreaming
* sod,*
Unto us lowliest sometime sweep,
* descend*
And of the curveship lend a myth to
* God.*

—HART CRANE, "THE BRIDGE"

41

In the Year of the Bridge

Here are some things that happen in 1883, the year the Brooklyn Bridge opens:

• **President Chester A. Arthur signs the Chinese Exclusion Act, which aims to keep Chinese laborers out of the United States.**

• **The electric iron is patented.**

• **Korea and the United States sign a friendship treaty.**

• **The University of North Dakota is founded.**

• **The Mississippi River floods, leaving 85,000 people homeless.**

• **Congress sets the cost of delivery for a first-class letter at one half-cent.**

• **New York and Chicago are linked by telephone lines.**

• **Philadelphia beats Providence 4–3 in the first National League baseball game.**

• **Thomas Edison's Pearl Street power station lights up New York City.**

• **In Fort Wayne, Indiana, a baseball game is played at night—under electric lights!**

• **The University of Texas opens in Austin.**

• **The U.S. Supreme Court rules that the Civil Rights Act of 1875 is unconstitutional and that racial segregation (except for jury duty and interstate travel) is legal (see Book 7 of *A History of US*).**

courage: from financiers who believed in the idea and raised the money (some were corrupt and made scandalous profits); from workmen who risked their lives; and from John Roebling, who lost his life after his toes were crushed in a construction accident and gangrene set in.

His son, 32-year-old Washington Roebling, took over. He was a Civil War hero and an engineer. It was he who figured out that to build the gigantic stone towers, workers would have to go underwater, into special chambers filled with compressed air. Roebling went right along with the laborers; then he was stricken with an illness that afflicts deep-sea divers. It is called the *bends*, and it left him partially paralyzed. He was unable to move about and had to supervise from his bed, using binoculars to watch the workmen. His wife, Emily Roebling, went back and forth to the bridge with his daily instructions. When it was finally done, the bridge was called a "wonder of the world." Its towers were bigger than any other manmade structure except for the Egyptian pyramids. The bridge was so high that tall ships could glide easily beneath it. Horse-drawn carriages, railroad trains, pedestrians, and an electric tram each had a special roadway on the Brooklyn Bridge.

It was the first bridge lit by electricity. People came from all over just to see it. It towered over the buildings on both shores and linked the separate cities of Brooklyn and Manhattan into a united New York. Americans felt that if they could build a wondrous bridge like this one, they could do anything.

In 1883, New York City had its biggest party ever. It was even bigger than the one at the opening of the Erie Canal. Fireworks filled the sky. New York's governor, Grover Cleveland, said some words, but it was President Chester A. Arthur who cut the ribbon that officially opened the bridge. Then the president went to Washington Roebling's bedside to thank him on behalf of the nation.

The Brooklyn Bridge was not only useful, it was gorgeous. Like Louis Sullivan and Frank Lloyd Wright, the Roeblings had used steel, stone, and concrete artistically.

For New Yorkers, the wait for the ferry was over.

A few people wondered if the big bridge was really safe—but after circus man P. T. Barnum led a herd of elephants across it, there were no more doubters.

7 Lady L

The face that was destined to welcome a thousand ships; somehow she managed to look solemn and dignified even sitting on the ground with no neck.

The woman was big. *Colossal,* they called her. The biggest ever. Why, her nose was four feet long. She had almost sunk on the voyage from Europe. Now she was in New York harbor, with no place to go. Her home wasn't ready. Some said it would never be ready. She was patient. She would wait.

It was June 1885, and workmen prepared to unload 214 wooden cases. They held the body of the handsome woman. She was a gift from the people of France to the people of America.

America in the 19th century held out the possibility of hope, freedom, and prosperity to immigrants who came from all over the world.

Some Americans were prepared to turn their backs on the gift. A pedestal was needed to hold her, and that would cost money. So the wooden crates (36 of them just held nuts, bolts, and rivets) were stacked on an island while Americans fussed and worried about who was to pay for the pedestal.

She was, of course, Lady Liberty —the Statue of Liberty—and she was about to become a *metaphor* (MET-uh-for).

A metaphor? Yes. A metaphor is a symbol. Something that represents

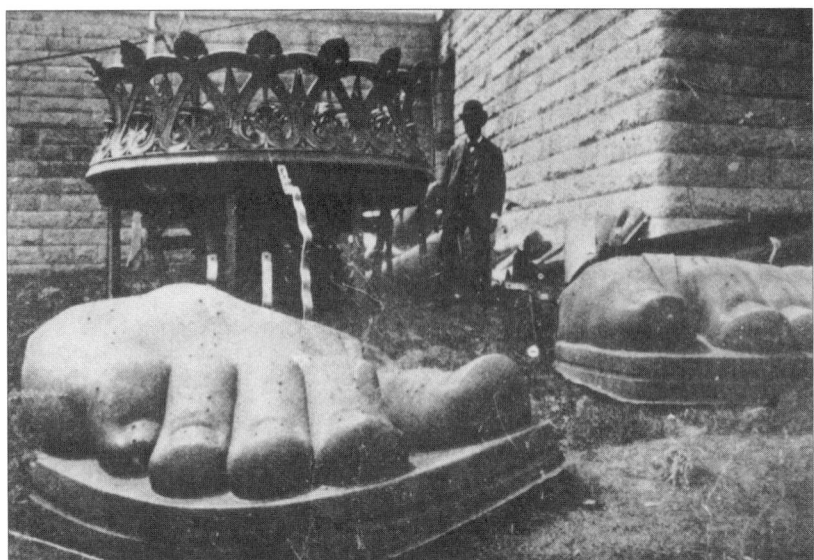

For a while the statue could be viewed from top (her crown) to toe (her feet) on the same level—the ground.

Laboulaye (luh-boo-LAY) believed that a republic was the best form of government. In a republic the citizens themselves hold power and (usually) elect officials to represent them.

Selflessness is the opposite of selfishness. *Awry* (uh-RYE) means wrong or twisted.

something other than itself. Usually, metaphors are words. But this metaphor was a copper-skinned giant of a lady. She would soon come to represent two things: the spirit of freedom and America's policy of welcome to people from around the world. That welcoming policy was called America's *golden door*. (Yes, the door is another metaphor.)

But who wants to talk of metaphors? They are dull figures of speech. This lady had a real figure. She was 151 feet from tip to toe, weighed 225 tons, had a waist 35 feet thick, and could hold 40 people in her head.

Where and how was she conceived? It happened in France, at a dinner party in 1865. Edouard de Laboulaye, the scholarly host at that dinner, was talking about liberty and America. He had a passion for liberty, and, although he had never been to the United States, he was filled with praise for the young nation. Laboulaye saw the recent Civil War, terrible as it had been, as a triumph for forces of liberty. That awful paradox—slavery in the land of the free—was no more. How could people in France join with Americans to celebrate their ideal of freedom, liberty, and justice for all?

The people at the dinner table talked about the long friendship of America and France. When they were children they had heard their parents and grandparents talk of the time when Benjamin Franklin and Thomas Jefferson lived in France. Laboulaye was proud of the role France played in America's revolution. He was proud of the French hero of the American Revolution, the Marquis de Lafayette.

Laboulaye, and the others, wanted to do something that would be a symbol of selflessness as well as of liberty. They decided to contribute much of their own money and time.

They would be doing it for France as well as for America. France had had a freedom revolution, but that rebellion had gone awry. Now France had an emperor: Louis Napoleon Bonaparte, who was the nephew of the first Napoleon, and a dictator. Laboulaye was a fierce republican. He didn't want to have anything to do with monarchy. He wanted to create a symbol of liberty for the whole world to admire.

Among the guests at his dinner party was a young sculptor named Frédéric Bartholdi. Bartholdi was swept away by the conversation. Laboulaye encouraged him to visit the United States. Bartholdi did. He went to Newport, Pittsburgh, Chicago, St. Louis, Denver, Salt Lake City, Sacramento, San Francisco, and Niagara Falls. "Everything is big here," he wrote to Laboulaye, "even the green peas."

When he sailed into New York, Bartholdi was struck by the beauty and openness of its harbor. He saw it as a symbol of the openness of America. In the harbor he found a small island—Bedloe's Island—and he knew almost at once that this was where he wanted his statue to stand. By now he had a great statue in his mind. On Bedloe's Island he could view rivers, ocean, and land—all at the same time. Bedloe's Island belonged to the government, Bartholdi wrote to Laboulaye. "It is land common to all the states."

Bartholdi decided he would build a statue bigger than the Colossus of Rhodes. That huge statue had been built to show Greece's power. Bartholdi's woman would be a symbol of liberty and welcome, not of power. "Trying to glorify the republic and liberty over there [in America]," he wrote to Laboulaye, "I shall await the day when they may be found here [in France] with us."

But those in France who believed in kings and military power certainly didn't want to help build a statue of liberty. It was the liberty-loving French people —ordinary people giving small amounts of money— who built the statue. So many of them gave money that soon those small amounts added up to a large amount.

A large amount was necessary. This was an expensive project. Consider the problem of building a huge statue that would stand unprotected in a harbor where it would be buffeted by winds, rain, snow, ice, lightning, perhaps even an earthquake. An engineering genius was needed.

France happened to have one. His name was Gustave Eiffel. (He would soon build a famous tower in Paris.) Eiffel designed a skeleton of iron bars. It was

Still in Paris, the hand and torch are finished by Bartholdi's workers. French businessmen used the statue's image in advertisements even before it was built, which also helped Bartholdi raise money.

The Glory That Was Greece

Bartholdi was not a small thinker. He studied the world's greatest monuments. The most renowned of all had been the Colossus of Rhodes. The Colossus, a statue of the sun god, Helios, was one of the seven wonders of the ancient world. It was fashioned of bronze and placed at the entrance to the great Greek harbor of Rhodes. According to legend, the Colossus stood astride two islands, and ships sailed between its legs. That wasn't true. Actually, the 100-foot-tall statue-god stood on a high promontory and looked down on the harbor. But the Colossus did hold a torch to light the way for vessels entering and leaving the harbor. To the ancient Greeks, Rhodes seemed the center of the universe. Then, in 224 B.C.E, a mighty earthquake toppled the giant. The power of Greece was tumbling, too. Rome became the center of the universe to those in the Mediterranean world.

The $250,000 that the statue cost was paid in by the masses of the French people…irrespective of class or condition.…It is not a gift from the millionaires of France to the millionaires of America, but a gift of the whole people of France to the whole people of America.

—*THE NEW YORK WORLD*

Between 1890 and 1910, some 20 million Europeans came to the United States. Many came for religious freedom. Others hoped to find economic opportunity. Some came for the political freedom that democracy promised. And some came for all those reasons. After 1945, large numbers of immigrants from Latin America and Asia arrived in America, attracted by the same American ideals and opportunities.

elastic enough to bend with the wind, and strong enough to support the giant lady and the people who would climb up inside her body. The lady's skin was to be made of delicate sheets of copper.

Bartholdi began work in his studio, but the great statue soon outgrew that home. Before long Liberty's head and arm could be seen towering over the rooftops of his Paris neighborhood. People were curious. Some 300,000 came to watch (and donate) as she was built.

But when Liberty was finished she needed a place to stand. No pedestal had been built on Bedloe's Island, and there was little money and little interest—or so it seemed—for the project in America.

What was needed was another kind of genius, a public-relations genius—one who could tell the story of Lady Liberty and make people listen. America just happened to have that kind of genius. His name was Joseph Pulitzer.

Pulitzer had come to the United States from Hungary when he was 17. He fought in the Civil War and then settled in St. Louis, Missouri, where

Bartholdi was not only an artist of amazing imagination, he was a great publicist. As he toured America, he sold the idea of his statue to everyone, from President Grant on down.

Joseph Pulitzer

"Let us not wait for the millionaires to give this money," wrote editor Pulitzer. "Let us hear from the people."

In 1907, Edward Corsi, an Italian who went on to become U.S. Immigration Commissioner, was watching from the deck of the *Florida*. "A steadily rising din filled the air. Mothers and fathers lifted up babies so that they too could see, off to the left, the Statue of Liberty....Looming shadowy through the mist, it brought silence to the decks....This symbol of America...inspired awe."

he became a reporter for a German-language newspaper. There isn't room in this book for the whole story of Joseph Pulitzer. There is too much to tell; he was a remarkable man.

He arrived in America speaking only German and Hungarian, but he soon learned English and bought an English-language paper, the *St. Louis Post*. Then he bought the *St. Louis Dispatch*, and merged them and created a great newspaper: the *St. Louis Post-Dispatch*. That was before he went to New York and before his greatest success, which came when he bought the *New York World*.

He turned the *World* into a reform-minded, crusading newspaper. He attacked the wealthy and powerful: he accused them of being greedy. He discovered that the wealthy citizens of New York would not give money to build a pedestal for the Statue of Liberty. Well, fie on them. He would show that ordinary people would support liberty. He announced

Joseph Pulitzer would be an interesting person to read or write about on your own.

47

A HISTORY OF US

The statue's head waiting on Bedloe's Island to be reunited with its body. The hand and torch sat in New York's Madison Square for four years in an effort to keep up public enthusiasm for the project and bring in money. Before long the hand blended into the city until most New Yorkers had forgotten what it was altogether. Then Joseph Pulitzer came along and took up the cause.

Below, the original manuscript of "The New Colossus."

Emma Lazarus

that anyone who donated money—any amount—would have his or her name printed in the paper.

A girl named Jane sent 50 cents. "I am only a poor sewing girl," she wrote. A 10-year-old sent "my pocket-piece—20 cents in silver." Twelve public schools in Trenton, New Jersey collected $105.07 from their students.

Pulitzer made the statue a patriotic cause. The children in one family wrote that they were now studying French. "We don't like it," they said, "but we love the good French people for giving us this beautiful Statue and we send $1."

All across America, people began to respond. Some gave things besides money. A group of artists and writers gave their work to be auctioned to raise money for the statue. Mark Twain was one of them. A 34-year-old woman named Emma Lazarus was another. Her first book of poems had been published when she was 16. The renowned poet and philosopher Ralph Waldo Emerson had encouraged her.

48

Lazarus had ancestors who came to the United States in the 17th century. They were Jews fleeing religious oppression in Europe. That was many generations before her time. Emma Lazarus led a sheltered, comfortable life; she knew nothing of hardship or trouble.

But, beginning in 1879, she began to hear about the *pogroms* that were sweeping Russia. Pogroms were mob attacks on Jews. Thousands of Jewish men, women, and children were killed; thousands more came to America.

All of that touched the young poet. It made her think about liberty and religious freedom. In America oppressed people have always been welcomed. So Emma Lazarus wrote a poem—a *sonnet*—about what the Statue of Liberty meant to her. She called the poem "The New Colossus." What she didn't know, and never learned during her short life (she died at age 38), was that her words would help give the statue a second meaning. It became not only a statue to celebrate liberty; it also became a symbol of America's policy of welcome—its golden door—its unusual decision to embrace people of all colors, races, and religions.

The last five lines of Lazarus's poem are engraved on the pedestal of the statue. Millions of immigrants, sailing into New York harbor, have been welcomed by those words. Today, when most immigrants come by air, Emma Lazarus's lines can also be seen in John F. Kennedy Airport. Here they are:

> *Not like the brazen giant of Greek fame,*
> *With conquering limbs astride from land to land;*
> *Here at our sea-washed, sunset gates shall stand*
> *A mighty woman with a torch, whose flame*
> *Is the imprisoned lightning, and her name*
> *Mother of Exiles. From her beacon-hand*
> *Glows world-wide welcome; her mild eyes command*
> *The air-bridged harbor that twin cities frame.*
> *"Keep, ancient lands, your storied pomp!" cries she*
> *With silent lips. "Give me your tired, your poor,*
> *Your huddled masses yearning to breathe free,*
> *The wretched refuse of your teeming shore.*
> *Send these, the homeless, tempest-tost to me.*
> *I lift my lamp beside the golden door!"*

Sarah Asher, who had come from Russia, said, "We had been sinking and we survived and now we were looking at the Statue of Liberty."

8 Presidents Again

"We are plain people," said Johnson's daughter of her family, "called here for a short time by a national calamity. I trust not too much will be expected of us."

NOTICE: this chapter may be BORING.

Now, there is something you can do about it.

You can skip it.

However, beware, some of the information in this chapter is IMPORTANT. So if you skip it, you do it at your own risk. It is a chapter about PRESIDENTS. Some of it is review and some of it is new, but if you don't know about the presidents you might fail a school test. Or, someday, you might be on a TV quiz program and get asked, "Who was the president who came after Chester Arthur?" If you don't read this chapter YOU MAY NEVER KNOW.

People will tell you that the presidents after Lincoln were weak and that Congress wasn't so strong, either. In fact, some people say that after the Civil War it was the new, rich businessmen who ran the country. Now there is something to that—but it's not the whole story. So when you read of the nine men who sat in the White House after the Civil War, keep an open mind. Some of these presidents were stronger than they may seem.

But not *Andrew Johnson (1865–1869)*. It probably would have been better for the country if

The dates given after the presidents' names do not indicate their births and deaths. What do they mean?

Grant was said to smoke 20 cigars a day. This may have had something to do with his eventual death from throat cancer.

someone else had been vice president when Lincoln was shot. You may already know that. In case you have forgotten the details, here is a review.

After the war, the United States needed a president who could tell leaders from both the North and the South to behave. But Johnson couldn't get Congress to respect or even listen to him. He wasn't a bad person, he was just stubborn.

You do have to admire him for a few things. A tailor-shop foreman taught him to read when he was 14 (he wasn't lucky enough to go to school). First he was a tailor; then he became a mayor, a U.S. representative, governor of Tennessee, and a U.S. senator. He was the only southern senator to support the Union when Lincoln was elected (that was in 1860).

After the Civil War, Johnson had a rare opportunity. The country needed to solve its racial problems now that slavery was abolished. Most people believe that President Lincoln would have attempted to solve them. President Johnson didn't even try. Partly because of that failed opportunity, racial hatreds continued to haunt the nation through the rest of the 19th and the 20th century.

Andrew Johnson let the same men who had seceded from the Union and started the Civil War take power in the South. He seemed to approve of Jim Crow, the spirit behind segregation and white people's hatred of blacks. He snubbed some of the moderate leaders in the North and South who wanted to compromise. He vetoed a civil-rights bill aimed at helping the freed slaves. (It was passed over his veto.) He opposed the 14th Amendment to the Constitution. (What did the 14th Amendment say?) Andrew Johnson was a backward-looking president at a time when the nation needed to go forward. He was so unpopular that some congressmen accused him of crimes and tried to throw him out of office. He was impeached, but saved from conviction by one vote.

The country needed a strong, capable president. Unfortunately, the next president was another failure.

He was the great Civil War general *Ulysses S. Grant (1869–1877)*. Being a general isn't at all like being president. In fact, the very things that made him a good general worked against him as president. Like Johnson, he was stubborn. That's not a bad trait for a general who has to keep fighting. It doesn't help a president who needs to be flexible enough to compromise.

There was something else that worked against Grant. He was too nice

During Grant's administrations, Reconstruction in the South was enforced by federal troops. In 1875 the Conservatives—white Democrats—in the Louisiana state legislature tried to seize power from the Republicans. The Conservative speaker snatched the gavel from the black Republican clerk and pushed him off the platform. Troops restored order, but two years later Rutherford Hayes abolished martial law—and with it any hope of an integrated South.

Rutherford and Lucy Hayes. *Puck*, a humor magazine, wrote of her: "How wine her tender spirit riles, while water wreathes her face in smiles."

Where is the campus of the electoral college? That's a joke: there isn't one. Can you find out why?

and trusting. He trusted men who weren't trustworthy; they got rich stealing from the government. There was much corruption and dishonesty when Grant was president, and he didn't realize it until too late.

During the Johnson and Grant presidencies, Congress sent troops south to see that elections were open to everyone. Male former slaves were able to vote. Black men were elected to state office and to Congress.

Some white southern leaders didn't like that. So when the next presidential election came along they decided to take charge. They wanted to take the vote away from black men, and they began to do it. President *Rutherford B. Hayes (1877–1881)* didn't do anything to stop them.

Hayes's election was one of the closest in our history. More people voted for his opponent than for him. He won in the electoral college by one vote, and that made him president. His supporters made a deal to pull the government troops out of the South in return for that vote. That was the end of congressional Reconstruction, and of most attempts to be fair to black people in the South.

Actually, if it hadn't been for that, historians would look kindly on Hayes. He worked hard at being president; he ended the corruption of the Grant years; he was an honest man.

Hayes's wife was a supporter of the growing *temperance* movement. Temperance supporters wanted to prohibit (ban) the drinking of alcohol. So did Lucy Hayes. She was known as Lemonade Lucy because she served only lemonade at White House parties. And that wasn't a bad idea. This was a time of extremes, when some people drank too much. President and Mrs. Hayes set a good example.

James A. Garfield (1881) was our 20th president. He was born in a log cabin in Ohio. As a boy he had a job driving a horse that pulled boats along the Erie Canal. Garfield got a fine education at Williams College, became a school principal, and then a congressman. He might have been a good president, but a man with mental problems shot and killed President Garfield soon after he was elected.

Chester A. Arthur took over as 21st president *(1881–1885)*. "Gentleman" Arthur, as he was known, was over six feet tall and good-looking. He wore stylish clothes and had whiskers that bushed down the side of his face, though his chin was shaved. He was a reformer: he wanted to make the government as efficient as possible. He did that by making the Civil Service Commission powerful. Civil-service jobs are government jobs. Politicians had been giving government jobs to their friends, usually as payoffs for favors. That was a terrible practice. It meant that the jobs often went to the wrong people. The Civil Service Commission made people take examinations for government jobs. Arthur's reforms angered some congressmen, and he was not nominated for a second term.

Grover Cleveland, the next president, was a big man with a neck like a bull and the body of a wrestler. He had common sense, courage, and integrity. When he was running for office some opponents told about mistakes he had made in the past. His advisers wanted to pretend they hadn't happened. Cleveland wired his campaign manager: WHATEVER YOU DO, TELL THE TRUTH.

Cleveland was 49 and a bachelor when he was elected. He soon married young Frances Folsom. When they started having children—they had five in all—they really livened up the White House. No president before had ever had a baby while in office.

Cleveland was another reformer. The reforms he had in mind had to do with money and organization and honesty. He didn't concern himself with social justice or fairness. He didn't understand the new problems faced by industrial workers or the old problems of racial injustice.

During Cleveland's presidency, in the southwest, the Apache chief Geronimo surrendered to army forces. That was the end of the Indians'

The campaign banner for the 1880 Republican presidential team of James Garfield and Chester Arthur—Civil War veterans who defeated another veteran, Winfield Hancock.

Higgledy-piggledy,
Benjamin Harrison,
Twenty-third
*   President,*
Was, and, as such,

Served between
*   Clevelands, and*
Save for this trivial
Idiosyncrasy,
Didn't do much.
        —JOHN HOLLANDER,
        "HISTORICAL REFLECTIONS"

Before he married, Grover Cleveland was forced to steer between the Scylla of friends who wanted jobs—and the Charybdis of matrons hoping to become his mother-in-law. (You'll find Scylla and Charybdis in Homer's *Odyssey*.)

Cleveland and Frances Folsom were married in the Blue Room of the White House. They honeymooned in Maryland, where newspaper reporters trained spyglasses on their rooms and bribed servants to show them what the presidential couple were having for breakfast.

freedom to live as they wished. At the time, hardly anyone—except the Native Americans—seemed to care.

When Cleveland ran for a second term he lost the election. The man who beat him was *Benjamin Harrison (1889–1893)*. Harrison was born in Ohio, but his family had roots in Virginia and Indiana. His father was a member of Congress; his grandfather, "Old Tippecanoe," was the nation's ninth president; his great-grandfather signed the Declaration of Independence.

During Harrison's administration the Sherman Antitrust Act was passed. It outlawed the monopolies that suppressed competition. Six new states were admitted to the Union while he was president. (See if you can find out which ones.)

Harrison had a problem that today's presidents wish they had. There was too much money in the Treasury! At least some economists thought so. Congress and Harrison's appointees decided to go on a spending spree. Harrison just let it happen. A lot of money went to modernize the navy. But when Harrison left office the country was in trouble financially.

The next president was a man you have met before: *Grover Cleveland*. He was our 22nd *(1885–1889)* and 24th president *(1893–1897)*. Cleveland came into office at the start of a big, five-year-long depression, one of the nation's worst ever (see Chapter 12). The stock market went way down, lots of people lost their jobs, and the times were awful for many Americans. Cleveland and his government didn't do much to reverse the depression, but governments then weren't expected to do that.

Benjamin Harrison with his daughter Mary and grandchildren. Harrison's wife died while he was in office; Mary took over the duties of first lady for the rest of his term.

54

Grover Cleveland always seemed to be puffing on a cigar. That probably caused the sore he discovered in the roof of his mouth. The sore was cancerous. It needed to be operated on at once. President Cleveland was afraid that if people knew he was dangerously ill it might make the stock-market panic even worse. He left Washington. Everyone thought he was going to Cape Cod for a vacation. Secretly, he went to New York. A yacht was waiting in the East River. Inside, in a specially equipped operating room, surgeons removed two teeth and the cancer.

"My God, Olney, they nearly killed me!" said Cleveland, to his attorney general, Richard Olney. Actually, the doctors saved his life. The president was soon back at work. Almost no one knew about that operation. Could that kind of secret be kept today? Should it be?

The next president, *William McKinley (1897–1901)*, was chief executive at the turn of the century. He was the first president since Andrew Johnson without a beard or mustache. McKinley had volunteered to fight during the Civil War; that helped make him popular. (Many wealthy men paid a substitute to fight for them.)

He was a lawyer, and smart, with good manners and a kindly way. He liked people and they liked him.

The United States fought a war with Spain while McKinley was president. Spain's time as a world power was ending; the United States' time was beginning. After the war—which lasted for 100 days—the United States controlled the Philippine Islands, Guam, the Samoan Islands, and Puerto Rico. During the war we annexed Hawaii. There were native leaders in each of those places who would have preferred independence to U.S. control (see Chapter 28 for details).

McKinley was elected to a second term. Six months after the election he was at a world's fair in Buffalo, New York, shaking hands with citizens who wanted to meet their president. A young man stepped up; one of his hands was wrapped in what looked like a bandage. No one realized it, but the man was an anarchist. He believed all governments were bad. Besides that, he may have been insane. The anarchist pressed the "bandage" against the president's stomach. Inside was a revolver. He fired twice.

McKinley fell to the floor. The assassin was caught and beaten. "Let no man hurt him," cried McKinley. Eight days later the president was dead.

"I told William McKinley it was a mistake to nominate that wild man," said McKinley's friend Mark Hanna when he heard the news. The "wild man" he was talking about was Vice President *Theodore Roosevelt*.

Geronimo

After the massacre of the Sioux by U.S. cavalry at Wounded Knee in 1890, the body of one of their leaders, Big Foot, lay frozen in the snow. Geronimo, who led guerrilla bands of Chiricahua Apache on raids and battles against the U.S. Army for over 30 years, finally surrendered in 1886. Last of the leaders in the Indian wars, he died in 1909, in his eighties.

McKinley falls, shot by Leon Czolgosz of Cleveland, Ohio, whose gun was hidden by a bandage. Later, Czolgosz said that the country's government needed changing and he wanted to get it started.

When Roosevelt took office, the time of weak presidents was over. Theodore Roosevelt acted as if he had swallowed a tornado. He had incredible energy. He also had a sense of fun. The American people had a good time with Roosevelt as president.

Did this chapter bore you? Well, you've just about finished it. Now all you have to do is find a way to remember the names of those nine presidents between Abraham Lincoln and Theodore Roosevelt. How are you going to do it?

One idea is to memorize a sentence that will use the first letters of each of their names. You can make up your own or use my sentence. Here it is: Joe Got His Gun And Chased His Crazy Mule.

Yes, that is a dumb sentence, but you know what it means: Johnson, Grant, Hayes, Garfield, Arthur, Cleveland, Harrison, Cleveland, McKinley.

Presidential Pets

Grover Cleveland had a pet mockingbird, several canaries, and a Japanese poodle. Benjamin Harrison, with his pointed beard and small eyes, looked a lot like a goat. He gave his grandchildren a real goat; its name was Old Whiskers. The goat was hitched to a wagon and often pulled the three grandchildren across the White House lawn. One day the goat ran away, pulling the kids and the wagon. The president—holding his top hat and cane—went chasing after it. Theodore Roosevelt was a real animal lover. Among the pets that he and his six children brought to the White House were: a small bear named Jonathan Edwards, a guinea pig named Father O'Grady, a badger named Joshua, a blue macaw named Eli Yale, a pig named Maude, a hen named Baron Spreckle, and a rabbit named (of course!) Peter. William Howard Taft

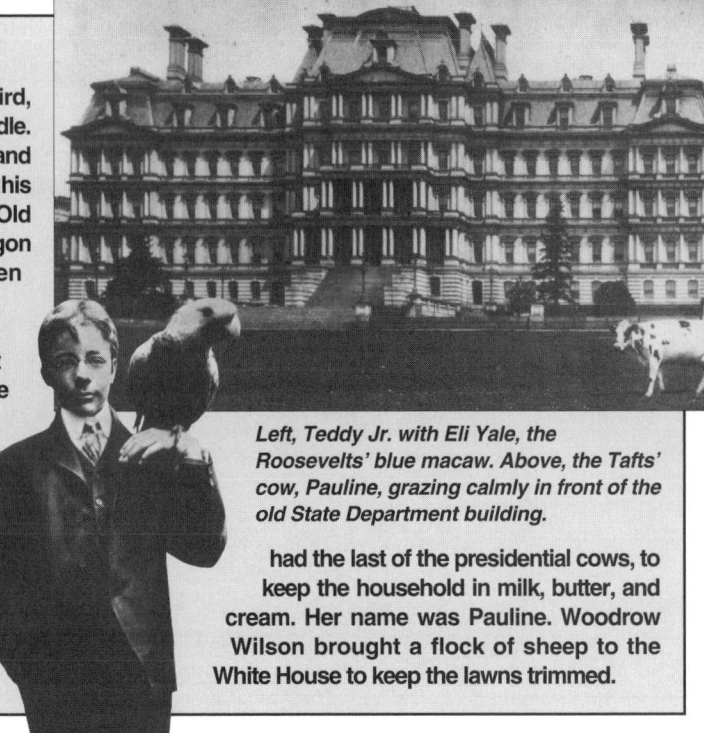

Left, Teddy Jr. with Eli Yale, the Roosevelts' blue macaw. Above, the Tafts' cow, Pauline, grazing calmly in front of the old State Department building.

had the last of the presidential cows, to keep the household in milk, butter, and cream. Her name was Pauline. Woodrow Wilson brought a flock of sheep to the White House to keep the lawns trimmed.

9 The People's Party

Tom Watson got Congress to pass the first ever resolution to have rural mail delivered free. Until then, farmers paid the mailman themselves.

The place is Georgia; the time, 1892. A small, redheaded man—his name is Tom Watson—is standing on a wooden platform under tall pines. A crowd of men tries to hear what Watson has to say—he is a fine orator—but they are having a hard time of it. Watson, a congressman, is running for reelection. He is a member of a new political party, the People's Party, also called the

Benjamin Harrison is president in 1892.

This cartoon—which was supposed to show what the Supreme Court would look like if the Populists ran it—sneered at them as a bunch of old fogeys and hayseeds.

The U.S. as a huge cow fed with the produce of hardworking western farmers while Wall Street types siphon the results into bank vaults and high tariffs.

White Southerners will not vote for Republicans. The Republican Party is the party of Thaddeus Stevens and the hated Radicals who sent northern soldiers south. (See Book 7 of *A History of US*.) Southerners call it a "Yankee" party.

When a man picked a ballot, everyone knew if it was a Democratic ballot, a Republican ballot, or another party's. Some employers fired workers who voted the wrong way. Bribery was common.

Populist Party. The Democrats have sent a brass band to his rally. They are playing loudly —very loudly. They are doing it on purpose.

There is something unusual about this southern crowd. It is both black and white. The people are mostly poor whites and poor blacks. Watson believes they have something in common: their poverty. If they stand together perhaps they can do something about it. "You are kept apart that you may be separately fleeced," he tells them.

His listeners know that on election day, they will be under much pressure to vote for Democratic candidates. Voting is not private. The Democrats have become the only party with power in the South. They have been known to stuff ballot boxes with false votes to ensure their victories. They have paid voters for their votes. Those who attempt to vote for any other party risk losing their jobs, or worse. Watson wants to change things. The People's Party is campaigning for secret ballots.

Watson and his Populists want to change other things, too. They see themselves as the party of the common man. They believe the government is working for the rich and powerful and taking advantage of the poor and weak. They believe that the people—ordinary people—must take control of the government. They are considered radicals. They want to change the system.

A Democrat on horseback rides into Watson's Populist crowd. He is inviting everyone to a free dinner. "These men are not going to be enticed away from free, fair discussion of great public questions by any amount of barbecued beef," shouts Watson. No one moves.

Tom Watson is no common man. He is a skilled lawyer, and the largest landowner in all of Georgia. But he can identify with people in need. He has seen trouble.

Tom's grandfather—whose name was also Thomas Watson—was a planter, a slave owner, and a man who was always true to his word. When the Civil War came, Grandfather Watson watched his three sons march off to battle. One son died; one became an invalid; the third, Tom's father John, was wounded. The Watson farm was ruined. Old Tom had a stroke and lost his mind. In Georgia, it was not an unusual story.

Maybe John Watson wanted to show that things in the South hadn't changed; maybe he was crazy, because he set to work and built a great white-columned southern mansion in front of his father's raw-timbered house. But he didn't have the money to pay for the house, so it had to be sold. His family—including his son Tom—moved to a small farm and lived in poverty. John drank.

Tom Watson was made of stronger fiber. He decided to make something of himself, and did. He was elected to Congress, and he built a home finer than any Watson before him. But he, too, did unexplainable things and ended his life with too much whiskey in his brain.

That was when he was old, frustrated, and angry. By then he had accomplished more than he realized. He helped guide a third party that flashed

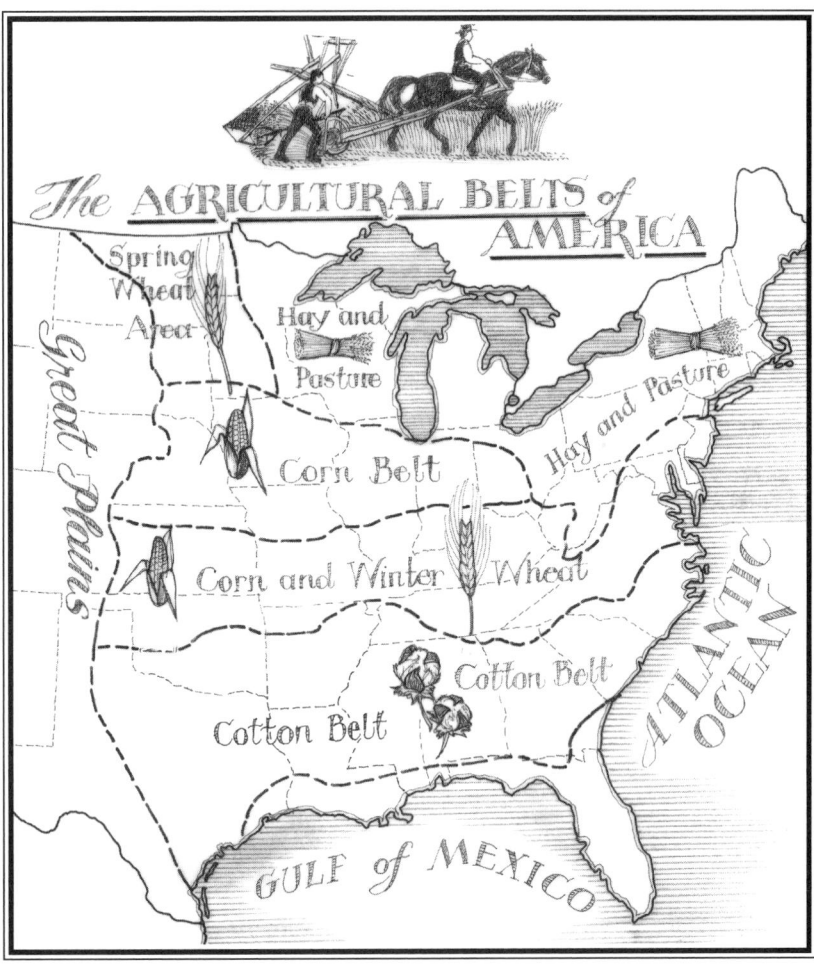

across the nation like a brilliant comet. That party—the People's Party—elected five senators, ten representatives, and three governors. It championed ideas that were laughed at—at first—but later became law. And though the Populists faded away, their ideas keep reappearing, in cycles, as most comets do.

Those reformers spoke for ordinary Americans who didn't want to be left out of the good times that were being enjoyed by others. They demanded rights. Some people called them "communists"; some people called them "hayseeds." But they weren't either thing. They were just people who wanted to take part in the governing process; they wanted their ideas heard. And it wasn't long before there were secret ballots and woman's suffrage and many of the other things the Populists supported. They demanded that government be strong and

We believe that the powers of government should be expanded… to the end that oppression, injustice, and poverty shall eventually cease in the land.
—POPULIST PARTY PLATFORM

*And there came a dark day on us when the interest wasn't paid,
And there came a sharp foreclosure, and I kind o' lost my hold,
And grew weary and discouraged and the farm was cheaply sold.
The children left and scattered, when they hardly yet were grown....*

*My wife she pined and perished, an' I found myself alone,
What she died of was a mystery, and the doctors never knew;
But I know she died of mortgage—just as well as I wanted to.*
—WILL CARLTON, FARMER, IN *ALLIANCE HERALD*, STAFFORD, KANSAS

active and help people—which was, and still is, a controversial path, but one the American government soon took.

What were some of their other ideas? The Populists wanted a graduated income tax. That means they wanted people to be taxed according to how much money they made. Wealthy people would pay more than poor people. They wanted senators directly elected by citizens—instead of by state legislatures, as the Constitution then directed. They wanted the government to lend money to farmers. They wanted the government to protect the consumer from unsafe goods and unfair practices.

All of those, and some other Populist ideas, would be adopted by the other political parties and eventually become law. "The land," said a Populist declaration, "including all the natural resources of wealth, is the heritage of all the people and should not be monopolized for speculative purposes." That was a conservation idea before most people thought about conserving land and resources.

But let's get back to Tom Watson. Remember, he is standing on a wooden platform talking to farmers; they are angry. Farm prices are low. In 1865, cotton sold for a dollar a pound. It is 1892 and cotton is 7 cents a pound. How would you like to be a farmer? It costs more than 7 cents to grow a pound of cotton! In the Midwest, wheat prices have tumbled from $2.50 a bushel in the 1860s to 50 cents a bushel in the 1890s. Farmers can't pay their bills.

When the farmers read the newspapers they learn how good life is for America's millionaires. Some people are calling this time "the gay Nineties." William Vanderbilt has just thrown a big party for his friends in ritzy Newport, Rhode Island. They sat on red damask chairs and dug with silver shovels in a play sandbox filled with rubies and diamonds. The society columns are full of that story. It is enough to make anyone angry. The farmers can't understand what is happening. They are working hard and helping to feed and clothe the world. Yet while some people are getting very rich, they are losing their farms.

The Populist leaders tell the farmers that there is a conspiracy. They say the eastern bankers, the railroad magnates, and the grain-elevator owners are plotting against them. They are keeping the

In the 1890s, as farmers' economic problems got worse, Populist agitators like Mary Lease went all over the western states making speeches. "You have to raise less corn and more hell," she told the farmers.

farmers poor so they can get richer.

That isn't really true. No one is plotting against the farmers on purpose. The big-money powers care only about themselves. They are working *for* their own interests—not *against* the farmers'. But their interests hurt the farmers. And their money gives them political power. The farmers have little money and little political power. Populism has arisen out of frustration.

Before the Civil War, life seemed simpler. Most people, then, were farmers who grew their own food, spun their own yarn, chopped their own timber, and had to buy little outside. Now farming has changed. Railroads and new equipment—and millions of acres of new farmland in the Great Plains—have led farmers toward larger farms and single-crop production. Farmers are growing big crops—of wheat, or cotton, or corn. Those crops are not just for themselves and their neighbors: the

It was a religious revival, a crusade...of politics in which a tongue of flame sat upon every man, and each spake as the spirit gave him utterance....The farmers, the country merchants, the cattle-herders, they of the long chin-whiskers, and they of the broad-brimmed hats and heavy boots, had also heard the gospel of Populism....Women with skins tanned to parchment by the hot winds, with bony hands of toil and clad in faded calico, could talk in meeting, and could talk straight to the point.

—ELIZABETH S. BARR, "THE POPULIST UPRISING," IN *A STANDARD HISTORY OF KANSAS AND KANSANS.*

Fat-cat industrialists stuff themselves on profits from high tariffs, while the poor farmer is excluded from the good life.

A Georgia woman scratches out a living from a hilly cornfield.

Populism brought together black farmers as well as white. But it did not have a deep impact in the South, and blacks remained second-class citizens.

American farmer is now competing in the world market.

That farmer is amazingly productive. But the more grain he produces, the more he floods the market. Because he farms so well, he is helping to drive prices down.

There is more to it than that. The farmer is no longer independent. In the South after the Civil War, everything seems changed. Many of the large plantations have been broken up. For the old aristocrats, losing their slaves has meant losing their wealth. A new merchant class wields power. Farmers must buy their goods and farm supplies from the merchants. When they are overcharged, they can do nothing about it. They are often in debt to the merchants. They must grow what the merchants wish. Many of the merchants are also bankers. Soon they own much of the farmland. Proud former planters have become tenants.

You can't be a modern farmer without modern equipment, especially on the big farms of the Middle West and Far West. Combines are needed to cut, thresh, and stack wheat. They are much faster and more efficient than human labor. To buy the new equipment, farmers must borrow from the banks. That puts them in debt. In order to pay the debt on farm equipment, to pay the mortgages on their property, and to pay railroad fees for shipping their crops, the farmers need cash. They need to sell their crops at a profit. They aren't doing that. They feel trapped.

In Kansas, 11,122 farmers lose their farms to the banks between 1889 and 1893.

Even those who hang on are angry. After all, they want to enjoy all the new things—bicycles, electricity, and so on—that other Americans are enjoying. They don't have enough money to do so.

If there were more money in circulation it would help, they believe. And they are right. The Populist platform includes a monetary plan. Many bankers make fun of it. They don't think these farmers are smart enough to know anything about money.

The bankers are wrong. Farmers come by the thousands to farm meetings where they sleep in their wagons, or under the stars, share barbecues, and listen to speakers who talk of economic and national problems. The farmers listen, argue, and learn. Populism is a democratic movement, and an impressive one.

It would be easier for the farmers to pay the interest on their loans if more dollars were circulating and prices were higher. The Populists know how money can be used to help or hurt groups of people. If you read the next chapter, you will, too.

10 Making Money

The government often encouraged industry with its policies. When industries were struggling "infants," that was helpful. But sometimes these "babies" went on getting special breaks when they were quite big enough to look after themselves.

Put on your thinking cap. You will need it. This is a complicated chapter.

Let's start with a checkbook. Write a check for $100. Now, can you get it cashed? You can if you have $100 in the bank. A check is just a promise to pay money that you already have.

Dollars (paper money) printed by the government are like that check. They are our government's promise that it has something of equal value. That something used to be gold.

In the 19th century, anyone in the United States could exchange paper dollars for gold coins. (Most people didn't bother to do that because gold is heavy and paper is convenient.) A country that backed its money with gold (that's called a *gold standard*) usually had a sound currency. The price of gold had to be fixed for this to work. The government said how many dollars it cost to buy an ounce of gold and stuck to that. Now other nations would accept its currency instead of lumps of gold or other real goods because they knew that they would be able to use the currency to buy things. No one wants money from a nation that will not guarantee its currency.

But a country on the gold standard can't print a lot of money. Gold is scarce, and it is *finite*—only a certain amount exists in the world, so there is only a limited amount to go around. If you were on the gold standard, you couldn't print more money than you had gold to back it with in your bank vaults.

In an anti-greenback cartoon, the paper greenback is only a shadow of *specie*, the "real" money backed by metal.

Currency is a country's actual money in circulation —its paper bills and coins. The first paper money is said to have been printed in China.

Finite (FY-nite) means *limited*.

In this 1878 anti-silver cartoon, Uncle Sam puts his foot in the trap when Congress votes to back U.S. government bonds with silver.

During the Civil War, Abraham Lincoln needed money and he needed it quickly. There wasn't enough gold. He issued a special kind of money, called *greenbacks*. There was no gold to back them. The government gave its promise to pay the value of the greenbacks. Because people had faith in the government—and the value of its land and people— they accepted the greenbacks.

But that extra money in circulation created *inflation*. Inflation means rising prices. The more money people have, the more they can pay for goods and services. The people selling the goods put their prices up. Then it takes more money to buy something than it did before. So the more dollars there are in circulation, the less each dollar is worth.

After the war, Lincoln's greenbacks were gradually taken out of circulation. In 1873 the nation returned to the gold standard. There was less money around. That caused *deflation*. That was natural too. There wasn't much money to pay for things, so people couldn't sell them. There were goods but no *demand* for them. Prices dropped. When there's no demand, prices drop until goods are cheap enough for people to start buying them again. (*Depressions* happen when many people are out of work, and so broke that they don't buy things no matter how low prices go.)

Falling prices meant less income for people like farmers, who needed to get a fair price for their produce. So farmers were unhappy. They wanted more money in circulation. But there wasn't enough gold to let the government print more bills. The farmers thought the government should use silver to back its currency—in addition to gold. Naturally, silver miners also wanted the government to buy silver to back dollars. They wanted a *silver standard*.

In 1878, Congress listened to the farmers and miners. It voted to buy silver to back the nation's currency. People now had a choice: paper dollars, gold, or silver coins. At the same time, the Treasury—where the government keeps its money—had a *surplus*: gold and silver piled up, because the government had more money coming in (from tariffs and taxes) than it was spending. Since it now had a lot of gold and silver, the government could print more money. Prices went up—including the price of farm produce. It was a time of prosperity and excellent harvests; many farmers associated good times with the new silver coins (though there was really a lot more to it than that).

The economic health of a nation depends on many, many different

ILLION - DOLLARISM > HOLE

Benjamin Harrison (whom cartoonists always showed dwarfed under his famous great-grandfather's hat) unloads the national surplus.

things, and some things were going on in this nation's capital that would prove unhealthy for the United States economy.

For instance, during Cleveland's first presidency the nation began building a new navy of steel ships. The government paid extra-high prices for Andrew Carnegie's steel. That helped Carnegie, but it didn't help the economy. Those high prices were paid by the American people.

The cost of borrowing money is called *interest*. If you borrow $100 and pay the lender $10 a year for lending you the money, your annual *rate of interest* is 10 percent. If you pay $5 a year, the annual interest rate is 5 percent.

Then, when Benjamin Harrison was president, Congress went on a spending spree. It was called "the billion-dollar congress." It gave away most of the surplus in the form of pensions to Civil War veterans. It also raised tariffs (taxes on imported goods) so high that the government's income from those taxes almost disappeared—people weren't willing to buy expensive foreign goods. That was the end of the surplus.

Soon money was scarce again and there was deflation. Farmers were earning less money because prices were dropping. That really hurt the farmers who had borrowed money for farm equipment. Many lost their farms.

Because money was in short supply, people who had money to lend could charge a lot of interest to those who wanted to borrow it—even though the price of other goods was falling.

In a Frankenstein-style anti-greenback comic strip, "The great experimental money doctor succeeds in making a rag baby; 'Bless its dear little heart, it is as good as Gold!' But the little pet grows rapidly, and becomes too heavy to carry; the creature arises and pursues its parent, and—The End."

65

Benjamin Harrison's pensions commissioner gives the billion-dollar surplus away to Civil War veterans—a lot of whom were not real veterans.

Deflation is hard on people who have borrowed money. They have less income but they still have to pay back loans at interest rates based on the old, higher prices.

The Populist leaders understood this. Since they were speaking for *debtor classes* (people who have borrowed), they wanted more money in circulation. They supported the *bimetal* (silver and gold) standard. Then the Populists came up with a radical suggestion. They wanted money to be backed by crops that would be put in government storage. It would be money based on real production—not gold or silver.

The Populists went even further. They felt the money supply should be controlled, not as it was in the 1890s—by private financiers like J. P. Morgan—but by an elected board. They were asking for a new monetary system that would create money "in the name of the whole people." Respectable thinkers called the Populists idealists. Their central concept—a democratic money system—was a huge break with tradition. The financiers hated the idea. Most Americans didn't understand it.

In the 20th century some of those Populist notions became law. A Federal Reserve System came into being, with a board (independent of political parties) that controls the supply of money. It had many elements of the plan the Populists proposed.

Before there was money there was *barter*, which means trading one thing for another. Do you remember Jack (of beanstalk fame)? It wasn't easy bartering a cow. Today, cash money is used less often than checks and credit cards.

What was Congress to do about the enormous Treasury surplus problem?

11 Hard Times

While their parents worked, some children stayed home and took care of younger brothers or sisters instead of going to school.

When Grover Cleveland stepped into the presidency for the second time, he walked into a beehive. It was 1893, and he got stung by a depression.

Remember, in those days, anytime you wanted to exchange your paper money for gold or silver, you could. But the supply of gold in the Treasury was way, way down. When Americans realized that, it created a money panic. People began turning in paper money for gold. Everyone preferred gold to silver. The gold reserve was being emptied.

Then the stock market went zooming down. (So many people were selling the shares they owned in companies that the companies quickly lost value.)

Farmers had been in trouble for at least five years, what with droughts, a grasshopper plague, and falling prices. Now the rest of the nation began hurting. Badly.

When farmers stopped buying goods, because they had no money, manufacturers began to suffer. Soon the banks were in trouble, too. The banks took farms from farmers who couldn't

Poor immigrants in New York City who had no families sometimes slept in "five-cents-a-spot" lodgings—as many as 12 people jammed into a room 13 feet square.

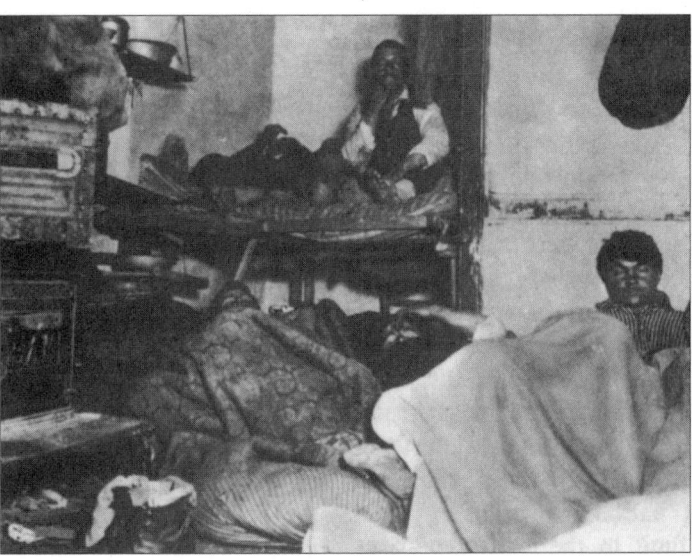

Child workers were cheaper than adults. In 1900, 14,000 children worked in Pennsylvania's coalmines. Many were under 14, the legal limit, but no one made them prove their age.

Say MOR-gidge

When a farmer borrows money from a bank to buy a farm (or when anyone borrows money to buy a house or piece of land), the money he borrows—his debt—is called a *mortgage*. It is a form of loan. (Many farmers who do own their farms completely—*outright*—may take out mortgages on them anyway, in order to buy expensive equipment or seeds for next season's planting.) The farmer has to pay back the bank for the loan in *installments*, a little at a time. If the farmer can't make his mortgage payments—if he *defaults*—the bank *forecloses*: it takes the farm instead of the payments. Now the bank has to sell the farm to someone else to make back the money it lent to the first farmer.

pay their mortgages; then they tried to sell the farms. Someone had to pay back the money that the banks had lent. But no one was buying farms. That put the banks in trouble.

In the first nine months of 1893, 172 state banks, 177 private banks, and 47 savings-and-loan associations closed. By the end of the year the total was 500 banks. More than 15,000 businesses failed. And that was just the beginning. Railroad earnings were way down, and then the unthinkable happened: railroads began closing. The Union Pacific, and the Atchison, Topeka and Santa Fe were two of the 156 railroads that folded.

Mines were shut down, steamers stayed in port, factories closed their doors, and companies went bankrupt.

Many of the people who had worked in those banks, railroads, and factories were out of work, which made the depression more frightening.

Farmers could usually eat, but unemployed city workers were desperate. Unemployment in 1894 is said to have been higher, in relation to the country's population, than at any time in our history. It was worse in some areas than others. The manufacturing states of Pennsylvania, New York, and Michigan were hit hard. One out of four people in Pennsylvania was reported out of work. In Michigan the figure was

43.6 percent. Nationally, one out of every five workers was said to be idle. In Chicago, 100,000 men were sleeping on the streets.

Even those who had jobs faced cuts in pay and work.

What was going on in America? Was this the land of promise?

A journalist described life in the Appanoose County mining camp near Cincinnati:

> The 500 mine families in this locality…have little to eat…and their clothing…is in utter tatters. All have a sickly appearance. Many have been confined to bed with illness.

"Carpenters, brick masons, stone workers, plasterers, and various other crafts depending upon finding work in house construction are experiencing…five or six months of inactivity," reported the popular magazine *Review of Reviews*.

Congress passed a high tariff law (remember, a *tariff* is a tax on goods that are imported from abroad). That high tariff helped the business trusts by keeping foreign competitors out of the country. But it made goods expensive for most people. In addition, foreign countries, like England and France, weren't going to sit back and accept the tariff. They got even by not buying American wheat and corn. That, of course, hurt the American farmer again. First farmers had to pay high prices for home-produced goods that didn't have to compete with outside imports. Then they couldn't find markets to sell their crops in because foreign countries were mad at them. And the high tariff stopped most imports from abroad, so the government got less income from taxes on foreign goods, just when the nation needed more money.

The business trusts weren't the only ones who wanted high tariffs. Most industrial workers believed that tariffs protected their jobs by making foreign goods more expensive than American-made goods. Without foreign competition, things made here were more likely to sell.

But the farmers were mostly Populists, and they were enraged by the high tariffs and high prices. The bankers and industrialists thought the tariff was needed to protect American industry and jobs. It wasn't easy for anyone to know who was right.

An anti-tariff cartoon has Uncle Sam left behind by the ships of other countries. Without foreign trade, the U.S. was stranded in a goose pond.

I believe in general that that government is best which governs least, and that interference with trade or manufactures is very undesirable. Yet I recognize the fact that evils may and do exist which require correction by the force of law.

—FRANCIS A. WALKER, PRESIDENT OF THE MASSACHUSETTS INSTITUTE OF TECHNOLOGY, AT A SENATE COMMITTEE IN 1883.

12 Gold and Silver

To **strike** means to stop working in order to force an employer to pay higher wages or to meet other demands. If all the employees of a company go on strike at the same time, it may force the company to shut down, or find other workers (*scabs*), or pay the higher wages.

The title of this 1878 illustration in the *Daily Graphic* was "The Financial Balance and How to Keep It." But should a nation's economy move like a dancer on a tightrope?

By the 1890s, Pullman stockholders were receiving an 8 percent annual dividend. Land that Pullman had paid $800,000 for in 1880 was now worth $5 million. However, the return on his investment on that land, mostly rents from workers, only brought Pullman 4.5 percent a year. (He was miffed over that, though his rents were 25 percent higher than comparable ones in Chicago.) In 1893 he slashed wages 25 percent, and the company's dividends went up. (Rents stayed the same.) In the model town, children were without shoes, homes without heat.

Eighteen ninety-three was an awful year; 1894 was worse. Some 1,400 strikes were called in 1894. Workers were protesting low wages and poor working conditions. Many of them lost their jobs when they went on strike. You know they had to be hurting to risk that.

In 1894 an army of unemployed men marched peacefully to Washington. They wanted the government to help them. President Cleveland refused to see them. Crowds cheered the marching men; the police arrested their leaders.

President Cleveland didn't believe it his job to do anything about the unemployed. Most leaders agreed with him. Employment and working conditions were thought to be the responsibility of business.

That summer, the highly profitable Pullman Company cut workers' wages for the fifth time. Pullman made railroad sleeping cars in a town near Chicago. When the company cut wages, it didn't cut the fees it charged workers for rent, heat, and lights, or to use the company church. The workers were angry; they went on strike. Soon the strike spread to 50,000 workers, throughout the railroad industry. The governor of Illinois said he could handle the situation, but Grover Cleveland's attorney general didn't agree. (The attorney general had been

George M. Pullman

a railroad lawyer.) He insisted that the government take action against the workers and their union. Federal troops were sent to Illinois, which led to violence, deaths, and arrests.

The president did feel that it was his responsibility to keep government money sound. And it did not seem to be sound. Businesses and banks were failing everywhere, and there was a run on gold as people tried to make sure their money was in the safest currency—gold. The government's gold reserves were disappearing. President Cleveland thought he knew exactly what had caused the country's money problems. He thought it was an act of Congress: the Silver Purchase Act of 1890. That act said that the government had to buy so many million dollars' worth of silver every year.

"The people of the United States are entitled to a sound and stable currency," said Cleveland. "Their government has no right to injure them by financial experiments opposed to the policy and practice of other civilized states." That experiment was silver. Cleveland

One of the aims of Coxey's out-of-work army was to get the government to hire the unemployed to build roads. Forty years later, Franklin D. Roosevelt did almost exactly that.

The army's weapon against the Pullman strikers was the butt end of the rifle.

In the 20th century the Federal Reserve System will give the nation better control of its currency.

1894: Riots break out among striking miners in Connellsville, Pennsylvania. 11 men are killed. In Columbus, Ohio, some 136,000 coal miners are on strike. In Plymouth, Pennsylvania, a mine collapses and 13 miners are buried alive.

Cheese Sandwiches in the Klondike

George Washington Carmack stood on top of a wrinkled mountain called the Dome, near where the Klondike and Yukon rivers come together in western Canada, not far from Alaska. Looking down, he saw that "the bald hills seemed to be painted in bands and stripes of green, yellow, and red, showing that they were highly mineralized." He was gazing at some of the oldest rock on our planet. The Yukon is a geologist's treasure house. Some of that rock is four billion years old.

Carmack wasn't interested in old rocks. He was looking for stones that would make him rich. He had inherited prospector's genes from his father (who dug for gold in California and died broke). When the younger Carmack heard rumors of strikes in Alaska, he headed north, married a Tagish native, wrote poetry, read *Scientific American*, hunted moose, prospected, and fished.

One night he dreamed of a huge salmon—it had gold nuggets for eyes. Would he catch a big fish?

It was just after that that Skookum Jim, Carmack's Tagish brother-in-law, found some glittering rock. Jim got Carmack and their nephew, Dawson Charlie, and they headed for Rabbit Creek. There, Carmack said, "I took the shovel and dug up some of the loose bedrock. In turning over some of the flat pieces I could see the raw gold laying thick between the flaky slabs like cheese sandwiches."

It was August of 1896, and the three friends staked out claims, named their stake Bonanza, and went off to record their find at a place called Forty Mile. Then they headed for Bill McPhee's saloon and told everyone what they'd found. They didn't realize that it was the richest gold strike ever. It would change the history of western Canada, Alaska, and the whole Pacific Northwest. Naturally, everyone in Forty Mile and thereabouts got out their shovels and headed for the hills.

Almost a year later, a squat, rusty ship, the *Excelsior*, docked at San Francisco. Small, wiry Tom Lippy, who had been a gym teacher at the YMCA in Seattle, struggled down the gangplank, barely able to drag his suitcase. It was heavy—about 200 pounds—and it was filled with gold. Lippy was just one of a score of newly rich men on the *Excelsior*. Two days later, another ship—bigger, dirtier, and filled with even more gold—landed in Seattle. There had been rumors of gold to the north, but now people could see the gleaming stuff for themselves. What would you have done if you'd heard the gold news? A whole lot of people headed for northern Canada and Alaska.

What happened to them is a great story—actually, it is many stories. Getting to the gold meant trekking over the hazardous Chilkoot Pass. About 100,000 adventurers set out for the Klondike; about 30,000 made it. Their goal was Dawson City. (It didn't exist in 1896, but was soon the largest town north of San Francisco.) Once you got there? Well, Dawson was a wild place. But the Canadian Mounted Police kept good order. They wouldn't let anyone carry a gun, so there were no killings—but there were some fights, like the time Mountain Molly got hit on the head by a jealous friend. At first it looked as if she might be on her way to the great goldfield in the sky, but Molly recovered. Dawson's first newspaper (it was handwritten) carried the good news. "Women are few and we can't spare any," wrote the editor.

Only a few prospectors got rich in the Klondike. To find gold in a stream, you had to be an early prospector—and lucky. Later, finding gold meant digging through frozen earth. To do that you needed to build a fire, melt the ground, shovel out the muck, build another fire, and keep going through 20 feet of frozen ground.

So when word reached the Klondike that gold had been found in the beach sands at Nome, Alaska (up near the Arctic Circle)—a lot of diggers headed west for another gold rush, this one on the Alaskan coast facing Russian territory. All this activity brought more new people to Alaska—and some stayed.

Few were prepared for what they found. Alaska, which became the 49th state in 1959, is huge. Put a tracing of Alaska on top of the lower 48, and you may be astonished at the size of our largest state. It has a coastline longer than that of all the lower states combined. Some other surprising things: Kodiak's lowest temperature is about the same as that at Little Rock, Arkansas. The climate at Anchorage (Alaska's biggest city) is similar to that in the Great Lakes region. Alaska's Mount McKinley is the tallest mountain in North America. (Who was president when gold was discovered?) Temperatures in northwest Alaska are the lowest recorded on the continent (close to -80° F). But this land with big-size statistics has only about half a million people.

Juneau (on the coast, off British Columbia) is its capital. Sitka, a city the Russians called "the Paris of the Pacific," is older than San Francisco. In 1942, U.S. Army engineers hacked a 1,388-mile road through wilderness from Dawson Creek to Delta Junction, near Fairbanks. That engineering marvel, known as the Alaska Highway, has, for better and worse, brought trucks, oil rigs, and and new people into a land of totem poles, caribou, and native cultures.

led the nation back to a strict gold standard. The Silver Purchase Act was repealed. The President became known as a "gold bug." But it didn't help a bit. The gold reserves kept going down. And down. And down. That led to a crisis. The nation was in danger of going bankrupt.

Finally, in desperation, President Cleveland went to the country's leading financier—J. P. Morgan—and asked for his help. (See Chapter 4.) Morgan, with other bankers, gave the government gold in return for U.S. government bonds (which they soon sold at a profit). That helped stabilize the currency. But many Americans thought it was humiliating for the president of the United States to have to go to a private banker for help. The financiers seemed to have more power than the United States government!

Prosperity would soon return. Within a few years there were jobs and confidence in abundance. The experts would not agree on what had brought on the depression, or what brought recovery. The discovery of gold in South Africa, Canada, and Alaska helped. It put more money in circulation worldwide.

But in 1894 and 1895, everyone in the nation was concerned about money. No one knew that the hard times would soon disappear. People argued a lot about what was needed to bring back prosperity. Farmers and silver miners associated the bimetal policy with good times. If the Treasury were full of silver, it could print more money and mint more coins. More money in circulation, they believed, would bring happy days. Others—who called themselves "sound money" people—thought silver was the road to financial disaster.

J. P. Morgan (again)

Just as in the California gold rush, there were very few women among the first settlers in the Klondike. It was a lonely life.

Silver *versus* gold became the big political issue of the 1890s.

> *The dollar of our daddies,*
> *Of silver coinage free*
> *Will make us rich and happy,*
> *Will bring prosperity.*

ran the words of a popular song.

Now, a stockpile of gold or silver in the Treasury isn't the only thing that determines a country's wealth. Its industry, resources, and people have much more to do with it. But you wouldn't have thought that back in 1895.

Gold and silver divided the nation. It was silver farmers against gold-bug industrialists and industrial workers. The fight got hot—very hot. Then into the fray marched a silver-tongued orator. He was young, handsome, and sincere. He wanted to be president.

The silver question—what to do when your bicycle wheels are different sizes and seem to go in opposite directions.

Making a Mint

Just imagine that you're a Colorado gold prospector—an average kind of prospector. You don't strike a thick vein of gold, but you do turn up a lot of gold dust. Well, that gold dust is valuable stuff. But in a mining town, what do you do with it? You can send it east, to an *assay* office, to have it weighed, valued, and purchased. It will take at least three months to get money for the gold. So what you'll probably do is just spend it at local stores and hope you're not getting cheated over its value.

That was the way things were in Colorado until three eastern businessmen—Emanuel Gruber and the brothers Austin and Milton Clark—arrived in Denver and opened a private mint at the corner of Market and 16th streets. A *mint* is a place where you make coins. Clark, Gruber & Company had a grand opening when the assaying equipment, the dies, and the punches were ready. The editor of the *Rocky Mountain News* was there. This is part of what he wrote:

The little engine that drives the machinery was fired up, belts adjusted, and..."mint drops" of the value of $10 each began dropping into a tin pail with the most musical "chink." About a thousand dollars were turned out at the rate of 15 or 20 coins a minute, which was deemed very satisfactory.

After two years (in 1862), the U.S. government bought the private mint and turned it into its own. There's been a U.S. mint in Denver ever since.

Today, U.S. coins are made there, and at the Mint in Philadelphia (which was created in 1792). The U.S. Bureau of the Mint has gold warehouses (they're called depositories) at Fort Knox, Kentucky, and at West Point, New York. Some commemorative coins are minted at West Point and at a mint and museum in San Francisco. Gold and silver coins (called bullion) are minted at West Point. Paper currency is made by the Bureau of Engraving and Printing in Washington, D.C.

13 A Cross of Gold

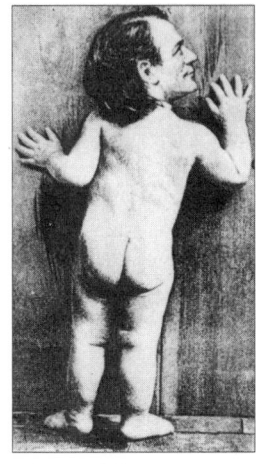

A Republican cartoon jeers at Bryan's effort to grasp the presidency in "Little Billy Bryan Chasing Butterflies."

If you were in school in the 1890s, and you wanted to impress your friends, you worked hard at oratory. Good speakers were heroes, even more than good athletes. Schoolchildren memorized Daniel Webster's speeches, and Abraham Lincoln's too. They learned long poems and recited them at school assemblies. Boys and girls joined debating teams. They learned to speak out—loudly and clearly—and to make their speeches interesting.

Even with all that competition, William Jennings Bryan was the outstanding speaker in his grade school, high school, and college. He was a farm boy, and, like most of his Illinois neighbors, a devout Protestant who believed in the absolute truth of the words of the Bible. (Because his father was Baptist and his mother Methodist, Willy Bryan attended Sunday school *twice* every Sunday.)

Along with religion, something else was central to his being. It was a belief in the values of the American Constitution and of American democracy. William Jennings Bryan believed in democracy with the same intensity and purity he brought to his religion. People quickly realized that.

Bryan became a lawyer, moved to Lincoln, Nebraska, and soon impressed people there with his honesty and his sincerity. When he was just 30 years old, in 1890, he got elected to Congress. Bryan was a Democrat, and Nebraskans usually voted Republican, so it was a surprising victory.

In Congress he asked questions, and learned. It was money and its distribution that concerned him and his constituents (the people he represented). Why do some people who work hard have lots of money,

The night before he gave his most famous speech, Bryan watched the delegates at the Democratic presidential convention cheering another candidate. "These people don't know it," he said, "but they will be cheering for me just this way this time tomorrow night."

At the turn of the century, when it most needed to be said, when it took real courage, he spoke the meaning of America in words of fire. He kept insisting—and history will remember him for it—that America is not really America unless the lowliest man feels sure in his bones that he has free and equal opportunity to get ahead.

—CLARENCE DARROW,
SPEAKING OF W. J. BRYAN.

North Dakota,
South Dakota, Montana, and Washington all became states in November 1889. In July 1890, Idaho and Wyoming were admitted to statehood. And in January 1896, Utah entered as the 45th state.

Campaigning for the presidency on one big idea—that silver could save the country—Bryan tried to hold on to voters from both sides, an impossible job.

and other people, who also work hard, have little? Bryan went to the Library of Congress, got books, read them, thought about gold and silver, and formed opinions. When the Democrats, under Grover Cleveland, repealed the Silver Purchase Act, Bryan refused to go along with his party. He spoke out, he gave his reasons, and people listened.

Then he ran for the Senate, and lost. It was no disgrace for a man as young as he. It didn't slow him down a bit. He decided he would run for president.

Now that seemed laughable. After all, Bryan would only be 36 on election day in 1896. He was good-looking, and he spoke well, but he was unknown in most parts of the country. The Democratic Party leaders ignored him.

Bryan set to work. Someone said he had "superlative self-assurance." He took a job as editor of the *Omaha World-Herald*. That gave him a platform—a chance to write editorials that could be sent around the country. Then he went on a speaking tour: North, South, East, and West. When he spoke—well, he was magnetic. People were attracted.

These were the days before microphones. You needed a big voice to be heard. William Jennings Bryan had one. He discussed issues intelligently. He smiled and shook hands. He was always pleasant and friendly. He made complicated ideas seem simple. When he talked about gold and silver, people understood what he was saying. He was a silver man. He supported many of the reforming ideas of the Populists.

The Democratic convention gathered in a packed auditorium in Chicago. The delegates were to pick a candidate for president: someone to follow Grover Cleveland (who, as you know, was a gold bug). No one could agree on a candidate. Few even considered the young man from Nebraska—until he got up to speak about silver.

He began quietly, but even Bryan's soft tones carried to the farthest corners of the big hall. He was clad in the armor of a righteous cause, he told his listeners. Then he led them through the history of the struggle between the forces of silver and gold. On Bryan's tongue it became a struggle between good and evil. He was dividing the country between East and West. Between *hardy pioneers* and *financial magnates*. Between *city* and *country*. Between *labor* and *management*.

The crowd was caught in the energy of his words. He controlled them as a great actor controls an audience. He said:

> Burn down your cities and leave our farms, and your cities will spring up again as if by magic. But destroy our farms and the grass will grow in the streets of every city in the country.

Cheers bounced off the walls like thunder off mountains. He wasn't finished. Now, when he spoke again, the audience was hushed. He talked of farmers and workers, and of the unfairness of an economic system that left the working classes burdened with debt. Then he came to the end of the speech and to words soon to be repeated around the nation. He was using religious images when, in a ringing voice, he said, *You shall not press down upon the brow of labor this crown of thorns; you shall not crucify mankind upon a cross of gold.* The convention went crazy.

The next day the Democratic Party nominated William Jennings Bryan for president of the United States.

The Populists, too, were swept up in the Bryan fever. They nominated the silver-tongued orator as their candidate for president.

This cartoon suggested that Bryan was a rabble-rousing cousin of anarchists who ruthlessly exploited the words of the Bible in his speeches.

Bryan came down to the sun-scorched, dried-up, blown-away little village of Red Cloud.... There, with an audience of some few hundreds of bronzed farmers who believed in him as their deliverer, the man who could lead them out of the bondage of debt, who could stay the drought and strike water from the rock, I heard him make the greatest speech of his life. Surely that was eloquence of the old stamp that was accounted divine, eloquence that reached through the callus of ignorance and toil and found and awoke the stunted souls of men. I saw those rugged men of the soil weep like children. Six months later, at Chicago, when Bryan stampeded a convention, appropriated a party, electrified a nation....one of those ragged farmers sat beside me in the gallery, and at the close of that never-to-be-forgotten speech, he leaned over the rail, the tears on his furrowed cheeks, and shouted, "The sweet singer of Israel." —WILLA CATHER

What a disgusting, dishonest fakir Bryan is! When I see so many Americans running after him, I feel very much as I do when a really lovely woman falls in love with a cad.

—ELIHU ROOT, OCTOBER 31, 1900.

It has become the custom nowadays, among supercilious people, to depict Bryan as a clown, or a fool, or a mountebank. He was nothing of the kind. In many respects, he was one of the shrewdest men I have ever known....His friendships were sincere; one could depend implicitly on his word....anyone who pictures him as a grumpy, sour, muddled fanatic is wholly wrong....to keep hating him, one had to avoid meeting him.

—WILLIAM G. MCADOO,
CROWDED YEARS

Mellifluous means sweetly or smoothly flowing; its roots are two Latin words, *mel* (honey) and *fluere* (to flow).

But not all the Populists were happy about it. Tom Watson was furious. He thought the nation needed a third party and that the Populists should have their own candidate. If the Populists fused (joined) with the Democrats, Watson said, it would be the end of the Populists. So when he was asked to run for vice president on the Populist ticket, Watson was reluctant. But he finally agreed.

In the meantime the Republicans chose an Ohioan, William McKinley, as their candidate. He was an honest man, and sincere, too. He looked distinguished and presidential. But his beliefs were different from Bryan's. He supported the gold standard and high tariffs. He was conservative and moderate. He was a quiet man, able to bring people together. He believed the future lay with the new business interests. He saw no reason for government to attempt to regulate or control business. If business prospered, he thought it would also benefit the poor and the farmers.

William McKinley

This election of 1896 was one of the most important in all of our nation's history. Americans had a real choice in 1896. Their decision set the direction the nation took in the 20th century. Here are some of the positions they took about issues:

DEMOCRATS, POPULISTS	REPUBLICANS
farmers	businessmen, some workers
silver	gold
"expanding money"	"tight money"
8-hour day, child labor laws	leave-alone labor policies
income tax	no income tax
farm	city
Jeffersonian	Hamiltonian
liberal	conservative

What a campaign it was! Bryan had little money for his campaign, but he had his remarkable energy and that mellifluous voice. He crossed the nation by train and in just a few months gave more than 600 speeches. Sometimes he spoke 30 times in a day. Once, while he was shaving, a few people wanted a glimpse of him, so he opened the train window and spoke through the lather. Often he talked from a platform at the end of the train. He was so interesting that the trainmen would rush to listen to him—over and over again. Mostly he talked about silver—he

needed a simple theme for these brief *whistle stops*—but the other reform issues were not forgotten.

In Canton, Ohio, William McKinley was engaged in a very different presidential campaign. He didn't go anywhere at all. He stayed on his front porch. People came to him. The railroads—which were supporting his candidacy—ran low-cost excursion trains to Canton. The corporations and banks sent money, lots of money. McKinley's good friend, Mark Hanna, organized things. Hanna was a brilliant organizer.

More than 120 million Republican pamphlets—printed in 10 languages—were distributed to voters. They made Bryan sound like a dangerous quack; 1,400 paid speakers went out around the nation speaking for McKinley and against Bryan. McKinley articles were sent free to newspapers. McKinley buttons, banners, and posters turned up everywhere. Theodore Roosevelt said that Mark Hanna "has advertised McKinley as if he were a patent medicine." (In 1896 the Republicans spent $4 million on the presidential campaign; the Democrats spent $300,000.)

Today we are used to big, costly presidential campaigns. That was something new in 1896. (Advertising a president wasn't new—that had begun with William Henry Harrison's campaign of "Tippecanoe and

Most Republicans saw Bryan's audience as a bunch of hick farmers who wanted easy money—unlimited silver coins at a ratio of 16 to 1 with gold—and who had been totally taken in by Bryan. Bryan, they said, told these ignorant people only what they wanted to hear. (The 16 to 1 ratio meant that 16 ounces of silver would buy 1 ounce of gold.)

Bryan traveled 18,000 miles on his campaign and spoke to 5 million people—and all before there were microphones.

Mark Hanna

A lot of people believed the idea in this cartoon (right): that tycoon Mark Hanna was the real Republican leader and that he had McKinley in his pocket. Hanna thought it was the government's job to help business, because if business did well the whole country would do well. Do you think he was right?

Tyler Too" in 1840—it was the spending of big money that was new.)

Maybe it was the money that made the difference. Maybe not. The American people had some tough issues to decide. To begin, there was the idea of democracy. Americans have never been decided on how far to take democracy. Thomas Jefferson and Andrew Jackson had faith in the people. They wanted democracy to be as broad and direct as possible. They wanted the American people to make decisions for themselves. Others, like Alexander Hamilton and the McKinley Republicans, favored a more limited democracy, with decision-making power in the hands of the elected, the appointed, and the leaders of business, industry, and other interests (today we call them *special interest groups*).

Many Americans wanted those reforms the Populists called for. They wanted laws to improve working conditions. They wanted shorter working hours; they wanted laws to prevent employers from hiring children for adult jobs. Many believed the railroads and the big utilities should be owned by the government and run for all people. Most wanted to see farmers helped.

But there were some things that were worrisome about Bryan. He was dividing the country into warring groups. He wasn't trying to bring the corporations and the common people together. He was picking a fight with the money interests. And he was supported by nativists and some other hate groups.

The business interests fought back and won. It was the corporation that would dominate the 20th century. Some say that the American people made that choice in 1896.

14 Some Bad Ideas

When times got hard, it was easy for workers to blame newer immigrants for accepting low wages and taking their jobs away.

The election of 1896 was history. Bryan went on to run for president again and again and never made it. He became better known than some of the men who did become president.

And what of the Populists? What happened to them?

Tom Watson was right. Their party was dead. Not quite buried, but almost.

And Tom Watson? Ah, if only I didn't have to write the truth about Tom Watson. For his is a tragic story.

Remember young, idealistic Tom Watson, who began his political career by doing something no other party leader was doing: calling on blacks and whites to unite? For a while it happened. He brought the races together. When a black Populist leader was threatened by the racist Ku Klux Klan, Watson called for help. More than 1,000 farmers came in buggies and on horseback. This was the 19th-century South, and these were white farmers rushing to the aid of a black man. The farmers stacked their guns on Tom Watson's porch and made it clear they would not allow a lynching. The Klansmen got the message. There was no more trouble.

But the People's Party failed. It was too bad, since so many Populist ideas were soon accepted by both Republicans and Democrats. Perhaps that irony was something Tom Watson couldn't accept. He took eight years off from politics, and wrote books, and thought, and

> **This is not a political fight, and politicians cannot lead or direct it. It is a movement of the masses, an uprising of the people....The people need spokesmen—not leaders—men in the front who will obey, not command.**
> —TOM WATSON
> ON THE PEOPLE'S PARTY

What did Tom Watson mean by that? Do you agree with him?

By the turn of the century the Ku Klux Klan was a large, powerful, and widespread organization. It was not confined to the rural South, as some people imagined. This Klan parade took place in Long Branch, New Jersey.

Racism and bigotry were appearing in other nations too. Japanese hated Chinese; Chinese hated Vietnamese; Greeks hated Turks; Turks hated Armenians; Germans hated the French; the French seemed to think they were superior to everyone. And that wasn't all. People with different religions and different-colored skins looked down on each other. It was sad and stupid, but not to people who believed that way.

brooded, and came out a lesser man. Tom Watson ended his days as a bigot. He had been a champion of the common people; he became enamored of "white supremacy," prestige, and power. When he died, the largest bunch of flowers at his funeral came from the Ku Klux Klan.

Watson wasn't the only Populist leader to take up bigoted theories. Sadly, it was a time when many Americans—and people in other nations, too—took racism seriously.

They were grappling with difficult problems. Life was unsettling in this age of extremes. In America, everyone could see that something was wrong, and not just on the farm. People were becoming too materialistic, too concerned with money and things. The economic system wasn't working well. Industry was ravaging the nation's resources. Thomas Jefferson's agrarian (farm-centered) world was vanishing, and the new world of corporations and capitalists

AN AGE OF EXTREMES

didn't seem very noble. For the most part, presidents and congresses were weak and money magnates and city bosses strong. Railroads and new industries had changed the nation; laws and ideas hadn't caught up.

Some people had a simple solution to the new problems. They blamed others. First, they blamed the rich. Actually, the rich industrialists were no different from the poor farmers. Many were greedy, but so were many ordinary people. Some industrialists, like Carnegie and Rockefeller, who had abused and exploited others to gain power and wealth, were doing a surprisingly good job of sharing their wealth.

When blaming the rich didn't work, people looked for other scapegoats. Unfortunately, many turned racist. Some were anti-Catholic. Others were anti-Semitic (which means they blamed Jews for their problems). Many Americans became anti-immigrant. (Immigrants were competing for jobs. One Populist leader called them *foreign scum*.) Some were anti-black. (It was at this time that the southern states wrote new constitutions that took the vote away from most blacks and poor whites.) On the West Coast, many citizens were anti-Asian.

Some Americans lost their way. Their wrongheadedness would hurt the nation. They didn't mean to be wrong. Few do. They were trying to define America. But it was as if they had decided to look through a telescope the wrong way. They narrowed the vision. They were looking backward to a past they thought was ideal. But things had never been quite the way they imagined them.

They thought America had once been just a nation of Protestant English farmers. They forgot all about the Native Americans—who had been a majority, and who had arrived on the continent thousands of years before the first Europeans. They forgot about the Spaniards who had settled in Florida and South Carolina and New Mexico and Texas and California.

A Jewish immigrant in New York celebrates the Sabbath. The photographer, Jacob Riis, wrote a book called *How the Other Half Lives*, which helped make people realize the terrible conditions that many poor immigrants endured.

Shtetl is a Yiddish word meaning *village*.

There's irony in this cartoon. Can you figure out why those shadows from the past are standing behind each of the tycoons? And why are they trying to stop the poor immigrant stepping off the boat? What have they forgotten?

They forgot the Poles, Italians, and Africans who had helped to create Jamestown. They forgot the Swedes in Delaware and the French in Louisiana. They forgot the Catholics in Maryland and the Jews in New Amsterdam. They didn't know their American history.

Those 19th-century bigots—whom we call *nativists*—were ignorant. They forgot that it was our English ancestors who had come up with the idea that all people are created equal. It was that revolutionary idea that was attracting immigrants to America from all over the world.

Because of that idea, America was attempting something amazing. We were taking peasants from German farms, children from Poland's shtetls, laborers from China's countryside, Italians from Naples fishing boats, and former slaves from southern plantations—and expecting them all to get along together. Of course it wasn't easy. Revolutionary ideas never are.

One thing neither the Populists, nor the Democrats, nor the Republicans understood was that the emerging political forces—the immigrants and the newly freed blacks—were helping to build a more fair and far richer America. But that wasn't clear to anyone at the end of the 19th century.

15 Producing Goods

Sears, Roebuck's Consumers Guide "tells just what your storekeeper at home pays for everything he buys—and will prevent him from overcharging you on anything you buy from him."

What do you do when you need a shirt? You go to a store and buy one.

Before the Civil War, you couldn't do that. Your mother, or someone in the family, had to make your shirt. If you had plenty of money, you could go to a tailor and have a shirt made especially for you. (Today you are lucky if someone in your family is talented enough to sew.)

Look around and notice: some of us are tall and some short, some fat and some thin. How can you make clothes in advance and have them fit? In the old days, no one believed that clothing could be made to fit unless it was made to measure. Then, during the Civil War, soldiers' uniforms were needed in a hurry. So uniforms were made in many sizes in factories. It was amazing—almost everyone could find something to fit. After the war, manufacturers started making clothing for civilians (people who weren't in the military). In the cities, new department stores began selling factory-made clothes, shoes, and things for the house and garden.

Do you remember how you felt when you were little and went into a big toy store for the first time? That's the way most Americans felt when they first entered a department store.

The people who couldn't get to the big-city stores weren't left out. They could buy factory goods, too, because of Montgomery Ward's smart idea. Ward decided to sell merchandise through the mail. He printed a catalogue that showed pictures of the items he had for sale. Soon another

Once the postman (this one had his own driver) delivered to remote farms and villages, country people could shop in the cities—by mail.

85

Say the worst that can be said about the evils of the machine age, early and late, in America; admit the social irresponsibility of the early captains of industry, the brutality with which the factory system ground men down and used them up....when all is said that can be said, the fact remains that what was done here meant...a more abundant life for all the people.

—BRUCE CATTON, HISTORIAN

In a time and place when buying a newspaper was an event, the mail-order catalogue's arrival made a red-letter day. By 1899 the Montgomery Ward "book" was 1,036 pages!

We cannot all live in the city, yet nearly all of us seem determined to do so.

—HORACE GREELEY, NEWSPAPER EDITOR

company, Sears, Roebuck, was doing the same thing.

The new department stores and the new catalogues brought wonders to the American household. Suddenly everyone wanted products from American factories. Those factories soon led the world with their good products and low prices.

That did some marvelous things for our country. It made life better for many people. Now most Americans could wear fashionable clothing and have attractive furniture in their homes. It made the United States more democratic.

More democratic? Yes, in the old days only the rich could afford the latest fashions. Now anyone could go

"NOW I GUESS I'VE GOT THE BULGE ON THE MIDDLEMAN."

Montgomery Ward had lost his savings in the Chicago fire, but the next year he scraped together enough to send out his first catalogue—a single price sheet.

into a store and buy a fine suit or dress. When immigrants got off their boats, all they had to do was go into a store to look American. Factories changed the way people lived and the way they worked.

Thomas Jefferson had wanted America to stay agrarian. That word *agrarian* means "farm-based." *Those who labor in the earth are the chosen people of God*, said Jefferson. He wanted the United States to be a nation of small farmers who would have little need for government regulations. It was a nice dream, but it wasn't the way the world was going. Alexander Hamilton knew that; he foresaw an industrial America.

Jefferson had seen what the Industrial Revolution did in Europe—he had seen poor working people, and the homeless,

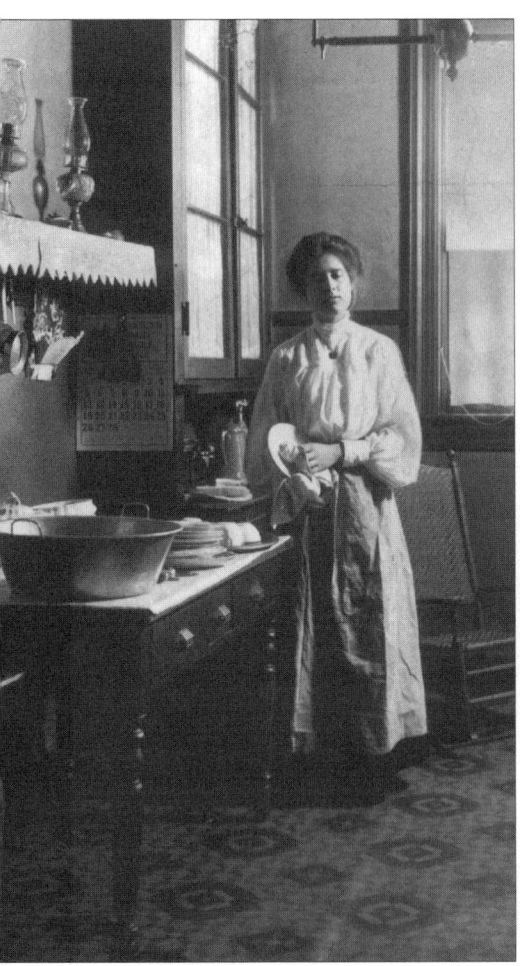

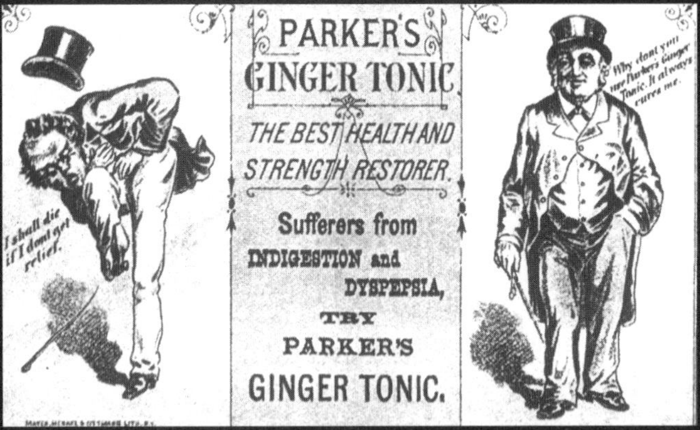
PARKER'S
GINGER TONIC
THE BEST HEALTH AND
STRENGTH RESTORER.
Sufferers from
INDIGESTION and
DYSPEPSIA,
TRY
PARKER'S
GINGER TONIC.
I shall die if I don't get relief.
Why don't you use Parker's Ginger Tonic. It always cures me.

Left, a turn-of-the-century housewife in her modern kitchen, with linoleum on the floor and gaslights on the ceiling. The makers of patent medicines and lotions claimed they cured almost anything; they also used almost anyone to sell them, from cute grandchildren to frogs. "Before-and-after" pictures were as popular as sales tools in the 1890s as they are today.

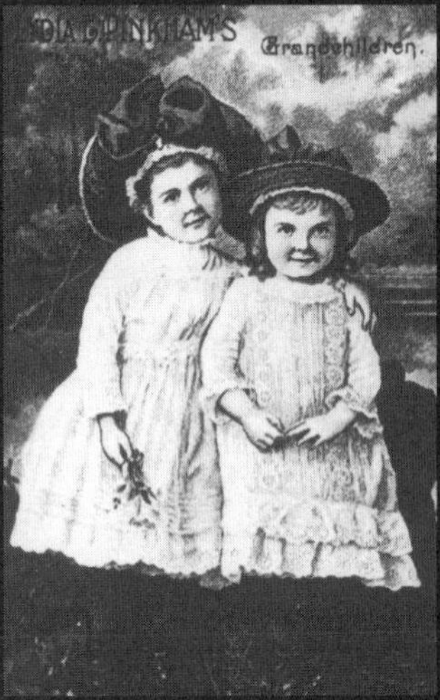
PINKHAM'S
Grandchildren.

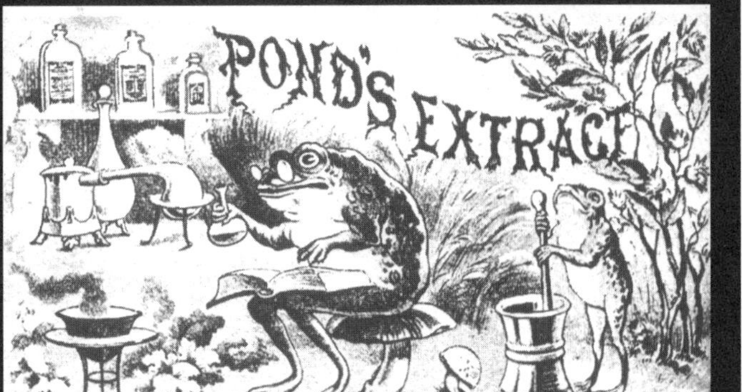
POND'S EXTRACT
OINTMENT
CATARRH CURE
PLASTER
The PEOPLES REMEDY
"Over."

and children who spent their days in factories instead of at school or play. He knew factories and cities brought problems. *While we have land to labor, let us never wish to see our citizens occupied at a work bench*, wrote Jefferson. But there was no keeping the Industrial Revolution out of America. (In 1920, half of all Americans lived in cities or towns. By then the United States was the leading industrial nation in the world, with nine million factory workers.)

Inventions That Changed Things

In 1880, George Eastman patented roll film for cameras. Five years later, he was selling a box camera that had film sealed inside. You sent off the loaded camera to the Eastman Company in Rochester, New York, to have its film developed. Six years after that, in 1891, Eastman came up with film that could be loaded in normal light, and, in 1895, the first pocket Kodak was in use.

George Eastman

When the Kampfe Brothers of New York City invented the safety razor in 1880, beards were in trouble. Without safety razors, most men went to a barber shop to get shaved—or risked cutting themselves. The safety razor was the start of do-it-yourself shaving. (Change came slowly; for many men, the barber shop was a kind of social club, as well as a place to get shaved.)

A drawing made in 1900 predicted what New York City would look like a century later, in 1999. What do you think of its predictions? How do you think a city like New York will look 100 years from now?

Many Americans found they liked living in cities. Cities were full of excitement. People filled the streets. There was music, and shopping, and entertainment. And there were jobs. Most of the factories were in cities or big towns. A new immigrant could get off the boat at Ellis Island, head for New York or Chicago or Cincinnati, and quickly find a job.

A farm boy or girl, from Iowa or Wisconsin, could head for the city and find a world of activity—and a job, too.

So Alexander Hamilton was right: we chose to become an urban, industrial nation. Hamilton was right about something else: an industrial nation needs the regulations of an effective government. But how do you find a balance between an interfering government and a helpful one?

Those gentleman farmers—Washington, Adams, Jefferson, Madison, who devised most of the founding rules for our nation—didn't foresee the new industrial age. Even Hamilton would have been astounded by it. No one was prepared for the era of big business. The United States wasn't ready for the changes that cities, industry, and inventions brought. The industrial age needed its own rules and regulations. There were new situations and problems that had not been faced before. It was hard to plan ahead.

NEW YORK CITY
—AS IT WILL BE—
IN 1999
PICTORIAL FORECAST OF THE CITY
AS APPROVED BY
ANDREW. H. GREEN, H.H. VREELAND
and JOHN.B. McDONALD

16 Harvest at Haymarket

Anarchists, who were often active in labor politics (and some of whose leaders were foreign-born), were terribly feared by many in the late 19th century.

When Cyrus Hall McCormick opened the McCormick Harvester Works in Chicago in the 1840s, he worked alongside his 23 employees. Of course, he knew them all by name. He cared about them.

A few years later, the McCormick factory was making more than 1,000 reapers a year. Cyrus still knew all 200 of his workers.

By 1884, the year Cyrus McCormick died, his plant was enormous. It covered 12 acres; 1,300 men worked 10-hour days, six days a week. Two huge steam engines supplied power in the modern factory. That year the company showed a profit of 71 percent. And McCormick no longer knew his workers.

That was typical of what was happening in America. Many of the new factories were owned by corporations—big-business companies. The owners of the corporations sometimes didn't even live in the same town as their workers. Some of those owners got very rich but refused to pay their workers a fair wage. Often they treated

In 1900, the average American worked 59 hours a week for 22 cents an hour. (You figure his weekly wage.) But then a new bike cost $14.65, a watch $3.65, and a pair of shoes $1.95. You could have dinner in a good restaurant for less than a dollar.

Harvesting on a New Mexico ranch in 1916. Most large farm machinery was still pulled by horses.

We forget, looking at pictures of factories, what deafening, dusty, smelly places they can be. Would you like to change places with the boy on the left?

workers as if they were commodities, like coal or lumber. They seemed to forget they were human beings. Steelworkers were expected to work 12 hours a day, six days a week, for little pay. Textile workers—many of them children—worked 60 to 80 hours a week. Conditions were often dangerous. Miners worked underground with explosives, but without safety regulations. In one year, 25,000 workers died on the job; many more were injured. Child workers had three times as many accidents as adults. If a person lost an arm in a job accident—and many did with the new machines—no one helped with doctor's bills. If a worker complained, he was fired.

Workers organized themselves into *unions* to try to fight for better conditions

It is easy to give free speech to those with whose ideas you agree. But in America we believe in free speech for all, which isn't always easy. Should anarchists—or neo-Nazis, or people against abortion, or people for abortion—be allowed to speak?

These mining boys worked 10 hours a day, 6 days a week. Imagine working those hours every day, in the dark, bent double, deep underground.

and better pay. The union was like a club for workers. People who worked together tried to help each other solve the problems they had in common. Sometimes they decided not to work unless they were paid better wages. In other words, they went on strike. Naturally, the owners hated strikes. They often fired anyone who joined a strike. Sometimes they hired police or soldiers to break a strike. Sometimes strikers were shot. Businessmen often took the law into their own hands. If they were powerful enough, they got away with it. Cornelius Vanderbilt was blunt when he said, "Law! What do I care about law? H'aint I got power?" He wasn't the only one who felt that way: Carnegie and Rockefeller hired their own police forces.

Workers began to demand their own power. The unions grew. Many Americans—especially the new immigrants—learned about democracy in the unions. Writer Upton Sinclair said the union was "a miniature republic; its affairs were every man's affairs and every man had a real say about them."

The top-hatted man here seems like a mean trouble-maker; but this is an anti-labor cartoon, and the man is supposed to be a union offi-cial, inciting innocent workers to unnecessary strikes.

Workers (labor) and business owners (management and capital) often had opposing interests. Workers wanted good wages and own-ers wanted to keep their labor costs low. (There wasn't much long-range thinking. With good wages, workers could buy the products the industrialists were making, and everyone would profit.)

Sometimes the relationship seemed like war. It was big business versus the unions. And, be-cause the situation was new, it was confusing.

Many people distrusted unions, especially because some unions were organized by so-cialists, who wanted the government to take over the businesses that affected most citi-zens, like railroads, electrical power, and tele-phones. (America had a tradition of individu-alism and private ownership; socialism seem scary.) Some unions were led by *anarchists*. They didn't believe in any government at all, which wasn't a very helpful idea. And some

An artist's idea of a mining dis-aster. Owners had little or no legal responsibility for acci-dents—and definitely did not have to compensate anyone who could not work because of injuries on the job.

A poster (in English and German) rallying workers to the fateful May 4, 1886, meeting in Chicago's Haymarket Square.

unions did abuse their growing power. Many strikes were poorly planned and hurt workers more than owners. But some business leaders just wanted capitalism without regulations. And some got angry at the idea of workers having any rights and power.

In 1884, soon after his father died, Cyrus McCormick II announced that he was cutting his workers' pay. (Remember, his company made an enormous 71 percent profit that year.) A few months later the workers went on strike.

McCormick hired other workmen to take their places. (They were called *strikebreakers* or *scabs*.) Striking union men attacked the strikebreakers. McCormick hired armed guards. A crowd captured and burned the guards' rifles. A police captain (who was on the side of the workers) did nothing. Chicago's mayor wouldn't help either, so McCormick finally agreed to go back to the old pay scale.

In a letter to her daughter, Mrs. Cyrus McCormick, Sr., wrote about the strike.

> *Hatred and fierce passions have been aroused; and an injury has resulted to our good name....It ended by our conceding the terms demanded.*

But young Cyrus wasn't finished. The next year he installed expensive machinery that was designed to eliminate the most troublesome of the workers. At first the machines seemed to do just that. McCormick wrote his mother that the machines, "are working beyond our expectations...two men with one of these machines can do an average of about three days' work in one."

But he didn't plan on machinery problems. The machines broke down. The parts they turned out weren't as good as the handmade parts. The cost—to keep the machines operating—was more than double the old labor cost. McCormick didn't care; he thought he had broken the union and that seemed important to him now.

But the union wasn't finished. Myles McPadden, a union leader, convinced McCormick's workers to join two national unions: the Metalworkers Union and the Knights of Labor. The workers went to McCormick demanding higher pay and better working conditions.

In the meantime, McCormick had been busy. He gave money to the mayor and the police (that's called *bribery*). Then he closed his plant rather than meet the workers' demands. Four hundred city policemen protected the plant. McCormick hired strikebreakers so the factory could start production again. Now he was in desperate need of workers, so he agreed to let the scabs work an eight-hour day, which was one of the major demands of the strikers. Naturally, that enraged the strikers.

One day, some strikers attacked a group of strikebreakers as they left work. Police started shooting. Two men were killed and several wounded. The next day a mass meeting was called to protest the shootings at the McCormick factory. The meeting was held in Chicago's Haymarket Square. Most of the speakers were journalists, and socialists, and peaceful—although some of them suggested that working men should arm themselves.

The meeting was just about over—it was smaller than predicted—when 180 policemen marched into the square and demanded the meeting be ended. There were only a few hundred people left, and the speaker was ready to go home. "We are peaceable," he said to the police chief and climbed down from his platform. Then something unex-

Nothing is so much to be feared as fear.
—HENRY DAVID THOREAU

Samuel Fielden, a teamster, was speaking to the Haymarket crowds when a cast-iron bomb filled with dynamite suddenly went off.

The Ultimate Victory of Liberty and Justice

Journalist August Spies (shpeez) was one of the four men hanged after the Haymarket riot. Here is part of what he said to judge and jury during his trial (Grinnell was the state's attorney for the prosecution):

Grinnell's main argument against the defendants was—"They were foreigners; they were not citizens." I cannot speak for the others. I will only speak for myself. I have been a resident of this state fully as long as Grinnell, and probably have been as good a citizen—at least, I should not wish to be compared with him. Grinnell has incessantly appealed to the patriotism of the jury. To that I reply in the language of [Samuel] Johnson, the English littérateur [man of literature], "an appeal to patriotism is the last resort of a scoundrel."...There was not a syllable said about anarchism at the Haymarket meeting. At that meeting the very popular theme of reducing the hours of toil was discussed. But, "Anarchism is on trial!" foams Mr. Grinnell. If that is the case, your honor, very well; you may sentence me, for I am an anarchist. I believe that the state of castes and classes—the state where one class dominates over and lives upon the labor of another class, and calls this order—yes, I believe that this barbaric form of social organization, with its legalized plunder and murder, is doomed to die and make room for a free society, voluntary association, or universal brotherhood, if you like. You may pronounce the sentence upon me, honorable judge, but let the world know that in A.D. 1886, in the state of Illinois, eight men were sentenced to death because they believed in a better future; because they had not lost their faith in the ultimate victory of liberty and justice!

pected happened. A bomb was thrown at the policemen. No one has ever discovered who threw the bomb. One policeman was killed (six others died later of wounds). Police began firing their guns. Four civilians died. Many were wounded.

The nation was outraged. Most people were angry at the strikers. They seemed to believed that the union workers were all anarchists who were plotting to overthrow the government. Many Chicago workers were immigrants. Stories circulated about foreign conspiracies.

The Chicago police rounded up suspects. They arrested people without warrants to do so. Eight men were charged with conspiracy and murder. Four of those men had left Haymarket Square before the bomb was thrown. One of them reported that "there was not a syllable said about anarchism at the Haymarket meeting." It didn't matter. Fear was in the air. As someone said, "anarchism was on trial." The nation was afraid of foreigners and socialists and anarchists. No one wanted to hear the truth.

All eight men were found guilty. Four of them were hanged. One was sentenced to 15 years in jail. Two had death sentences changed to life in prison. One committed suicide in prison.

At the McCormick factory, workers returned to a 10-hour day.

"You may strangle me," said August Spies when he was hanged, "but my silence will be more terrible than speech."

17 Workers, Labor (and a Triangle)

Gompers put aside ideas of personal wealth and spent his energy building a strong labor movement. He disagreed with the socialists of the day.

American labor laws lagged far behind those of almost every other industrial nation. Working conditions were often unsafe, factory pay was rarely fair, and workers had few if any benefits. In 1900, only one American worker in 12 belonged to a union.

Unions were feared by workers as well as managers, because many early labor leaders seemed too radical for most Americans. Then, near the turn of the century, a labor leader appeared who was a conservative thinker. No one could accuse Samuel Gompers of being a radical. He used American business methods to organize and negotiate for labor.

Sam Gompers came to this country from England when he was 13. His family was actually Dutch—they were Dutch Jews—but they had moved to London, where Sam's father tried to make a living as a cigarmaker. He didn't have an easy time of it, especially as his family kept growing.

Sam was a bright boy and did well

Horace Greeley said that a cigar was "a fire on one end and a fool on the other."

"Making old-fashioned 'stogies,' Pittsburgh," wrote photographer Lewis Hine. Like the wagons, *stogies* were named for Pennsylvania's Conestoga Valley, where cigars were made.

The **Talmud** is a collection of ancient writings on Jewish laws and traditions.

When the Irish Land League issued orders forbidding the Irish from supplying British land agent Captain Charles Boycott with provisions, it added a new word to the English language. That word came to America and became a tactic used by American labor. You know what the word is, don't you?

in school. After classes he went to Hebrew school and studied the Talmud, which he said "develops the more subtle qualities of mind, the student learns to deal with abstract problems, to make careful discriminations, to follow a line of reasoning from premise to conclusion."

He liked school and wanted to go on, but the family was desperately poor. Sam had to go to work. At age 10 he was apprenticed to a shoemaker. But he decided he'd rather be a cigarmaker, so he helped his father make cigars. Even that wasn't enough. The Gomperses were hungry when the Cigarmakers' Society (a union) came to the rescue. They had an emigration fund that helped members go to America. A civil war was being fought in America, but that didn't stop the Gompers family. They boarded a ship and headed for the New World.

On the first day, we found a home in Houston and Attorney Streets [in New York]. Those four rooms signified progress from the little London home. Our neighbors were chiefly American, English, and Holland Dutch. I was then thirteen years, six months, and two days old.

Father began making cigars at home, and I helped him. Our house was just opposite a slaughterhouse. All day long we could see the animals being driven into the slaughter pens and could hear the turmoil and the cries of the animals. The neighborhood was filled with the penetrating, sickening odor. The suffering of the animals and the nauseating odor made it physically impossible for me to eat meat for many months—after we moved to another neighborhood.

Back of our house was a brewery which was in continuous operation, and this necessitated the practice of living-in for the brewery workers. Conditions were dreadful in the breweries of those days, and I became very familiar with them from our back door.

Our little home was not far from the shipyards of John Roach. Every morning at eight o'clock a bell rang the beginning of the workday. I remember the incident vividly for the great majority of workmen had been at work at least an hour. John Roach was one of the first employers to establish the eight-hour day.

The Gomperses lived in a New York City

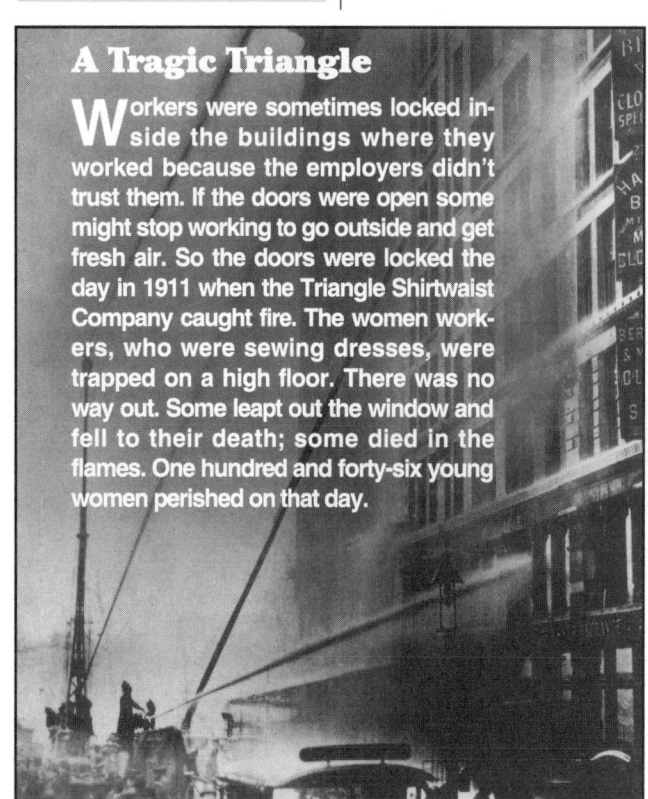

A Tragic Triangle

Workers were sometimes locked inside the buildings where they worked because the employers didn't trust them. If the doors were open some might stop working to go outside and get fresh air. So the doors were locked the day in 1911 when the Triangle Shirtwaist Company caught fire. The women workers, who were sewing dresses, were trapped on a high floor. There was no way out. Some leapt out the window and fell to their death; some died in the flames. One hundred and forty-six young women perished on that day.

tenement. Tenements were apartment houses for the poor. Many were used as factories. Sometimes they were called *sweatshops*, because they were usually hot and airless, and workers were "sweated"—forced to work long hours in cramped, dirty rooms with no provisions for safety, rest, comfort, or refreshment.

Sam and his father rolled cigars at home. Sam joined a debating club and began taking courses at New York City's Cooper Union, where he studied history, music, mechanics, economics, electric power, geography, astronomy, speechmaking, and more.

When he was 16, he got a job in a cigar factory. While the cigarmakers rolled the tobacco they liked to have someone read to them. The reader had to be smart. The cigarmakers wanted to educate themselves. They kept up with the latest news, they had lively discussions, and they listened to good literature too. Sometimes Sam Gompers did the reading.

After he got married and started his own family, he began to take an interest in the Cigarmakers Union. Gompers was short and square-jawed, with a bushy mustache. He was a good-humored, no-nonsense person who got results. His powerful voice and his good sense soon helped make him president of the Cigarmakers Union. It was a craft union, which means that all its members did

Left, a young boy rolling cigars at home, as Sam Gompers did with his father. Right, cigarmakers work while listening to their colleague read the news. They pooled their wages to pay the reader—the owner didn't provide such services.

Ideal *v.* Real

The anarchists and socialists were working for big changes; they wanted society to be organized in new ways. That scared most Americans. Sam Gompers stuck to labor issues such as working hours, wages, and job safety. He used strikes to get eight-hour working days, five-day work weeks, safety reforms in mines, and the right of workers to band together to negotiate (called *collective bargaining*). By 1901, the A.F. of L. had more than one million members.

"**Show me the country in which there are no strikes,**" said Gompers, "**and I will show you that country in which there is no liberty.**"

the same kind of work. In 1886, he persuaded other craft unions to band together with the cigarmakers and form the American Federation of Labor. Gompers was named president, and for the next 38 years he worked for the A.F. of L. He made it a major force in the American industrial world.

Sam Gompers was a practical man. He stayed out of politics. He knew that would divide the workers. He had only one goal—to improve working conditions in the United States. He wanted American workers to have the best possible wages and benefits. If workers earned good pay, he believed they would make everyone prosperous. Besides, he thought a fair labor policy led to a just society. "Show me the country in which there are no strikes and I will show you that country in which there is no liberty," said Samuel Gompers. (Do you agree with that statement? Why? Or why not?)

In one sweltering factory, the owner wouldn't let cigar rollers out to get ice from the iceman (who came in a horsedrawn cart with sawdust covering big chunks of ice, and was important in American urban life before refrigerators or air-conditioning).The workers had to strike to get the right to have cold water to drink.

In earlier days, businesses had been small. Usually owner and employee worked together. But in the industrial age, factories grew big and impersonal. Employers had almost unlimited power. They could lock employees in or out of the workplace. Their wealth often gave them the means to destroy unions, by hiring armed guards or by buying unfavorable and often unfair publicity. The courts almost always favored the employers. That changed when unions acquired power and respectability. Then American workers began to reap the benefits of their own productivity. It might not have happened without leaders like Samuel Gompers.

The founder of the American Federation of Labor voting in a union election.

Leaving Sicily: From Mediterranean Island to a New World

EUROPEAN EMIGRATION
1820~1920
numbers show emigrants to the United States

NORWAY 730,000
SWEDEN 1,000,000
SCOTLAND 570,000
DENMARK 300,000
IRELAND 4,400,000
HOLLAND 200,000
WALES 75,000
ENGLAND 2,500,000
BELGIUM 140,000
GERMANY 5,500,000
RUSSIA 2,000,000 JEWS
Poles
Czechs
Jews
FRANCE 530,000
AUSTRIA-HUNGARY 3,700,000
SWITZERLAND 258,000
Slovenes
Romanians
Croats
Serbs
PORTUGAL 120,000
ROMANIA 80,000
BULGARIA 60,000
SPAIN 130,000
ITALY 4,190,000
Armenians
Sicily
OTTOMAN EMPIRE 320,000
Greeks
GREECE 350,000

Most of the people of Santo Stefano were shepherds or cheesemakers or harvesters of nuts or olives. But there wasn't enough of any of those things, and you could reach Santo Stefano only by mule path. Wolves prowled the paths.

Something unexplainable was happening in Sicily: people were having more children than ever before. In 1800 there were a million Sicilians; by 1900 there were three and a half million. In Santo Stefano, as in many of the villages, there were just too many people to feed and house. On top of that, there was a worldwide surplus of wheat and grapes. The price of Sicilian farm products tumbled. In 1877, the mayor of Santo Stefano wrote that the village was "absolutely in a critical condition, actually in the most extreme misery."

If you look at the map and notice the boot that is Italy, you will see that the boot's toe is kicking a triangular rock. That rock is actually an island—the island of Sicily—and, back at the end of the 19th century, a fever spread across the island.

It was American fever, and almost everyone on Sicily got infected. Giuseppina Spoto was one of the early germ spreaders. She and her husband had gone to the United States. She fell in love with the place, but her husband felt differently. He was set in his ways, and homesick. (Besides, he'd met up with a *coccodrillo*—an alligator—in Florida, and it scared him.) So they came back to Santo Stefano, their mountain village. The money they'd saved in America made them rich in Sicily. But Giuseppina missed the United States. She missed the excitement, and, she said, in America "there was no scarcity of anything." In America you could live *una buona vita* (a good life), she told her neighbors.

The Sicilians formed mutual aid societies to try to help themselves, but when they couldn't pay their rents to the wealthy landowners (most of whom lived in Italy, not Sicily), Italian troops were sent to the island. Some Sicilians fought the troops. Squads of *bersaglieri* (sharpshooters) took care of the rebels. Are you surprised to learn that between 1891 and 1913, more than 7,500 villagers from tiny Santo Stefano climbed on mules and clopped down to the port of Palermo and then went on to the United States? And Santo Stefano was just one little, out-of-the-way village. The same thing happened all over the island. Between 1880 and 1920, more than three million emigrants left Sicily and sailed for America. It has been called "one of the greatest mass migrations in history."

18 Rolling the Leaf in Florida

Smoking Start

Cigarettes were first made from tiny pieces of tobacco swept up from the cigarmakers' floor. Some workers took those tobacco leftovers home and rolled them in paper—and made cigarettes. Tobacco companies began selling pocket-sized bags of tobacco so people could roll their own cigarettes. Then, in 1881, James Buchanan Duke worked on a cigarette-making machine that could turn out 200 cigarettes a minute. Duke's special talent was in marketing. He spent a lot of money advertising cigarettes, and it paid off. By 1889 he was selling more than 800 million cigarettes a year. A year later the five largest tobacco companies joined to form a trust called the American Tobacco Company. "Buck" Duke was president. He was just getting started.

Gentlemen often smoked outside, or at clubs; many people thought it improper to smoke around the house or where ladies were present.

It was in 1886 (the same year that Sam Gompers founded the A.F. of L.) that Don Vincente Martinez Ybor (say EE-bor) opened a tobacco factory in a section of Tampa that was to be called Ybor City.

Florida—with its hot, humid climate—was the perfect place for rolling cigars. The humidity kept the tobacco leaf soft and pliable. Ybor soon helped make Tampa the cigar capital of the world. By 1900, Tampa had an annual tobacco payroll of almost $2 million.

In those days, cigar smoking was popular, especially among men. It wasn't until the second half of the 20th century that people discovered that cigars and cigarettes are deadly and cancer-causing (although in 1604, King James I of England called smoking "loathsome to the eye, hateful to the nose, harmful to the brain, and dangerous to the lungs"). But in the 19th century, cigars were a big business. And the very best cigars were made from Cuban tobacco. Something about the soil and weather in Cuba seemed to produce a superior leaf. However, Cuba had placed a tax on its cigars, and that made them expensive in the U.S.

Some businesspeople decided to ship Cuban tobacco leaves to Florida, offer jobs to Cuban workers, and make the cigars in this country. They would be just like Cuban cigars, but American-made and much less costly.

So that was what they did. They began in Key West, an island off the

Mario Sanchez, the native Key Wester who painted this picture of a Key West cigar factory, was the son of the reader in his picture.

tip of the Florida peninsula; but things didn't go smoothly in Key West. There were labor strikes, a hurricane, two bad fires, and no railroad (it came to Key West later, over a long causeway and bridge).

Ybor and some other manufacturers decided to move halfway up the west coast of Florida, to a sleepy port town named Tampa. It had about 1,000 residents and a railroad; it soon became a "boom town." Workers came from Cuba, Spain, Italy, Germany, and Romania. Twelve thousand of them were soon working in some 200 cigar factories. They created an industrial community and an immigrant city—and both were unusual in the Deep South. There was something even more unusual: men and women, blacks and whites, Christians and Jews, all worked together around the cigar tables.

The Spaniards considered themselves the aristocrats and usually got the best jobs. Most of the Italian workers came from Sicily and were very poor, but willing to work hard to get ahead—and many did. The Cubans were agitating for a free Cuba (Cuba was a colony of Spain). Sometimes these different people argued fiercely—usually about politics—but, mostly, they lived and worked together with dignity and good will.

Ybor City was a planned, company town. Workers could buy their homes from the cigar company, if they wished. (The wooden houses were small and pleasant with high ceilings, front porches, backyard

In 1883 Oscar Hammerstein patents a cigar-rolling machine. Like many Americans, he is versatile. Hammerstein is known as an opera impresario, which means he puts together opera productions. In the 20th century, his grandson will become famous writing the lyrics for American musical comedies.

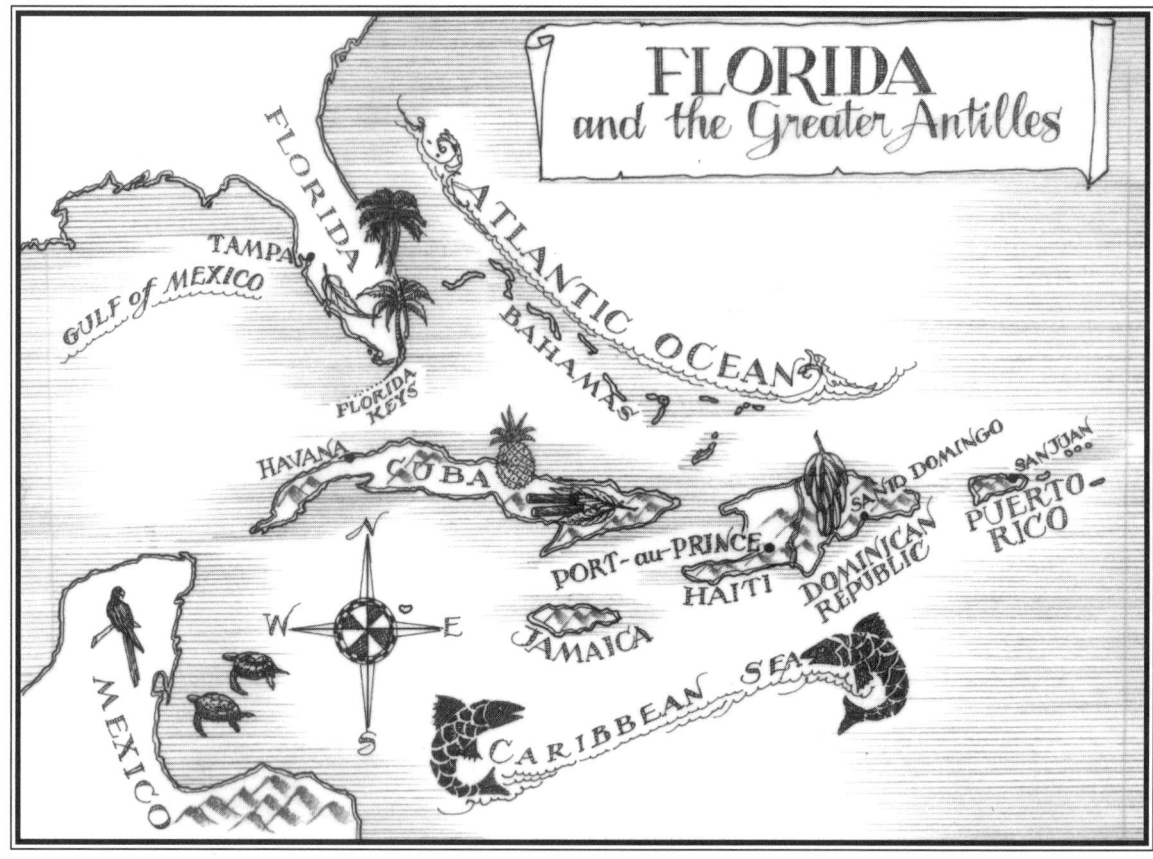

FLORIDA and the Greater Antilles

gardens, and outhouses.) Ybor's big, red-brick cigar factory had tall windows and stairs of wrought iron. Mutual-aid societies took care of most people in Ybor City. The societies provided medical care, burial insurance, and a place for parties and socializing. Each national group had its own society and its own society building. The Italians had a three-story building with marble columns in front. Inside were a theater, a bowling alley, a library, meeting rooms, and a big dance floor. (The building still stands today.) Stores and restaurants in the city were owned by individuals, not by the factory owners (as they were in many northern manufacturing towns).

If you walked down the red brick streets in Ybor City and sniffed the air, you'd smell the aromas of Cuban and Italian breads, roasted Cuban coffee, and pungent tobacco. There was plenty to do—actors even came from Spain to put on plays. The town's trilingual newspaper (it is still published) had articles in Spanish, English, and Italian. But it was Spanish culture that dominated.

Most of the workers spoke Spanish (and if they didn't, they soon learned that language). In the cigar factories the reader, who was called a *lector*, read in Spanish as workers rolled the fat cigars. It was a prestige job. The lectors were paid by the workers and made more money than any of the cigarmakers. They auditioned for the job, which means they had

The pleasant, red-brick cigar factory that Don Vincente Martinez Ybor built in Tampa, Florida.

Making cigars in Tampa, Florida, around 1910.

to try out the way an actor auditions for a play. Sometimes a committee of cigarmakers told them what to read. Usually that included the latest news and good books. The cigarmakers became very knowledgeable. While they rolled cigars they held discussions. They kept up with politics and, since many were Cuban, they worried and even got involved with what was happening in Cuba. A freedom movement was brewing on that island (more on that in Chapter 28).

A Hero for All the Americas

José Martí

José Martí was cut out to be a hero. He was both a poet and a man of action. He cared passionately about freedom and he dedicated his life to the cause of Cuba Libre ("free Cuba"). When he wrote essays and poems, he did it with a style that was vivid and clear and filled with beautiful images—and that was at a time when most Spanish writers were using stilted, pretentious language. He was a *modernista* (a modern writer) before the 20th century began. Martí is considered one of the greatest of Latin America's writers.

But it was politics and revolution that consumed most of his energy. At 16 he was arrested and kicked out of Cuba. He went off to Spain, studied, and earned a master's degree and a law degree. After that he lived and worked in Mexico, Guatemala, Venezuela, and the United States (mostly in New York City). He wrote for American magazines (articles on Emerson and Whitman as well as politics) and for Spanish publications. Martí said he was a citizen of the Americas.

When he appeared in Ybor City (as he did several times) and spoke on the iron steps in front of the Ybor cigar factory, his listeners were electrified. He was a man everyone admired (except for those who wanted to keep Cuba Spanish). Usually, in Ybor City, Martí stayed at the home of Ruperto and Paulina Pedroso, who were Afro-Cubans. Martí said Paulina was his "second mother." The lectors were sure to read whatever Martí wrote; he called their platforms "pulpits of liberty."

So when José Martí died in 1895 at age 42, on a battlefield in Cuba, people wept and called him a martyr and a great hero. Seven years later, Cuba became independent.

19 Telling It Like It Is

In Philadelphia, Mother Jones said the city's mansions were built "on the broken bones, quivering hearts and drooping heads of these children."

"Mother" Jones was a pugnacious little woman, and fearless. The worst things that could happen to a person had happened to her, so nothing else ever scared her. Her real name was Maria Harris Jones and she was living in Memphis, Tennessee, when her children caught malaria. In those days, before modern medicines, malaria was a killer. Maria Jones's four boys died. Then her husband died. She was all alone. She got her courage together, moved to Chicago, and opened a dressmaking shop.

Mrs. Jones had style, and she knew how to sew. She was becoming successful when, in 1871, Chicago had a great fire. Some say Mrs. O'Leary's cow kicked over a lantern and that started it. However it started, the whole city burned and Maria Jones's business with it. She was left with nothing. That decided her. If she was going to start over again, again, she wanted to do something important with her life. She wanted to help others. It was children she worked hardest to help.

Mother Jones was tiny—about five feet tall—with white hair (it turned white after her children died). She was called "mother" because she seemed like a nice old lady—until she opened her mouth. She swore like a trooper, had the energy of a battalion, and spoke in ear-splitting tones. Clarence Darrow, a famous lawyer, wrote of her, "Mother Jones's...fearless soul always drew her to seek the spot where the fight was hottest and the danger greatest."

She wanted people to know of the plight of child workers, so she marched a group of them from Pennsylvania to New York. The children were all millworkers. "Here's a textbook on economics," she said to a crowd in Philadelphia as she introduced little James Ashworth. His

Mother Jones was born in Ireland in 1830. In America, Andrew Jackson was president. She lived to be 100 years old. When she died, in 1930, Herbert Hoover was president and women, at last, could vote.

back was bent and he was all hunched over from carrying 75-pound loads in a factory. "He gets three dollars a week …working in a carpet factory 10 hours a day." Then she introduced Gussie Rangnew, "a little girl from whom all the childhood has gone." Gussie, whose tired face was like an old woman's, packed stockings all day long, day after day, summer, winter, spring, and fall.

The police said Mother Jones was a public nuisance. They arrested her. When the judge asked who gave her a permit to speak on the streets, she said, "Patrick Henry, Thomas Jefferson, and John Adams!" Mother Jones was sent to jail—more than once. In jail she spoke of George Washington as a "gentleman agitator" who had fought the powerful English establishment. Each time Mother Jones got out of jail she went right back

These children worked alongside their mothers and big sisters in a Maryland packing factory. "Those too small to work are held in laps or closed away in boxes," said the photographer.

The Chicago fire killed 250 people. Few people know that the fire spread to the forests of northern Michigan, where it killed 1,000 people.

In the 20th century, reformers and labor unions helped bring better wages and conditions to most of America's workers. Child-labor laws limited the hours that children could work. School laws made going to school compulsory.

A Letter From a Woman Homesteader

January 23, 1913

Dear Mrs. Coney,

When I read of the hard times among the Denver poor, I feel like urging them every one to get out and file on land. I am very enthusiastic about women homesteading. It really requires less strength and labor to raise plenty to satisfy a large family than it does to go out to wash, with the added satisfaction of knowing that their job will not be lost to them if they care to keep it. Even if improving the place goes slowly…whatever is raised is the homesteader's own….This year Jerrine [Stewart's daughter] cut and dropped enough potatoes to raise a ton of fine potatoes. She wanted to try, so we let her, and you remember that she is but six years old….

To me, homesteading is the solution of all poverty's problems, but I realize that temperament has much to do with success in any undertaking, and persons afraid of coyotes and work and loneliness had better let ranching alone….I am only thinking of the troops of tired, worried women, sometimes even cold and hungry, scared to death of losing their places to work, who could have plenty to eat, who could have good fires by gathering the wood, and comfortable homes of their own, if they but had the courage and determination to get them….

Yours affectionately,
Elinore Rupert Stewart

Many children Mother Jones fought for worked in difficult and dangerous jobs. These boys are operating a canning machine.

to speaking out for workers. "I'm not a humanitarian," she said, "I'm a hell-raiser." Actually, she was both. And she was very good at getting attention. Mother Jones made people think about America's working children. Here is part of what she wrote after going into a cotton mill in Alabama, where she worked along with the children:

Little girls and boys, barefooted, walked up and down between the endless rows of spindles, reaching thin little hands into the machinery to repair snapped threads. They crawled under machinery to oil it. They replaced spindles all day long; all night through…six-year-olds with faces of sixty did an eight-hour shift for ten cents a day: the machines, built in the North, were built low for the hands of little children….At the lunch half-hour, the children would fall to sleep over their lunch of cornbread and fat pork. They would lie on the bare floor and sleep. Sleep was their recreation, their release, as play is to the free child.

These children weren't slaves, but they might as well have been. This was another form of servitude. Something needed to be done. Laws were needed to keep children in school. Laws were needed to make working conditions safe for all workers. And there was something else—besides working conditions—that needed regulating: it was the products themselves.

Since there were no laws to prevent it, some meat packers put dangerous spoiled meat in hot dogs. Some manufacturers built toys that could hurt children. There

were no laws about these things, because in the early days people bought meat from a butcher they knew. Toys were usually made at home. Now, with big factories and modern transportation, people were buying things made far from their homes.

Mother Jones wasn't the only one concerned. Writers were writing about the problems of unregulated business. Theodore Roosevelt called those writers *muckrakers*, because they raked up muck and told people about it.

But you can't clean up the dirt unless you know where it is. (Read about the muckrakers in Chapters 22 and 23.) Eventually, laws were passed to protect children and make going to school compulsory. A pure food and drug act helped make our food safe. It was those who shouted out—like Mother Jones—who made those laws happen. "The militant, not the meek, shall inherit the earth," said Mother Jones. What did she mean by that?

Above, children sewing piecework in a New York tenement; below, a city newsboy. These boys had to pay for any papers they couldn't sell.

Inferno in Chicago

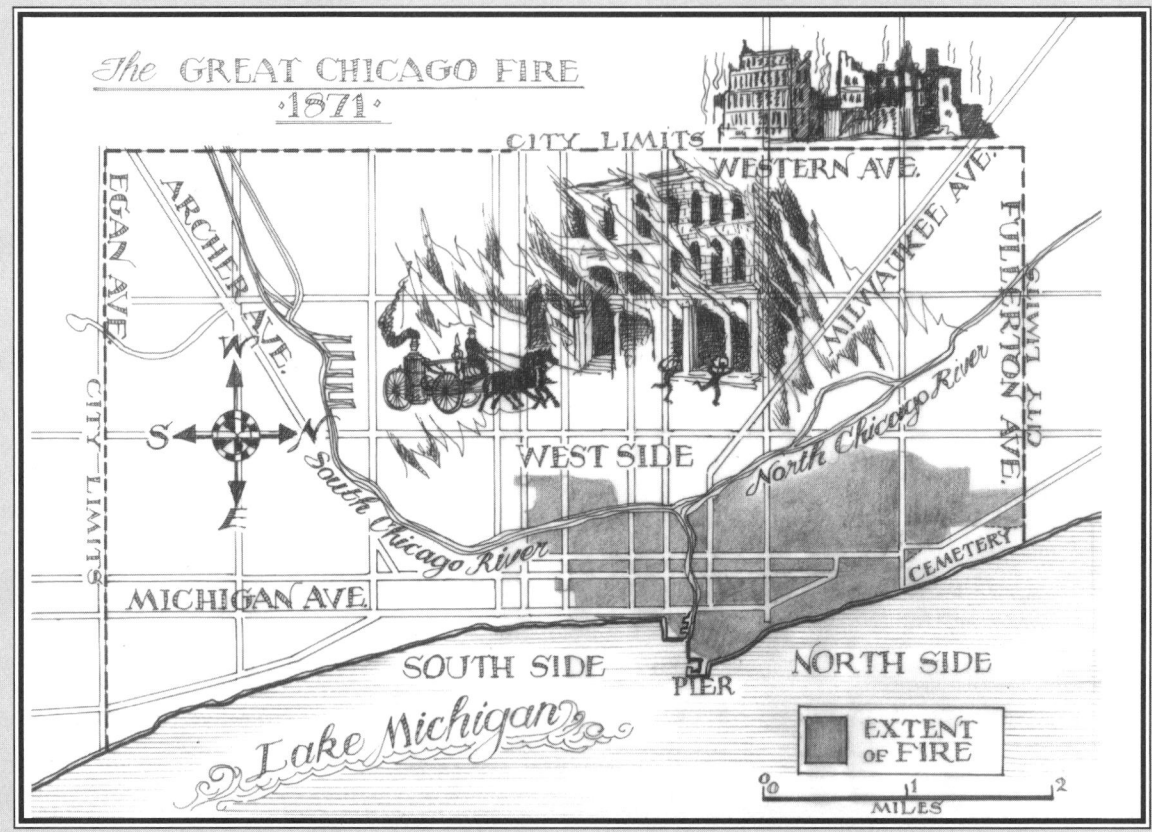

It was October 8, 1871, and Mrs. O'Leary left a kerosene lantern in her hay-filled barn on DeKoven Street. The cow kicked, the barn began blazing, and there was no stopping the flames. Chicago was then a rinky-dink, hastily built city. Wooden buildings were squeezed together. The city quickly became an inferno. By morning, 18,000 buildings were gone. The fire is said to have reached 3,000° Fahrenheit. Buildings of "fireproof" masonry melted away. Cast-iron buildings turned liquid. Ninety thousand people (out of a population of 300,000) were left homeless.

John R. Chapin, a reporter for *Harper's Weekly*, arrived in Chicago for the first time on a Saturday night and checked in at the Sherman House Hotel. He knew that a fire had turned part of the city to ashes, but urban fires were commonplace; he didn't think much of it—even though a wind was blowing. Then a friend took him to see the new, completely fireproof home of the *Chicago Tribune*—and he was impressed. He was fast asleep when someone banged on his door. "I rose and went to the window, threw open the blinds, and gazed upon a sheet of flame towering one hundred feet above the top of the hotel and upon a shower of sparks as copious as drops in a thunderstorm." Chapin ran toward Washington Street, joining a crowd of people, all fleeing. "Helping now a poor mother who was struggling along with an infant and half a dozen older children....assisting an old woman staggering under her burden of household stuff, we at length

"A torrent of humanity was pouring over the bridge," wrote a reporter. *"Drays, express wagons, trucks...of every conceivable species and size."*

reached the other side and emerged into a place of safety....As far as the eyes could see toward the south the flames extended in one unbroken sheet, while they were advancing (a wall of fire from one to two hundred feet in height) with terrible rapidity. One glance was sufficient to convince the most hopeful that the city was doomed." What about the "completely fireproof" *Tribune* building? It burned too.

After the fire: the heart of the city, at the corner of State and Madison streets.

20 Bread and Roses, Too

The emblem of a railroad union affiliated with the Wobblies. The Wobblies attracted many whom the regular unions weren't interested in: migrant workers, and unskilled laborers of all kinds.

For a small, disorganized group, Western Wobblies got a great deal of public attention. Some of that they asked for directly. Beginning in 1910, in rebellions that started as protests against manipulative employment agencies, the Wobblies staged a series of free-speech fights along the Pacific Coast. Seeing the Wobblies as the embodiment of social disorder, city governments passed ordinances prohibiting their public speeches. Some of these ordinances were extraordinary in their nullification of civil liberties.

—Patricia Nelson Limerick,
The Legacy of Conquest

What does "embodiment of social disorder" mean? How about "nullification"?

Officially they were the Industrial Workers of the World, but everyone called them *Wobblies*. Yes, you read that right: Wobblies. Utah's William "Big Bill" Haywood opened their founding convention in Chicago in 1905, when he took a loose board, pounded on a table, and proclaimed in his booming voice: "Fellow workers...this is the Continental Congress of the Working Class."

Lucy Parsons joined him on the platform. Parsons was Mexican-Indian and, like Big Bill, powerful-spirited and decent. Her husband, Albert Parsons, had been hanged after the Haymarket Square bombing. Lucy knew he had nothing to do with the bombing, so she took her two children and went off and spoke at hundreds of meetings until she sparked a worldwide protest movement. Finally, the governor of Illinois proclaimed that Albert Parsons and the others had been killed for their beliefs, not their actions.

Mother Jones, now 75 and feisty as ever, was an honored guest at the IWW founding convention.

Wobblies had the idea that all workers, not just skilled workers, should be in unions together. Their goal was one big union—all workers would belong to it—and they'd have one big strike

Big Bill Haywood

110

The IWW paper *Industrial Worker* had its own comic strip, "Mr. Block," about a poor worker (Mr. Block) who was too stupid to understand that the big bosses weren't on his side.

that would stop everything, and the workers could take over and make the country a better place. It was a dream that captivated them. They were idealists, and mostly sincere, but they were rarely in agreement with one another about just how that ideal country would be organized.

At first, most of the Wobblies were miners, from the West. There was an abundance of writers among them, and they wrote poems and songs about their problems and hopes. Just about every member had a copy of the little red IWW songbook; singing seemed to come naturally to them. (One of their songs was called "Solidarity Forever." It became a theme song for the whole labor movement.) If a local union needed help, Wobblies would hop into train boxcars, arrive, march, climb on soapboxes, speak, get thrown in jail, and sing.

They hated Sam Gompers's American Federation of Labor. It was the American *Separation* of Labor, said the Wobblies. AFL members were skilled workers—the aristocrats of the working world—and not everyone was welcome. The Wobblies were democratic: any worker could join.

Gentle Eugene Debs, a lanky railroad man from Terre Haute, Indiana, was another important Wobbly founder. (Later, Debs became head of the Socialist Party, was sent to prison for opposing World War I, ran for president from jail, and got more than 900,000 votes.) Yet another was tall, black-bearded Father Thomas J. Hagerty, a Roman Catholic priest who had fought some battles for Mexican railroad workers. Hagerty said, "The

Eugene Debs was pilloried by the press (here shown as "King Debs") for backing the Pullman strikers. He is the only presidential candidate ever to run from jail.

A textile working town is not a pleasant place to live in—dirty wooden buildings, dirty streets, unlovely looking people, cheap goods in the store windows, no good society. So the owners live in Boston and elsewhere.

—RAY STANNARD BAKER
(A MUCKRAKER) IN THE *AMERICAN*

working class and the employing class have nothing in common" (which didn't leave a whole lot of room for working out problems together).

But, while overthrowing capitalism was their long-range goal, the IWW (like the AFL) started out by fighting for shorter hours, better pay, and safer conditions for workers. It was in Lawrence, Massachusetts, that they had their finest moment.

The Massachusetts legislature passed a law saying that women and children were not allowed to work more than 54 hours a week. The owners of the textile mills in Lawrence weren't going to accept that! Women and children had been working 56 hours. The owners speeded up their machinery so the workers would produce as much in 54 hours as they had in 56 (workers had to work faster to keep up). Then they took two hours' pay (about 32 cents) out of each wage envelope. Since the average worker earned about seven dollars a week, 32 cents—the price of three

"What time is it?" said a Wobbly poster. "Time to organize." And at Lawrence, they organized. They ran separate committees for each nationality, so different ethnic groups wouldn't fight, and translated speeches and fliers into each language.

Elizabeth Gurley Flynn became a strike leader for the Wobblies at the age of 16.

loaves of bread—was a lot of money.

William M. Wood, president of the American Woolen Company, said, "To pay for 54 hours' work the wages of 56 would be equivalent to an increase in wages, and that the mills cannot afford to pay." (The American Woolen Company's Lawrence mill was the largest cloth-producing factory in the world—30 acres under one roof. The company's net profits in 1911 were close to $4 million.)

It was January of 1912, and bitter cold, and when they got those pay envelopes some Polish women left their looms. Before long 25,000 millworkers had walked off the job. Most were foreign-born—between them they spoke about 45 different languages. (None of the mill owners was foreign-born; none lived in Lawrence.) Many of the workers had come to Lawrence after reading advertisements in their native lands telling of opportunities in the mills. (One poster showed a Lawrence workingman leaving the factory with a suitcase full of gold.) When they got to Lawrence they found that their pay barely kept them from starving. Their housing was horrible. Their children worked because they had to (most would rather have been in school).

They wanted more than just barely enough to eat. So they picketed with big signs that said, "We Want Bread and Roses, Too."

But they didn't have a real leader—all those languages made leadership difficult—so they appealed to the IWW for help. Big Bill Haywood was soon on his way east. He had no trouble communicating with gestures and sign language and his big heart. Elizabeth Gurley Flynn (a slim, pretty Irish dynamo) came too. Flynn was well known. She had chained herself to a lamppost in Spokane, Washington, after city officials began throwing Wobblies in jail for having public meetings to protest job-hiring methods. Flynn called it an attack on freedom of speech. But it was 26-year-old Joe Ettor who turned out to be the leader in Lawrence. The son of an Italian immigrant family, Ettor grew up on the West Coast and spoke Italian and English fluently, with enough Polish, Hungarian, and Yiddish to get by. Joe was stocky, had a big grin, and was a terrific organizer.

In Lawrence, some leading citizens were calling the strikes

The Wobblies [used] a then novel nonviolent, passive-resistance tactic. They courted arrest, deliberately violating ordinances denying them free speech. Each time one speaker was arrested, another Wobbly would take his place. As more and more "footloose rebels" came to town, the process was continued. Arrested by the hundreds, one after another, the Wobblies continued to demonstrate in jail—singing, shouting, hunger striking...as obstreperously [obstinately] as possible. As they kept on coming, they filled the jails and the improvised bullpens—causing the city politicians maximum embarrassment and expense, until their right to meet, speak, and organize was conceded.

—LEN DE CAUX, *WOBBLY*

113

Joe Ettor (left), one of the most important Wobbly leaders in Lawrence, and Arturo Giovannitti were arrested for murder to get them out of the way.

A Woman with a Cause

Margaret Sanger

Margaret Sanger was in charge of getting the Lawrence children down to New York City. Later, she became famous—notorious, in fact —when she opened America's first birth-control clinic. She was arrested several times, but was determined not to give up—she herself was the sixth of 11 children; her mother died of exhaustion at the age of 49.

un-American and blaming "foreign influences." (They meant the immigrants.) The *American Wool and Cotton Reporter* (the mill owners' magazine) warned of "anarchy" and "socialism" and challenges to "the fundamental idea of law and order." (It meant the Wobblies.) Ettor tried to keep the workers calm. He said to them, "You can hope for no success on any policy of violence....violence...means the loss of the strike."

There was violence at Lawrence. It was police violence. Strikers were the victims. The mayor said, "We will either break this strike or break the strikers' heads." Richard Washburn Child, writing in *Collier's* (a popular magazine), quoted a wool-company stockholder as saying, "The way to settle this strike is to shoot down 40 or 50 of them."

Militia, special policemen, and Pinkerton detectives were brought to the city. Dynamite was discovered, strikers were arrested, and newspaper headlines screamed of anarchy. But it was soon found that the dynamite had been planted by the son of a former mayor, trying to frame the strikers. Then detectives—pretending to be striking workers—smashed streetcar windows and tried to start a riot; Joe Ettor kept the real strikers orderly.

Collier's wrote, "It is wrong to charge...that the doctrine of the IWW... at Lawrence...was...a doctrine of violence; fundamentally it was a doctrine of the brotherhood of man."

One evening a group of strikers found themselves surrounded by armed police. A shot rang out and Annie LoPizza fell dead. Joe Ettor and IWW poet Arturo Giovannitti were arrested for the murder—although they were two miles away at the time. They were kept in jail for months, and kept out of their leadership roles.

More was to come. Police bayoneted and killed 16-year-old John Rami, who wasn't even a striker (he was on the street watching the picketing). Newspapers and magazines were covering the strike. People all over the country began reading about Lawrence. Most Americans hadn't known about conditions in the mills. Some offered to care for strikers' children. A group of children sent to New York were all "found to be suffering from malnutrition." They hadn't been getting enough to eat. People's hearts were going out to the Lawrence workers.

On the 43rd day of the strike, 40 children and their parents were gathered at the Lawrence railroad station. The children had been invited to Philadelphia, where families had arranged to "adopt" them until the strike was over. Suddenly the police appeared. The *Boston Common* of February 28, 1912, reported what happened:

"Police, acting under orders of the city marshal, choked and knocked down women and children, the innocent wives and babies of the strikers."

That was too much. Congress investigated. Dr. Elizabeth Shapleigh of Lawrence said that "thirty-six of every 100 of all men and women who work in the mill die before or by the time they are 25 years of age." Fourteen-year-old Camella Teoli told of catching her hair in a machine and having it all pulled out. President Taft (whose wife attended the hearings) ordered a general investigation of industrial conditions. Finally, the mill owners agreed to raise wages, pay for overtime, and re-hire the strikers. The Bread and Roses strike was over!

That's the best story of the Wobblies. After that it was mostly down-hill. The Wobblies opposed America's entry into World War I. Most Americans didn't agree with that, or with some of their other ideas. But,

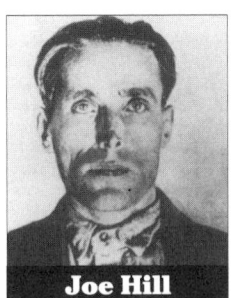

Joe Hill

in a free country, is that a reason for jailing and persecuting people? The First Amendment is all about respecting free speech even when you don't agree with the speaker. If you want to know more about the Wobblies and unions in the West, read about the workers' massacres at Ludlow, Colorado, and Everett, Washington (and see Chapter 2). Or find out about Wobbly songwriter Joe Hill. Or about Margaret Sanger, who started out as a Wobbly.

"They cannot weave cloth with bayonets," said Joe Ettor. "By all means make the strike as peaceful as possible."

21 The Fourth Estate

"They serve as chimneys to carry off noxious vapors and smoke," said Thomas Jefferson. What was he talking about?

Thomas Jefferson (left) was talking about the press. Noxious vapors? Could those be stinking ideas?

School Speech

On February 26, 1969, the U.S. Supreme Court handed down a decision on free speech that affects students in schools. In the case of *Tinker* v. *Des Moines Independent School District*, the majority decision said: *It can hardly be argued that either students or teachers shed their constitutional rights to freedom of speech or expression at the schoolhouse gate.*

What does that mean? Does it mean you can be irresponsible? Is lying protected? Invite a lawyer into your classroom and have a discussion. Better yet, invite two.

How many branches does our government have? Did you answer three?

Some people say you are wrong. They say we have four branches. The fourth is unofficial but very important. Thomas Jefferson wrote a letter to a friend in which he said that the fourth branch was the most important of all.

Later, when he became president, he got a bit irritated with that fourth branch. Can you guess what the fourth branch is?

Think for a minute before you read on. Then see if you can guess from the clues that lie ahead.

On January 16, 1787, Thomas Jefferson wrote a letter to his friend Edward Carrington. He began by saying, "The people are the only censors of their governors." What does that mean?

When Jefferson used the word *censors* he meant examiners or supervisors. In other words, it is up to the people to look carefully at those whom they have chosen as their leaders. How can the people do that? How can people make sure they are well informed about government and about those who govern them? It is with that fourth branch of the government. Read another clue from Jefferson's letter:

The way to prevent…[errors] of the people is to give them full information of their affairs through the channel of the public papers, and to contrive that those papers should penetrate the whole mass of the people.

Have you figured out the answer? Here is a very famous part of Jefferson's letter to Edward Carrington.

The basis of our government being the opinion of the people, the

very first object should be to keep that right; and were it left to me to decide whether we should have a government without newspapers, or newspapers without a government, I should not hesitate a moment to prefer the latter.

The fourth branch of our government is its *free press*!

The First Amendment to the Constitution, also known as Article I of the Bill of Rights, says:

Congress shall make no law…abridging the freedom of speech, or of the press.

Americans have been eager readers of newspapers and journals since the days of William Bradford and Peter Zenger. (Remember them?) But

Today we have electronic billboards. In 1898, during the Spanish-American War (see Chapter 28), the latest bulletins off the telegraph were written up by hand on New York City's Park Row, where many newspapers were printed.

To **abridge** means to cut, shorten, or edit.

Congress shall make no law respecting an establishment of religion, or prohibiting the free exercise thereof; or abridging the freedom of speech, or of the press; or the right of the people peaceably to assemble, and to petition the government for redress of grievances.

—THE FIRST AMENDMENT
TO THE CONSTITUTION

Today when we use the word *media* it usually means any or all of newspapers, magazines, radio, and TV.

America's leaders have often become exasperated with that free press. No one likes to be criticized, and that is exactly what good journalists do. John Adams tried to curb the press with the Alien and Sedition Acts. And, as you know, even Thomas Jefferson got annoyed at the press when he was president.

Sometimes the media can be irresponsible, though libel laws usually control deliberate lying. (You can sue a newspaper if it lies and that lie harms you. A public figure must prove that the newspaper, or TV program, knew that what it was saying was false and that it had reckless disregard for the truth.)

Jefferson never changed his mind about the importance of the press. And Americans have always understood that if we are to solve our problems we need *information*. A free press supplies that information.

At the turn of the century, America had unusually difficult problems to solve. The country was experiencing astonishing growth; industrialization and urbanization; an influx of many different peoples; and excessive government corruption. People needed to understand these phenomena to be able to deal with them. To understand them they had to have information.

Just when they were needed, some remarkable writers and editors appeared. They did exactly what Thomas Jefferson wanted them to do. They looked at America critically, fearlessly, and honestly—and they explained what they saw.

A Woman Named Nellie Bly

You don't have to get in a covered wagon to be a pioneer. Anyone who charts new territories is pioneering. So Elizabeth Jane Cochrane was a real pioneer—and famous, too—although hardly anyone knew her by that name. They called her *Nellie Bly*, which was the way she signed her newspaper articles. Nellie got started when she wrote a sizzling letter to the editor of the *Pittsburgh Dispatch* (after reading it he hired her). She was soon writing for the most talked-about newspaper in the country, Joseph Pulitzer's *New York World*. Most women who were reporters—and there weren't many of them—were assigned to the cooking or household beat. Not Nellie Bly. She was a daredevil reporter who went around the globe to see if she could outdo the exploits of a character named Phineas Fogg in a popular novel by Jules Verne, *Around the World in Eighty Days*. She did it. When she decided to write about the treatment of the mentally ill, she pretended to be insane, got herself committed to an asylum, and wrote the best-selling series of articles "Inside the Madhouse." Later, Bly became the first woman to cover the European front in World War I.

Nellie Bly in her traveling-around-the-world outfit in 1890. She loved stylish clothes.

22 Ida, Sam, and the Muckrakers

A fellow muckraker said Ida Tarbell was "beautiful with virtue—so generous, so modest, so full of kindness," and able "to infect her pages with her own shining love of truth."

Ida Tarbell was a *muckraker*—although she preferred to call herself a historian. Actually, she was both. And amazingly good at both callings.

Muck is dirt. Muckrakers were journalists who wrote about wrongs: about injustice, unfairness, and corruption. They went into slaughterhouses, where animals were killed and meat was processed, and they saw rats and dirt, and described what they saw. They wrote about city bosses and told how dishonest government cheated citizens of their rights and money. They wrote about the mighty industrial tycoons, about how some of them broke the law and got away with it, and why that cost the public great sums of money. And they wrote that in a democracy, all of these wrongs could be righted by the people; but only if the people are informed and take the time to vote.

The muckrakers had several things in common: they wrote unusually well, they did careful research, and they cared—really cared—about making this country a better place to live. They developed a new kind of journalism—*investigative journalism*—just at a time when publishing techniques made it possible to produce a good magazine, distribute it widely, and sell it for 10 cents. Everyone seemed to read the muckrakers' articles. And that made them very influential. They helped bring about change. Food-inspection laws were passed; antitrust laws were enforced; reforming mayors were elected to office.

Of all the muckrakers, Ida Tarbell was the most famous. When she was a little girl she heard women reformers say that if she wanted a career,

> Sensible, capable, and very affectionate, she knew each of us and all our idiosyncrasies and troubles. She had none of her own so far as I ever heard. When we were deadlocked we might each of us send for her, and down she would come to the office, smiling, like a tall, good-looking young mother, to say, "Hush, children."
> —LINCOLN STEFFENS ON IDA TARBELL

Idiosyncrasies (id-ee-o-SIN-kruh-seez) are special quirks.

119

In 1906, muckraker Upton Sinclair (above left) wrote a best-selling novel, *The Jungle*, about the city of Chicago, its horrible slums, and in particular its stockyards (above) and meat packers. He exposed factories' filthy ways of butchering and preparing meat.

Men with the muck-rake
are often indispensable
to the well-being of
society, but only if they
know when to stop
raking the muck.

—THEODORE ROOSEVELT

she would have to give up the idea of marriage. Tarbell vowed never to marry—and she never did. She wished to be a scientist.

She knew, if she was to do something with her life, that she needed an education, so she enrolled at Allegheny College, the only woman in her class. She soon discovered that a college degree and a passion for science were not enough; the world of scientific research, like most fields, was a men-only domain. Educated women were expected to teach. Ida did become a teacher, but she found she didn't want to teach, so she went off to Europe.

Sam McClure

She had a little money and a lot of adventurousness—and she could write. She believed she could write articles that would support her in France. That was what she was doing when the doorbell rang and Samuel Sidney McClure walked into her life.

Sam McClure was born in a two-room cottage in Ireland. When he was eight his father died. The family had relatives in Indiana, so his mother decided to take her three children to the United States. It was in Indiana, one Fourth of July, that young Sam heard a congressman give a speech. "He talked about the land of freedom...of

120

unbounded opportunities. I had never heard such a speech before....I felt that, as he said, here was something big and free—that a boy might make his mark on those prairies." But it wouldn't be easy for Sam. His mother worked as a maid and washerwoman. "I remember the hardship," he wrote later, "of having to eat frozen potatoes boiled to a kind of gray mush."

At age 14, with a dollar in his pocket, Sam McClure left home. He was determined to go to high school, but he needed to work to do it. He found a job, got room and board, and was up at 5:30 each morning to milk cows and feed horses. He had no winter coat, so he ran to school. "Speed was my overcoat," he wrote.

High school left Sam hungry for more learning. He headed for Knox College in Galesburg, Illinois. But he didn't have enough money to go to college; so he worked, went to college, dropped out to earn more money, went to college, and worked some more. By the time he graduated he was sure of one thing: he didn't want to do physical labor again.

> I had looked forward for eight years to graduating, and I had always thought that when I graduated I would be tall, that I would know a great deal, and that I would have all the plans made for my life. Here I was no taller, no wiser and with no plans at all. The future was an absolute blank ahead of me.

Sam went east, to Boston, where he saw an advertisement for a job at a bicycle manufacturing company. The job was to teach people how to ride. He'd never had a bike; he'd never even "been close to one," but he learned quickly. He got the job. Soon he was editing a biking magazine called *Wheelman*. Bicycling was a new rage; articles poured in.

Then he got a brilliant idea. He would start a syndicate (SIN-dih-cut) for writers. No one had ever done that before. He bought articles from very good writers and sold each article to several publications. The authors made more money than if they had sold to just one journal, and small papers and magazines were able to publish the best authors. McClure took the assembly-line method and applied it to journalism (read about factory assembly lines in Chapter 31).

By now he realized that what he really wanted to do was to be an editor. In 1892 he borrowed money and founded *McClure's* magazine. Not long after, he received an article from an unknown author. It was about paving the streets of Paris. That was an unlikely topic, but as soon as he started reading he said to an associate, "This girl can write. I want her to do some work for the magazine."

So he went to Paris, met the author, and established one of the most interesting collaborations in the history of journalism.

Enter Sam McClure: blond, tow-headed and mustached, blue-to-hazel eyes, oval face, short, that is five feet seven or eight, with a wire voice....He talked like a pair of scissors, clipping his sentences, sometimes his words; gave the impression of a powerhouse of energy.

—WILLIAM ALLEN WHITE,
MUCKRAKER

The cover of the issue of *McClure's* that made both Sam McClure and Ida Tarbell world famous.

23 A Boon to the Writer

"Miss Tarbell," said one paper, "has done more to dethrone Rockefeller in public esteem than all the preachers in the land."

Sam McClure could spot talent. Ida Tarbell was an outstanding writer. McClure suggested she write a book about Napoleon. When she did, *McClure's* ran a chapter each week. It was an inspired idea. People couldn't wait to read her chapters. McClure sold a lot of magazines.

Next, Tarbell wrote a *Life of Abraham Lincoln*. Again, *McClure's* ran chapters in each issue. And, again, people couldn't wait to get their copies of the magazine. *McClure's* circulation jumped from 120,000 to 250,000.

Then Ida Tarbell began looking at the world around her. She felt that the standards of her day were not at all the standards of her hero Abraham Lincoln. Many people—whether big business leaders, union leaders, political leaders, or ordinary citizens—seemed not to care about laws, or even about right and wrong. Money and power were their only goals. "A thing won by breaking the rules of the game is not worth the winning," she wrote.

McClure (most people now called him "S.S.") encouraged her to write a book about America's most powerful citizen, John D. Rockefeller, and about his giant trust, Standard Oil. Tarbell spent four years writing two books that shocked the American people. She showed how Standard Oil took unfair advantage of its competitors. She showed how its uncontrolled power

Ida
Tarbell

Rockefeller's son said Standard Oil was a rose that "can be produced …only by sacrificing the early buds which grow up around it." This cartoonist didn't think much of that idea.

had spread into railroads, mining, and banking, and how that power affected the lives of most Americans. Tarbell was always proud that nothing she wrote was ever proved wrong.

Three years after her books were published, the Supreme Court dissolved the trust of the Standard Oil Company.

Mr. Rockefeller has systematically played with loaded dice, and it is doubtful if there has ever been a time since 1872 when he has run a race with a competitor and started fair. Business played in this way loses all its sportsmanlike qualities. It is fit only for tricksters.

—IDA TARBELL

Ida Tarbell wasn't the only writer whom S. S. McClure encouraged. He had a knack for finding good writers. "I had to invent a new method of magazine journalism," he said. His method was to pay writers well and let them do careful, lengthy research. One of them, Ray

Rockefeller runs as the conservative magazine *Judge* tries to protect him from an ink-throwing gang of muckrakers.

Standard Oil goes after new oil finds in Kansas and tries to defend its policies to a shocked governor and two disbelieving muckrakers.

The misgovernment of the American people is misgovernment by the American people.

When I set out on my travels, an honest New Yorker told me honestly that I would find that the Irish, the Catholic Irish, were at the bottom of it all everywhere. The first city I went to was St. Louis, a German city. The next was Minneapolis, a Scandinavian city, with a leadership of New Englanders. Then came Pittsburgh, Scotch Presbyterian, and that was what my New York friend was. "Ah, but they are all foreign populations," I heard. The next was Philadelphia, the purest American community of all, and the most hopeless. And after that came Chicago and New York, both mongrel-bred, but the one a triumph of reform, the other the best example of good government that I had seen. The "foreign element" excuse is one of the hypocritical lies that save us from the clear sight of ourselves.

—LINCOLN STEFFENS,
THE SHAME OF THE CITIES

See Book 7 of A History of US *for the story of Boss Tweed.*

Stannard Baker, wrote:

> *What a boon to the writer! To be able to take his time, saturate himself with his subject, assure accuracy by studying the subject at first hand and consulting every possible expert.*

Lincoln Steffens, another of *McClure's* writers, decided to investigate America's growing cities. He wanted to compare "the theories of ethics" (how people should behave) with the "actual conduct of men in business, politics, and the professions." He did that in articles that became a book called *The Shame of the Cities.* It made him famous.

Lincoln Steffens

Steffens went to St. Louis, Minneapolis, and Philadelphia, and found corruption. Then he studied New York and found it the best-governed city in America. Remember New York's Boss Tweed and his Tammany Hall gang of crooks? New Yorkers had booted them out and had good government and schools. Most people assumed it was the poor who were the criminals in cities; Steffens showed that crime and graft were also found in the world of the middle class and the rich.

Steffens's boyhood wasn't at all like S. S. McClure's. Lincoln Steffens grew up in Sacramento, California, with his own pony and just about everything a boy could wish for. The house he lived in was so beautiful that it later became the California governor's mansion. Did he appreciate everything he had?

Magazines often used well-known illustrators, too; John Sloan was the artist for this cover for *The Masses* about the 1914 Colorado miners' strike. Police attacked the strikers, who were camped in tents.

Not a bit. He was a problem student, so his parents sent him to military school, hoping he would reform. He hated it there. When it was time to go to college he couldn't even pass the entrance exams. His parents got him a tutor, and, finally, he made it into the University of California at Berkeley. He still wasn't much of a student, but he was becoming interested in ideas and books.

After college he didn't know what to do with himself. He thought he'd like to write novels. So he went to Europe, studied some more, and tried to write. But his novels weren't any good and his father said he would no longer support him. Steffens had to go to work. He came back to America and got a newspaper job as a police reporter. He was good at that. New York City's police commissioner, Theodore Roosevelt, often called on him for advice.

When Steffens became a muckraker, he "set the pattern for investigative and advocacy journalism," wrote his biographer, who also said that his work is "marked by...ethical fervor, compassion, generosity, and good hope."

Jack London, Booth Tarkington, Rudyard Kipling, Stephen Crane, Hamlin Garland, and Willa Cather were others of McClure's writers. If you have not heard those names, you will. They are all exceptional writers.

Because *McClure's* was so successful, other magazines began doing the same thing: hiring good writers and paying them well. Most of those magazines sold for 10 cents. It was a fine time for America's readers.

Jack London

McClure came up with an idea he called "human documents." He wanted his writers to tell the personal stories of public officials. Journalists had not done that before. It was a good idea. The public loved reading about the private lives of public people.

24 In Wilderness Is Preservation

John Muir once said, "I only went out for a walk and finally concluded to stay out till sundown, for going out, I found, was really going in." What did he mean by that?

Sometimes too much of a good thing turns out to be not such a good thing. We Americans were so rich in land, we became wasteful. It was the existence of the frontier that was in part to blame. The frontier—empty, inviting land—had a bewitching effect on the nation. It seemed as if it were endless, and that there would always be new land to settle, plant, and use up.

Thomas Jefferson thought America a land "with room enough for our descendants to the hundredth and thousandth generation." After 1890, most people knew that was not so.

In 1890 the U.S. Census Bureau said there was no more frontier. That was a shock. What did it mean?

It meant that the great stretches of habitable empty land were gone. The country was filling up. The frontier had been what is called a mixed blessing. It made hard work, cooperation, and resourcefulness important American traits. On a frontier it is what you can do—not who you are—that people care about. The frontier made America more democratic. But that frontier also made us wasteful, and it wasn't only land we wasted.

Muir always hurried back to the mountains from the city shouting, "I'm wild once more!"

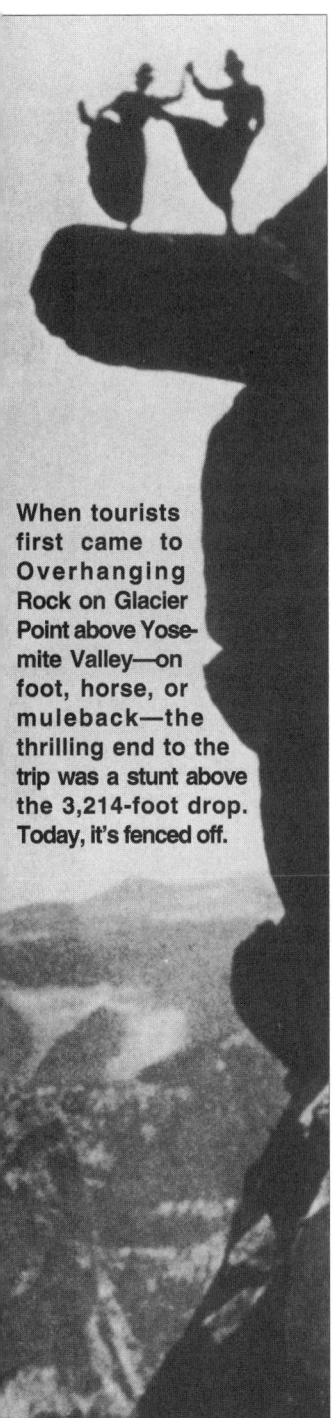

When tourists first came to Overhanging Rock on Glacier Point above Yosemite Valley—on foot, horse, or muleback—the thrilling end to the trip was a stunt above the 3,214-foot drop. Today, it's fenced off.

By 1890 the passenger pigeon was extinct; the endless herds of buffalo were being mowed down and would soon be gone; millions of acres of towering, ancient trees were gone or going; and mining was leaving mountainsides ravished and barren. A few citizens—a very few—began to talk of ways to preserve the land. One of them was John Muir.

Muir arrived in Wisconsin from Scotland at age 11. His new neighbors soon realized that he was a genius. It was his inventions that most impressed them. He invented a field thermometer so sensitive that it registered the heat of an approaching person or animal. He invented a wooden clock that struck the hours, started the fire in his stove, lit his lamp and—with levers and wheels—raised the head of his bed and woke him in the morning.

He might have been another Thomas Edison, but an accident set him on a different path. Muir was working in a factory when a file flew into his eye. For a while he was blind and believed he would never see again. When he recovered he said he would waste no more time, but would live with nature. "God has to nearly kill us sometimes," he said, "to teach us lessons."

It was 1867. Muir was 29, and he wrote, "I set forth...joyful and free, on a thousand-mile walk to the Gulf of Mexico...by the wildest, leafiest, and least-trodden way I could find." He was embarking on the life he most wanted to live. "I might have been a millionaire," he said. "I chose to become a tramp." He spent much of the rest of his life in the out-of-doors. He took other Americans outdoors with him in the journals he kept and the articles he wrote:

As long as I live I'll hear waterfalls and birds and winds sing. I'll interpret the rocks, learn the language of flood, storm, and the avalanche. I'll acquaint myself with the glaciers and wild gardens, and get as near the heart of the world as I can.

Come with me along the glaciers and see God making landscapes.
—JOHN MUIR

A *habitable* area is livable (as opposed to barren mountains, waterless deserts, soggy swamps, etc., which cannot support permanent human settlements).

Muir called himself a citizen of the "Earth-planet-universe," and went on "rambles," seeking knowledge, in Europe, Asia, South America, and Africa. When the elderly poet and philosopher Ralph Waldo Emerson met young Muir, Emerson added Muir's name to a list of great men he had met. (The feeling was mutual.)

John Muir was a naturalist; he studied nature (and loved it). Some other American naturalists were Thomas Jefferson, John James Audubon, and Henry David Thoreau.

The Sierra Club, dedicated to preserving and exploring the wilderness, was one of the results of its president John Muir's work. These picnicking ladies are early members.

Muir believed that it was in nature that one can best answer questions of life and its meaning. Disturbing the balance of nature, he said, leads to floods and drought. Disturbing the balance of peoples leads to war.

In California's rugged Sierra Nevada mountains he felt at home—although he rarely stayed in one place. He was always going off on hikes and adventures. He would "throw some tea and bread in an old sack and jump over the back fence." Muir climbed mountains, slogged through swamps, faced bears, panthers, and snakes. He never carried a gun; to kill was to disturb nature. He walked through much of Alaska, the Grand Canyon and California's Yosemite Valley. Yosemite, carved by glaciers (as Muir discovered), has mountains, meadows, waterfalls, and cliffs. It has giant sequoia trees. "God himself seems to be doing his best here," was what John Muir said of Yosemite. His writings helped make it a national park. That was in 1890. Do you think it a coincidence that it was the same year the census bureau reported that there was no more frontier?

Three kinds of people were deciding the future of our national resources. There were those, like John Muir, who loved nature so intensely that they wanted to leave vast acres just as they were created, untouched by man. Others, who also cared about the land, thought land should be used, but wisely. They wanted foresters to harvest timber and plant new trees so there would be woods and forests for the future. But others seemed to care only about using land and lumber to make money. A congressman, in that last group, voted against a conservation bill. "Not one penny for scenery," he said. Many people agreed with him.

John Muir was alarmed. America's timberland was rapidly disappearing. Using a scientist's eye and a poet's tongue, he began to convince Americans that trees and birds and animals were too precious to destroy.

> *Thousands of tired, nerve-shaken, over-civilized people are beginning to find out that going to the mountains is going home; that wilderness is a necessity; and that mountain parks and reservations are useful not only as fountains of timber and irrigation…but as fountains of life.*

Muir also said:

> *It took more than three thousand years to make some of the trees… trees that are still…waving and singing in the mighty forests of the Sierra….Any fool can destroy trees….They cannot run away.*

John Muir believed that all the world is interrelated. "When we try to pick out anything by itself," he wrote, "we find it hitched to everything else in the universe."

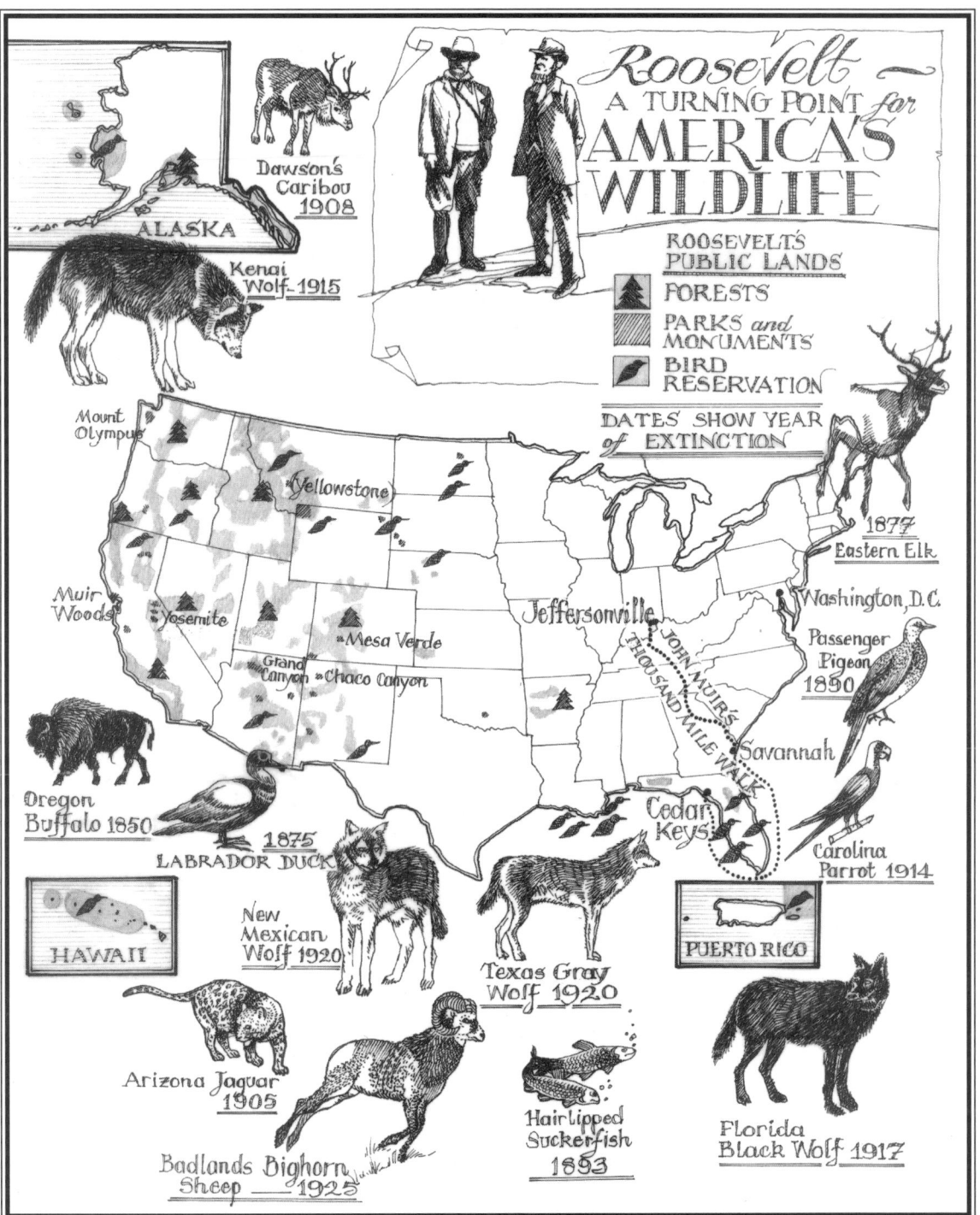

Roosevelt —
A TURNING POINT for
AMERICA'S
WILDLIFE

ROOSEVELT'S
PUBLIC LANDS
FORESTS
PARKS and
MONUMENTS
BIRD
RESERVATION

DATES SHOW YEAR
of EXTINCTION

Dawson's
Caribou
1908

ALASKA

Kenai
Wolf 1915

Mount
Olympus

Yellowstone

Muir
Woods

Yosemite

Mesa Verde

Grand
Canyon Chaco Canyon

Jeffersonville

JOHN MUIR'S
THOUSAND MILE WALK

Washington, D.C.

Passenger
Pigeon
1850

1877
Eastern Elk

Savannah

Cedar
Keys

Carolina
Parrot 1914

Oregon
Buffalo 1850

1875
LABRADOR DUCK

HAWAII

New
Mexican
Wolf 1920

Texas Gray
Wolf 1920

PUERTO RICO

Arizona Jaguar
1905

Badlands Bighorn
Sheep   1925

Hairlipped
Suckerfish
1893

Florida
Black Wolf 1917

129

Parks for a Nation

Back in 1832, after a trip to the Dakota region, the artist George Catlin is said to have come up with the idea of preserving some of America's land "in a magnificent park...a nation's park." Catlin could already see that the westward expansion of the American nation was threatening the land and its first inhabitants. Thirty-two years later, President Abraham Lincoln signed a bill granting California the Yosemite Valley on condition that it "be held for public use, resort, and recreation...for all time."

It was the beginning of an idea that would grow into national and state park systems. What do you think of that idea? Should some land be preserved from development? Do nations have a responsibility to the environment as well as to people? Could it be that preserving land, animals, birds, and insects actually makes a big difference to people, too?

Around 1870, some explorers wrote of the spectacular Yellowstone area (in Montana and Wyoming). They feared that it would be destroyed by homesteaders. Congress couldn't give the land to a state to preserve (Montana and Wyoming weren't states then), so, in 1872, when Ulysses S. Grant was president, Congress put one million acres under federal control as parkland. Settlers couldn't move in. There were a lot of howls about this, but it set a precedent. In 1890 some other big areas were turned into national parks (including Yosemite, which now came under federal control). The railroads were big supporters of the national-park idea. They built large, rustic hotels for tourists in the parks, to encourage their passenger business.

Besides the undeveloped lands, there were some other areas that needed protection: Indian mounds, cliff dwellings, pueblo ruins, early missions, and other historic places. These were national treasures. The first step toward protecting them came in 1889 (Benjamin Harrison was president), when the Casa Grande ruins in Arizona were reserved from settlement. Finally, in 1916, when Woodrow Wilson was president, the National Park Service was created "to conserve the scenery and the natural and historic objects and the wild life therein...by such means as will leave them unimpaired for the enjoyment of future generations."

By that time there were 37 national parks; today there are more than 360. They are places where we celebrate history, find delight in nature, or are awed by natural wonders. Some are spectacular sites; some are gentle places. They include mountains, canyons, seashores, volcanoes, and geysers. All are yours to enjoy—and preserve. They are part of your inheritance as an American citizen. So, if you feel like exploring, find out about *your* national parks.

Albert Bierstadt painted these giant California sequoias in 1858.

25 The Gilded Age Turns Progressive

"If only you would buy this gadget," the advertisements for the new labor-saving devices seemed to say, "your troubles will finally be over!"

Are you confused by all the things happening in this Gilded Age? That's not surprising. It was a mixed-up time: a time of optimism and hope; a time of delight with inventions; a time of worry about corruption; a time of poverty and wealth. It was, as you know, an age of extremes.

There was, for instance, all the new technology. It took the world by surprise. It changed the way people lived and worked. No one was prepared. Trains, telephones, electric lights, harvesters, and vacuum cleaners weren't around when the Constitution was written.

Remember early America? Here is how Ben Franklin described it:

> There are few great proprietors of the soil and few tenants; most people cultivate their own lands, or follow some handicraft or merchandise; very few are rich enough to live idly upon their rents or incomes.

America wasn't quite like that anymore. While most people still lived in rural areas, each year fewer and fewer Americans cultivated their own lands, and some people were able to live idly on their rents. Many Americans had moved to the cities, where they found jobs and opportunities—but also crime, poverty, and other problems.

That's what the whole Populist movement was about. Mostly the Populists were farmers, and they seemed to be saying, "Whoa," and "Hold on," and "Let's look at the old-time rural values."

The distinguishing thing about the Progressives was something [that] might be called "activism": they argued that social evils will not remedy themselves, and that it is wrong to sit by passively and wait for time to take care of them.... Conservatives generally believed in time and nature to bring progress; Progressives believed in energy and governmental action.

—RICHARD HOFSTADTER, HISTORIAN

Peaceful reform and change are difficult in any society. The powerful people in every nation are usually powerful because of the way things are. They don't want to see things changed. Besides, change is unsettling for everyone. All that makes the Progressive achievements especially impressive.

In Iowa of the 1890s, children celebrate the last day of school before the start of summer and harvest time. In cotton mills like this one in the South, six- and seven-year-old girls work 13 hours a day.

But there was no way to do that. The times were changing; America was changing with them.

Actually, by the year 1900, things were going well for most Americans. The depression had ended in the middle of the 1890s, and good times were back. Farmers were prospering, too.

Most Americans in the Gilded Age were better off than people anywhere ever before. Most weren't rich or poor. They were middle class, and they were beginning to have washing machines, sewing machines, kitchen appliances, mass-produced furniture, and factory-made clothing. In addition, many ordinary people could afford a great luxury that once only the rich enjoyed: leisure time. So most Americans had reason to be optimistic and confident.

But the Populists were right. Some people were being left out. For some people the dream was a nightmare. Some children—your age—were working 12 or 14 hours a day and not going to school. Miners

A Hundred Years of Leaps and Bounds

Back in 1800, when John Adams was president, the nation had 5.3 million citizens, 16 states, and territory that stretched all the way from the Atlantic Ocean to the Mississippi River. In those days, Americans were too busy settling the land to think about much else. They often spoke of "conquering" land because the vast forests seemed like enemies. Forests had to be cut down and destroyed to make room for houses and farms.

The 1900 census showed that America had 76.2 million people, 45 states, and territory that stretched from coast to coast. No other nation had ever grown so fast. We Americans were the most prosperous people in the world. We were confident we were entering a century when the U.S. would lead the world.

When William Vanderbilt canceled a fast mail train and was asked how it would affect the public, he replied, "The public be damned!"

were spending most of their lives underground, getting little pay, and often dying in accidents. Slums in the big cities were horrible: more than 2,000 people lived in one city neighborhood without a single bathtub! Spoiled food was being canned and sold; it sometimes killed people. City officials and police were often corrupt—and that means dishonest. America's forests were being cut down, its land destroyed, its rivers polluted. Beggars were dying on city streets while others, like William Vanderbilt, lived like emperors. Vanderbilt didn't do a thing to earn his fortune. He inherited it. And he didn't give to charity.

Why was all this happening? Some blamed the immigrants. Those millions of new people were certainly complicating things. Many of them came without any money. Most of them couldn't even speak English. Some people said it wasn't worth the effort to absorb them. Some people said America should close its gates. Those people said that the American dream should be just for those who were already here. Or those with a certain color skin, Or a certain religion.

It was a selfish idea, and surprising; after all, the older Americans all had ancestors who had been immigrants themselves. Besides, the

Two sides of New York City life: a young immigrant woman in her kitchen, with broken faucet and littered floor; and a comfortable family outing, complete with dog, to the beach on Staten Island.

Robert ("Battling Bob") La Follette, governor and senator of Wisconsin, was a reforming politician who got laws passed regulating railroads, banks, and the civil service.

Land and Trees

Land? In the 19th century few Americans worried that we might be destroying it. There was so much land that we didn't have to think about it, did we? And pollution? Why, the earth was vast, and if coal-burning furnaces and oil refineries were dirtying the air, people could just move somewhere else. Were loggers cutting down America's oldest and grandest trees? How silly to worry about that. There were more than enough trees, said the woodchoppers. Only a few people thought about keeping water pure or rivers and beaches clean. Only a few, that is, besides John Muir and the man you will read about in the next chapter. He wanted America to stay beautiful for you and your children.

Gifford Pinchot (head of the U.S. Forest Service in 1905) wanted to use forests wisely, but he and John Muir disagreed about how that should be done.

newcomers had the same dream as the older Americans. It was a dream of a free, democratic land.

It was that American dream that made us special. We were an experiment: a nation that would be different, a nation that would not repeat the mistakes of the Old World.

We were showing the world that a broad democracy—a government for all the people—could work. We were tackling our problems democratically.

This was a nation where all people were said to be created equal and endowed by their creator with the right to *life, liberty, and the pursuit of happiness*. That great idea had turned this country into a land where dreams came true.

But could we fulfill the dream of equal opportunity? It wouldn't be easy. Technology had changed the world; growth had changed the American people; the laws hadn't kept up. Besides, that old villain—bigotry—was still in residence.

The important thing to remember about democracies is that they are capable of responding to the wishes of the people. When the people are ready for change, it usually comes about.

And so the Progressive Movement was born. The Populists had made people aware of some of the nation's problems. The Progressives began to do something about them. They attempted to take the old rural values and make them work in the new urban order. For a while, Progressive ideas were accepted by both the Democratic and Republican parties. Intelligent, able people got involved with their government. They became mayors and governors and presidents. They became reformers and writers and lawmakers.

Progressives fought to see that children no longer spent their days working in fields and factories. They helped public schools grow until most children were assured of an education. For the immigrants pouring into the country, American public schools were a democratic wonder offering promise and hope for all.

Progressives attacked the problem of long hours and low pay for workers; the problem of business monopolies; and the problem of the waste of our national resources. In the next chapter you'll meet the first Progressive president.

But there was one problem the Progressives put aside. It was the problem of racial prejudice. That was saved for later generations to face.

Many people couldn't visit New York's Metropolitan Museum (paid for by public taxes) because it was closed on Sunday, most workers' only free day. It was finally opened to "the lower classes" in 1891.

Politically Speaking

WHAT IS A DIRECT PRIMARY?

Candidates for political offices were nominated at party conventions, and those conventions were often controlled by party bosses. Now, if the candidates could be chosen by the people in party elections before the main election, you'd have direct primaries and a more democratic process. In 1896, South Carolina adopted the first statewide primary. After that, the movement spread quickly to most other states.

INITIATIVES AND REFERENDUMS

South Dakota was the first state (in 1898) to try the *initiative* (in-ISH-uh-tiv) *and referendum*. That fancy-sounding phrase means

that voters get a chance to vote on some laws themselves (instead of leaving everything up to their legislators). If a specific number of voters petitioned to have a measure put on the ballot (the *initiative*), then voters could vote for or against it (the *referendum*). It was democracy expanding again. Can you think of good reasons why some people were against this idea?

AMENDMENT XVII

Article 1, Section 23 of the Constitution says: "The Senate of the United States shall by composed of two Senators from each State, chosen by the Legislature thereof, for six years." "Chosen by the Legislature there-

of" was a process that bothered many Americans. They wanted to choose their own senators directly. It would be more democratic, but the Constitution would have to be amended. The House of Representatives voted for such an amendment; beginning in 1894, they voted for it three times. Each time, the Senate defeated the measure. The senators liked the way they'd been chosen, but most Americans didn't.

Finally, on the fourth try, the Senate agreed; in 1913 the 17th Amendment was ratified by the states. It says: "The Senate of the United States shall be composed of two Senators from each State, elected by the people thereof, for six years."

26 Teedie

Teedie in Paris, aged 11, on his family's European tour. In Rome, "I...was given by Papa...a Roman vase and coin," he wrote. "Just think of it!!"

Theodore Roosevelt never went to school. At least, not the way you go to school. Theodore —who was called Teedie when he was a boy— was very rich and lived in a five-story house in New York City with his brother and his two sisters and his mother and father. Four or five servants (sometimes more) lived in the house, too. Uncle Robert and Aunt Lizzie Ellis Roosevelt lived next door with guinea pigs, chickens, a cow, a parrot, and a monkey. More Roosevelt cousins lived nearby.

If you looked out the front door of the big house, onto East 20th Street, you could see cobblestones and horse-pulled carriages and hear city noises; but in the quiet backyard, flowers and strutting peacocks filled a block-long garden.

The Roosevelts all seemed to have something in common: it was energy and high spirits. They liked having a good time. They enjoyed laughing, playing games, and riding horseback. When Teedie grew up and became president, he brought more laughter to the White House than any president before or since.

The Roosevelts were an old Dutch family, and had been New Yorkers since the days of Peter Stuyvesant. They were aristocratic and proper, and spent much of their time with wealthy families like themselves.

Their children didn't go to school, but they were well educated. Tutors, governesses, and relatives came to the house to teach the Roosevelt children. Young Theodore was a studious boy. He became an astounding reader. All his life he read at least a book a day. Often he read more than that. When he read he could block out all the distractions around him and concentrate intensely. He had an amazing memory.

When he became president he surprised people with the wide knowledge he had from books. He also loved to write, and before he died, at age 60, he wrote some 150,000 letters. He wrote all his presidential speeches himself (most presidents have speechwriters), and he wrote more than 30 books.

But when he was a boy, Theodore Roosevelt expected to become a scientist. His special interest was in nature, especially bugs and birds. He set up a natural-history museum in his house. He labeled all his exhibits with their scientific Latin names. A *Mepitis chinga* was a skunk.

Grownups paid a penny to see the museum; children got in free if they helped feed the animals. He had about 250 different specimens. Once his mother threw a litter of fieldmice out of the icebox and Teedie moaned about "the loss to science." Another time, a servant complained that she couldn't do the laundry with "a snapping turtle tied to the legs of the sink." On the streetcar one day he lifted his hat politely when he saw an elderly lady and "several frogs leaped gaily to the floor." But Theodore Roosevelt was serious in his scientific study, and kept detailed drawings and records of the animals he observed.

It was 1871, Teedie was 12, and the family headed for the Adirondacks. According to biographer David McCullough, "They all went—in true Roosevelt fashion, in a swarm—Theodore, Mittie, and the four children, Uncle Cornelius and Aunt Laura, Uncle Hilborne, Aunt Susy, and Cousin West. Theodore packed a copy of *The Last of the Mohicans* to read by the campfire after dark." Teedie wrote of "grand and desolate wilds," and of seeing a salamander, a mouse, and a bald-headed eagle.

When Teedie was five (left), his mother (center) wrote to his father (right), who was away: "Teedie was afraid last night there was a bear in your dressing room....He is brimming full of mischief and has to be watched all the time."

In this group portrait of family and friends taken during the Roosevelts' Egyptian tour in 1872, Teedie is sitting on the floor, second from the right. His brother, Elliott (far right), though 16 months younger, was always bigger and taller.

Who's the Dude?

Theodore Roosevelt usually wore a long coat and top hat, as other rich society men did. Most politicians were of another class and dressed differently. Some sneered when they first saw him. A member of New York's Assembly who met Roosevelt in 1882 wrote:

Suddenly our eyes and those of everybody on the floor, became glued on a young man who was coming in through the door. His hair was parted in the center, and he had side-burns. He wore a single eye-glass, with a gold chain over his ear. He had on a cutaway coat with one button at the top, and the ends of its tails almost reached the tops of his shoes. He carried a gold-headed cane in one hand, a silk top hat in the other, and he walked in the bent-over fashion that was the style of the young men of the day. His trousers were as tight as a tailor could make them, and had a bell-shaped bottom to cover his shoes.

"Who's the dude?" I asked another member, while the same question was being put in a dozen different parts of the hall.

"That's Theodore Roosevelt of New York," he answered.

He was born just before the Civil War began, and his first memories were of playing soldier. Teedie pretended he was a Union soldier; his brother and sisters were not so sure which side to take. Theodore's father—who was Theodore, Sr.—was a strong supporter of Abraham Lincoln and the Union cause. Theodore's mother, Mittie Bulloch, was a Georgia girl who grew up on a plantation. Her brothers were famous heroes of the Confederate navy. Mittie Bulloch Roosevelt sympathized with the Southern cause. Perhaps it was because of his wife's feelings that Theodore, Sr. chose not to fight in the war. He did what many other rich northern men did. He paid a substitute to fight for him. It was the only thing he ever did that upset his son.

The older Theodore was a philanthropist (fil-AN-thruh-pist), which means he spent much of his time and money helping others. He set up a program to help soldiers' families; he founded the Children's Aid Society; he helped start the American Museum of Natural History; he aided hospitals; he worked on other good government causes. He believed that his wealth gave him a special responsibility to be a helpful citizen. He was a glass merchant and a banker, but he spent most of his time helping others. Yet he always seemed to have time to romp and play with his children. His son called him "the best man I ever knew."

You can see that Theodore Roosevelt had an unusual childhood. When he wanted to learn more about animals and how to stuff them, his parents gave him lessons with a taxidermist who had hunted and worked with the famous artist and naturalist John James Audubon. When the Roosevelts wanted their children to learn about geography and art and history, they took the family on a year's trip to Europe. Teedie was 10. When he was 14, they spent a winter on a houseboat on the Nile River in Egypt. Teedie was given a rifle, and he shot and stuffed hundreds of birds. It would have been an idyllic (i-DILL-ick—it means "ideal") childhood, except for one problem. Theodore's health was poor. He had asthma—bad asthma—terrible eyesight, and stomach problems. He was frail and sickly, and no one thought he would live long.

"I was nervous and timid," he wrote. His father told him he needed to build his body to match his mind. At age 11 he began lifting weights and doing exercises. For the rest of his life he boxed, rode horseback, hunt-

ed, and rowed. Like a caterpillar who turns into a handsome moth, the weak, scrawny lad turned himself into a powerful, fearless man.

At Harvard, Teedie took up rowing (in a single-scull boat) and posed for his picture in his rower's cap and breeches, with a tough-guy scowl on his face.

Visiting History

Are you wondering what Theodore Roosevelt's house was really like? Well, you can actually go there, stand in his room, and pretend you are Teedie. You won't find peacocks in the backyard now, or carriages by the front door. East 20th Street is a commercial area today. But the house has been preserved and is open to the public. So is Sagamore Hill, the sprawling, 23-room house that TR built for his family on Long Island. In that comfortable house, among woodlands and fields, he spent most of his adult life. "There could be no healthier and pleasanter place in which to bring up children than in that nook of old-time America around Sagamore Hill," he wrote. You can walk through his rooms, see the stuffed animals he brought back from Africa, and look at his books, his furniture, and his children's pictures. Sometimes, when you are there, it seems as if the door is about to open and TR to walk in, which is just the way I like my history.

A great many historic places are open for you to visit, all over our nation. Many, like Theodore Roosevelt's homes, are run by the National Park Service. Thanks to that agency, when you go to Salem, Massachusetts, you'll see a world the whalers knew. Take a ferry to Ellis Island in New York Harbor and you can imagine yourself an immigrant, just arriving in

The Roosevelt house on East 20th Street.

the land of promise. Stand on the battlefield at Horseshoe Bend in Alabama and you'll see where Andrew Jackson fought the Creeks.

You can tour Frederick Douglass's home in Washington, D.C., or visit a house built at Sitka, Alaska, in 1842, by a Russian bishop (when Alaska still belonged to Russia). At Hopewell Village, Pennsylvania, you'll see a 19th-century blast furnace for smelting iron. If your experience is like mine, in each of those places you will find wonderfully informed tour guides, film programs, and some terrific National Park Service historic guidebooks. I'm telling you all this because (as I've mentioned before) the National Park Service belongs to you. Don't miss out on something you own.

27 From Dude to Cowboy

Theodore Roosevelt in a studio photo, the Tiffany knife and sheath in his belt.

The North Dakota cowboys chuckled when they saw the young dude who had come from the East to hunt and become a rancher. His name was Theodore Roosevelt, and he wore a huge sombrero, a fringed and beaded buckskin shirt, fringed leather pants, silver spurs engraved with his initials, and alligator boots. Tucked in his belt were a knife and scabbard, custom-made at Tiffany's, the finest jewelry store in the nation. A silk cord hung from his thick glasses. He was skinny, with a squeaky voice and a big toothy grin, and he carried books under his arm. One day out on the range, the cowboys figured, and the city slicker would hightail it back East.

So a guide took him buffalo hunting. They were gone seven days, riding the wildest, loneliest, most difficult trails the Dakota Badlands had to offer. It rained most of the time; the days were hot and the nights were frigid. They were charged by a wounded buffalo, their food ran out, the dude fell into a bed of cactus, wolves frightened their horses, the horses had to be chased, and they woke one cold morning to find themselves sleeping in four inches of water. The guide, Joe Ferris, was close to collapse from exhaustion. But the worse things got, the more the dude seemed to enjoy himself. "By Godfrey, but this is fun!" was what he kept saying.

"You just couldn't knock him out of sorts," said Ferris, who was surprised that "he had books with him and would read at odd times." When Roosevelt finally shot a buffalo he jumped, danced, and whooped. "I never saw anyone so pleased in all my life," Ferris remembered later. "I was plumb tired out," he added.

The Badlands is a high, dry region with deep gullies caused by heavy rain. That rain is nature's joke, because normally there isn't enough to make much of anything grow. When the rain does come, it is sometimes so hard it washes the land away. Badlands aren't good for agriculture or pasture, but they are hauntingly beautiful and full of tall earth columns and platforms.

Roosevelt had dropped his childhood name, Teedie, and was now signing his letters "Thee," or "Ted," or "Theodore." Later, when he became president, people would called him "TR," or "Teddy." But he was little Teedie when he first dreamed of the West after reading adventure books by James Fenimore Cooper. He longed for adventure himself. He went west for another reason, though. He went to forget and to begin again. He was 26, and he had lived through a series of tragedies that no young man should have to face.

The first tragedy came when he was a college student. He studied hard and passed the entrance exam for Harvard. He expected to become a scientist. Before he graduated, he began work on a book about ships and the navy in the War of 1812. Then his beloved father—the man all the family called "Greatheart"—died. That changed his life, and his career, too. He decided to go into politics—to become a responsible citizen, as he believed his father would have wished him to do. Few people with his wealth and education entered politics. They left government jobs to others. They were apt to look down their noses at the people who ran the the country, which wasn't helpful. Roosevelt was determined to be a reforming politician. When friends asked why he had gone into politics, he said he wished to be part of the governing—not the governed—class.

So when he left college, he became a legislator in New York's Assembly. He did something else. He got married, to sweet-natured Alice Lee. She was like a fairy-tale bride: blue-eyed, blonde, and beautiful. They were enchantingly happy. And then, less than four years later, on the same day, in the same house, Alice died giving birth to their first child, and Mittie, Theodore's mother, died of typhoid fever. Mittie was 48; Alice, 22.

After those tragedies, he went west and threw himself into cowboy

life. Later on, he wrote, "There were all kinds of things of which I was afraid at first, ranging from grizzly bears to 'mean' horses and gunfighters; but by acting as if I was not afraid I gradually ceased to be afraid."

Here is one of his adventures, in his own words:

"Nowhere else does one seem so far from all mankind," TR wrote of the plains.

Life, Not Legalism

After listening to Samuel Gompers, Congress passed a law prohibiting the making of cigars in tenement "sweatshops." (It was 1882 and Grover Cleveland was president.) The Supreme Court soon ruled the law unconstitutional. "It cannot be perceived how the cigarmaker is to be improved in his health or his morals by forcing him from his home…to ply his trade elsewhere."

Reformer Theodore Roosevelt had visited some of those sweatshops. In his autobiography he wrote, "It was this case which first waked me to a dim and partial understanding of the fact that the courts were not necessarily the best judges of what should be done to better social and industrial conditions. The judges who rendered this decision were well-meaning men. They knew nothing whatever of tenement-house conditions; they knew legalism, not life. This decision completely blocked tenement-house reform legislation in New York for a score of years."

"I do not think ever a man loved a woman more than I love her," TR wrote of Alice. "For a year and a quarter now (even when hunting) I have never gone to sleep or waked up without thinking of her."

I was out after lost horses…it was late in the evening when I reached the place. I heard one or two shots in the bar-room as I came up, and I disliked going in. But there was nowhere else to go, and it was a cold night. Inside the room were several men, who, including the bartender, were wearing the kind of smile worn by men who are making believe to like what they don't like. A shabby individual in a broad hat with a cocked gun in each hand was walking up and down the floor talking with strident profanity. He had evidently been shooting at the clock, which had two or three holes in its face.

…As soon as he saw me he hailed me as "Four Eyes," in reference to my spectacles, and said, "Four Eyes is going to treat." I joined in the laugh and got behind the stove and sat down, thinking to escape notice. He followed me, however, and though I tried to pass it off as a jest this merely made him more offensive, and he stood leaning over me, a gun in each hand, using very foul language.…In response to his reiterated command that I should set up the drinks, I said, "Well, if I've got to, I've got to," and rose, looking past him.

As I rose, I struck quick and hard with my right just to one side of the point of his jaw, hitting with my left as I straightened out, and then again with my right. He fired the guns [as] he went down…he was senseless. I took away the guns.

The skinny dude with the glasses had been on the boxing team at Harvard. Next day the bully left town on a freight train.

Another time, Roosevelt helped capture three thieves. Then he walked them 45 miles and turned them over to a surprised sheriff. After that, he limped off to a doctor to get his blistered feet bandaged.

TR learned to rope steers, wrestle calves, and ride bucking ponies. He could ride 100 miles a day and then sit up all night on watch. If he found someone who could talk about books or ideas, he would talk and talk and talk. A Scotsman who was in North Dakota in those days remembered him as "the most remarkable man I ever met."

Roosevelt fell in love with the bleak, haunting Dakota Badlands. He called it "the romance of my life." It was a strange place of cliffs, ravines, and flat tablelands where survival wasn't easy—even for birds and animals. He may have understood that his was the last generation that would enjoy that frontier in its natural state.

When Roosevelt became president he did everything he could to save wilderness areas for future generations. He increased the national forests by 40 million acres, created five national parks, 16 national monuments, four national game refuges, and 51 bird sanctuaries. After hiking with John Muir, he made sure that Yosemite's forests of giant sequoia and redwood trees were saved "for the people's children and children's children." He helped make conservation a popular idea.

His first trips west did exactly what they were meant to do. They helped him begin his life again. When he went back east, he was ready to accept a new job, as police commissioner of New York. (Some people said roping steers was easier.) Now he was out walking the streets of New York with writers Jacob Riis and Lincoln Steffens. At night he could be seen in dangerous areas, making sure the police were doing their job. No police commissioner had done that before.

And he married Edith Carow. Together they raised a noisy, happy family of six children.

Teddy (then president) with John Muir at Yosemite.

WELL, I HARDLY KNOW WHICH TO TAKE FIRST!

McKinley the waiter takes Uncle Sam's imperialist order.

Expansionism

Expansionism is a big word, which is appropriate, because it means the practice (by a nation) of getting bigger. Should nations grow and grow as much as they can? In the past, many nations have felt the only way to be great was to do just that. How does a country grow? Usually by getting land from others.

Isn't that wrong? Well, in the past, many good people believed that they were helping or improving the other nations that they grabbed. Besides, it was the way nations had always become powerful. At the turn of the century, many Americans thought expansion would bring glory, prestige, and power to the United States. They believed America's ideals were so great that they should be forced on other people. It was a popular way to think. Expansionism was also called

imperialism. Theodore Roosevelt was an imperialist. He always liked to do things in a big way.

But some people—like Mark Twain, Carl Schurz, and ex-President Cleveland—thought differently. They believed it was America's destiny to be different from other nations. They thought the United States should stick to its own affairs. Thomas Jefferson said, "If there is one principle more deeply rooted in the mind of every American, it is that we should have nothing to do with conquest." And they remembered George Washington's advice to the nation: "The great rule of conduct for us in regard to foreign relations is, in extending our commercial relations to have with them as little political connection as possible."

The people who were against expansion were called anti-imperialists. Their view was not very popular. America's citizens would do a lot of thinking about "imperialism" and "isolation" and "world responsibility." It would be difficult to find the right road.

Measured by McKinley for a suit stuffed with new territories, Uncle Sam ignores anti-imperialist Carl Schurz.

28 The Spanish–American War

This cartoon of the "Spanish brute" after the *Maine* disaster was a typical example of the racist attitude of Americans who wanted war with Spain.

> To that composite American identity of the future, Spanish character will supply some of the most needed parts. No stock shows a grander historical retrospect—grander in religiousness and loyalty, or for patriotism, courage, decorum, gravity and honor.
>
> —WALT WHITMAN, CAMDEN, NEW JERSEY, JULY 20, 1893

> I would give anything if President McKinley would order the fleet to Havana tomorrow....the *Maine* was sunk by an act of dirty treachery on the part of the Spaniards.
>
> —THEODORE ROOSEVELT, ASSISTANT SECRETARY OF THE NAVY IN 1898

Spain's time as a great world power was behind her. Still, she remembered the glory days of Queen Isabella and King Ferdinand and clung tightly to colonies in Cuba, Puerto Rico, and the Philippine Islands.

In Cuba there were those, like the Americans in 1776, who wanted freedom to run their own country, especially as many of the Spanish officials seemed cruel and corrupt. So the Cubans rose up against the Spaniards. Naturally, most Americans sided with the revolutionaries.

Now this freedom movement came at the very time two rival American newspapers were fighting each other for readers. The Cuban story made exciting reading. Every day the newspaper headlines would boldly tell of atrocities in Cuba. When there was no real story to tell, eager reporters would make one up. That's called *yellow journalism* (good papers don't do it).

Anyway, with all the scare stories, the American people began screaming for war with Spain. They wanted Spain to clear out of the American hemisphere. But Spain didn't want to leave Cuba.

Spanish, Cuban, and American diplomats began meeting; they were trying to solve their differences quietly. Maybe they would have done so, if the *Maine* hadn't sailed into the harbor at Havana, Cuba.

The *Maine* was a U.S. battleship, and it had been sent to pick up American citizens if any trouble developed. Trouble did develop—on the

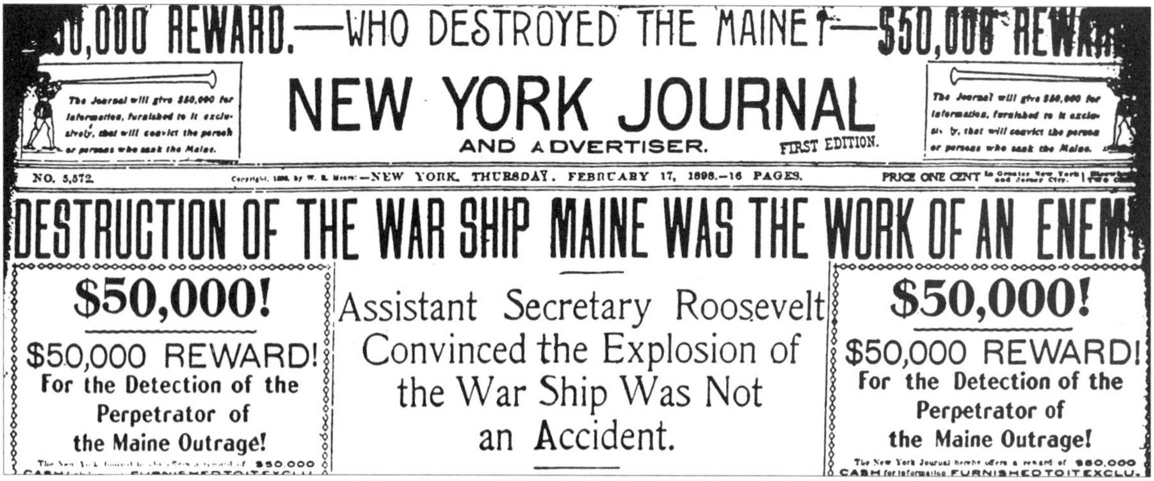

0,000 REWARD.—WHO DESTROYED THE MAINE?—$50,000 REWA

The Journal will give $50,000 for information, furnished to it exclusively, that will convict the person or persons who sank the Maine.

NEW YORK JOURNAL

AND ADVERTISER. FIRST EDITION.

The Journal will give $50,000 for information, furnished to it exclusively, that will convict the person or persons who sank the Maine.

NO. 5,572. —NEW YORK, THURSDAY, FEBRUARY 17, 1898.—16 PAGES. PRICE ONE CENT

DESTRUCTION OF THE WAR SHIP MAINE WAS THE WORK OF AN ENEM

$50,000!

$50,000 REWARD! For the Detection of the Perpetrator of the Maine Outrage!

Assistant Secretary Roosevelt Convinced the Explosion of the War Ship Was Not an Accident.

$50,000!

$50,000 REWARD! For the Detection of the Perpetrator of the Maine Outrage!

The New York Journal hereby offers a reward of $50,000 CASH for information FURNISHED TO IT EXCLU...

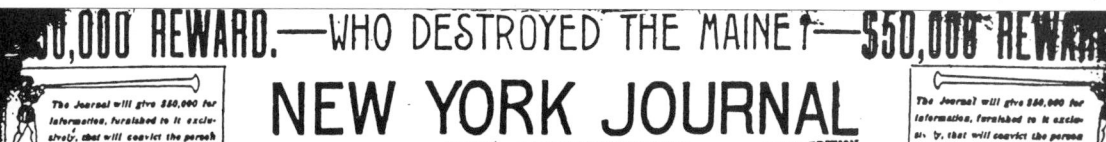

Maine! Wham-bang trouble! The *Maine* exploded! Sky high! Two hundred and sixty American sailors were killed.

A team of American experts said the *Maine* had hit a mine. Spanish officials said the explosion came from inside the ship. Seventy-eight years later, in 1976, an investigation proved the Spaniards were right. Internal combustion had started a fire that reached some gunpowder on the

The screaming headlines of the *New York Journal* sold more than one million copies a day when the *Maine* blew up. Joseph Pulitzer's *World* sent its own divers to investigate the wreck in Havana harbor.

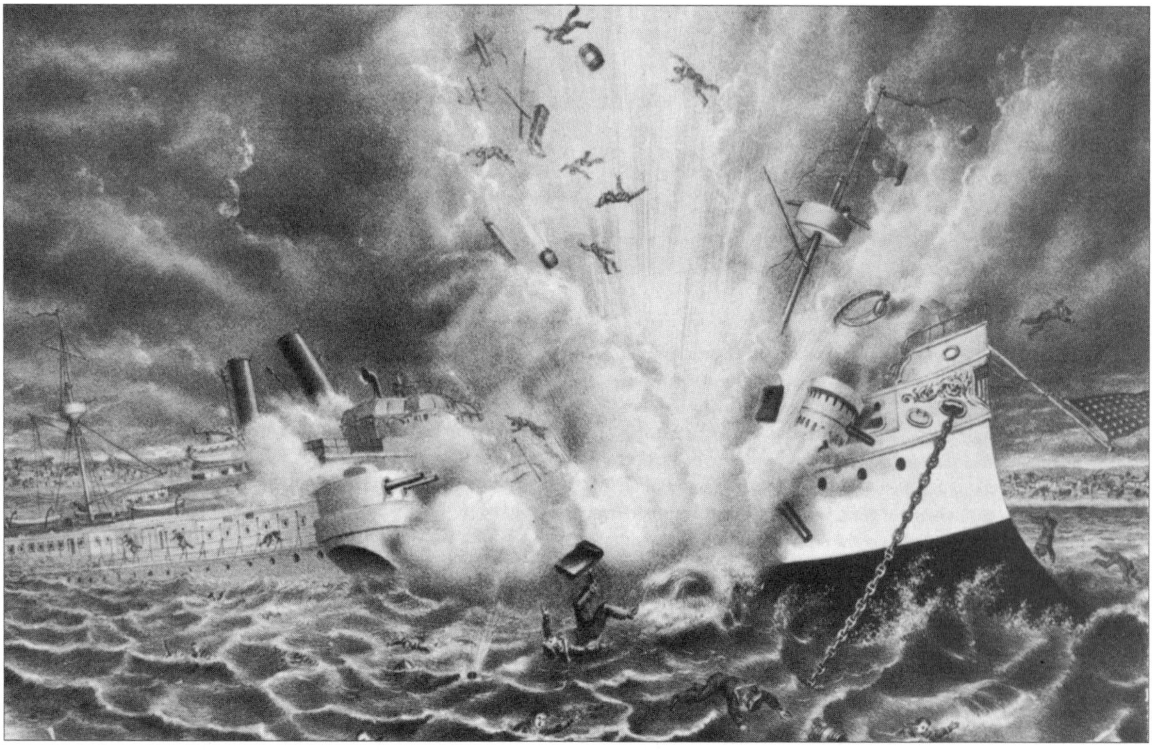

Teddy wrote about the Rough Riders: "Nine-tenths of the men were better horsemen than I was, and probably two-thirds of them better shots.... Yet...nobody else could command them as I could." Below, San Juan Hill.

Maine. In other words, it was an accident.

But in 1898 no one knew what had really happened. The newspapers played up the *Maine* story: they called it a Spanish attack. A headline in the popular *New York Journal* said WARSHIP MAINE SPLIT IN TWO BY AN ENEMY'S SECRET INFERNAL MACHINE. The American people went wild. They demanded war. Congress wanted war. Theodore Roosevelt wanted war. William McKinley was president, and he had fought in the Civil War. He knew the horrors of war; he wanted no part of one. People started calling him a coward. They didn't realize it usually takes more courage to say no than yes. Finally McKinley gave in. War was declared on Spain.

Theodore Roosevelt, who was now assistant secretary of the Navy, resigned at once. He wanted to get into this war. He organized a cavalry troop, which trained in Texas. The cavalrymen called themselves "Rough Riders." (They got that name from the old Pony Express.) But when they got to the docks in Tampa, Florida, they found there was room on the ship only for officers' horses. The Rough Riders wanted to fight, even if they had to be foot soldiers. So they called themselves Weary Walkers, and headed for Cuba.

In Cuba they fought fearlessly, TR most of all. He charged ahead with bullets flying around him. Along with the 9th and 10th Negro regiments, the Rough Riders fought their way up two important hills, Kettle Hill and San Juan Hill. The Spaniards were at the top of the hills, shooting down on them. When those Americans took San Juan Hill they went into the history books forever.

The war was short and popular. (It was over in 113 days.) Northerners and Southerners fought together; that helped heal some of the old Civil War wounds. Cuba won her freedom; Spain lost out. The United States took Puerto Rico as an American territory.

In the Pacific, Admiral George Dewey sailed into Manila harbor in the Spanish-held Philippine Islands and destroyed a Spanish fleet. The Philippines became American territory; so did Guam and Wake Island. At about the same time, American businessmen in the Hawaiian Islands asked the United States to annex those islands. We did.

Some native Hawaiians, and many Filipinos, wanted to be independent—they wanted to form their own nations. They weren't given a choice. American expansionists wanted the islands. The Filipinos decided to fight. They fought the United States valiantly. It took 75,000 soldiers— four times the number that fought in Cuba—to conquer the Filipinos.

Senator Henry Cabot Lodge said:

> We must on no account let the islands go: the American flag is up and it must stay....Manila with its magnificent bay is the prize and pearl of the East....it will keep us open to the markets of China.

A Harvard professor called the Philippine fight an "unrighteous war." Samuel Gompers called it "an unjust war."

Theodore Roosevelt came home from Cuba a hero. New Yorkers soon elected him governor. As governor, he worked

Admiral Dewey sank every Spanish ship in Manila Bay. Eight Americans were wounded and one died of the heat. Below, some troops resting during a lull.

We need Hawaii just as much and a good deal more than we did California. It is Manifest Destiny.
—WILLIAM A. MCKINLEY, 1898.

ALASKA 1867
BERING SEA
ALEUTIAN ISLANDS 1867
UNITED STATES
ASIA
PHILIPPINE ISLANDS 1898-1946
Manila
MIDWAY ISLANDS 1867
WAKE ISLAND 1899
JOHNSTON ISLAND 1898
HAWAIIAN ISLANDS 1898
GUAM 1898
PALMYRA ISLAND 1898
AMERICAN SAMOA 1899
AUSTRALIA
Sinking of the Maine
CUBA 1898-1902
PUERTO RICO 1898
PANAMA CANAL ZONE 1903-1979
SOUTH AMERICA

UNITED STATES and POSSESSIONS 1867 — 1903

Aloha, Hawaii

Liliuokalani, who wrote the song "Aloha Oe" and was the last queen of Hawaii.

Long before Columbus set sail, and more than 200 years before the Vikings' voyages, Polynesian sailors set out from the Marquesa Islands and discovered the Hawaiian Islands, more than 2,000 miles away. How they did it is still a mystery. They had no compasses or maps or sextants. But they were skilled navigators, and were soon sailing back and forth between the islands and perhaps to Samoa and Tonga, thought to be their original homes. A 17th-century buccaneer who saw their canoes at Guam called them "the best of any Boats in the World." For long voyages they lashed together two canoes, using cords made from coconut fiber, and rigged them with sails woven of leaves. Some of their vessels held 200 people. A member of Captain Cook's crew wrote: "These Canoes rund us nearly out of sight…they sail about 3 miles to our two."

so hard and did such a good job that the political bosses hated him. They didn't know what to do—TR was trying to put them out of business! Then one of them got a bright idea. Why not nominate TR as vice president of the United States? That way he would be out of New York and out of their hair. Roosevelt was ambitious; he was delighted to run for vice president on the Republican ticket with William McKinley (who was going for a second term). They were elected easily. No one knew that an assassin had a bullet ready for President McKinley.

Theodore Roosevelt was hiking in the Adirondack Mountains when a messenger ran puffing up the mountain with a telegram. McKinley was dead. Roosevelt was 42, younger than any president before him. His first day in the White House was his father's birthday. That, he believed, was a good omen.

The trusts tell McKinley what to do; nursemaid Hanna sits on TR to shut him up.

Mark Hanna didn't see anything good about it. He was a political insider who had been persuaded to help get TR out of New York and into the "safe" job of vice president. "Now look!" Hanna said to New York's Senator Platt. "That damned cowboy is president of the United States!"

Albert J. Beveridge

Our God has planted on this soil a mighty people. He has given a glorious history to His Chosen people. This history has been made heroic by our faith in our mission and our future. It is the history of soldiers who carried the flag across blazing deserts and through hostile mountains, a history of a people who overran a continent.

So said Albert J. Beveridge in a rousing speech he gave in 1898. Beveridge, a leading Republican, would soon be a United States senator from Indiana. He was an expansionist and he believed in Manifest Destiny. Here is some more from that speech:

Those who do not want the United States to annex foreign lands tell us that we ought not to govern a people without their consent. I answer, "That rule of government applies only to those people who are capable of self-government." We govern the Indians without their consent. We govern our territories without their consent. We govern our children without their consent....

Wonderfully, God has guided us. We cannot retreat from any soil where He has unfurled our flag. It is our duty to save that soil for liberty and civilization.

Carl Schurz, another leading Republican and a former senator, was an anti-imperialist. He didn't believe the United States should annex territories. This was what he said in 1899:

It is said that we should annex certain islands taken from Spain in the recent war. It is nearly time to make a decision on the matter.

Our government was, in the words of Abraham Lincoln, "the government of the people, by the people, and for the people." To make this republic the example and guiding star of mankind was the noblest of ambitions. Such was our ambition just a short year ago.

Then came the Spanish War. When our forces occupied foreign territory, a loud demand arose that the conquests, even the Philippines, should be kept. "Why not?" was the cry. Has not the job of the republic almost from its beginning been one of territorial expansion?

The question is not whether we can do such things, but whether we should do them. If we do we shall, for the first time since the abolition of slavery, again have two kinds of Americans: first-class Americans, who have the privilege of taking part in government, and second-class Americans, who are to be ruled by the first-class Americans.

29 Teddy Bear President

TR knocks down the trusts. But he wasn't as tough on big business as this cartoon makes out.

Roosevelt made a great president. But you knew he would. He was "dee-light-ed" to be president, he said. It was a "bully" job, he added. No president has ever had such a good time at it—and worked so hard, too.

Andrew Jackson had made people feel welcome in the White House, but not the way TR did. Remember when Jackson escaped out a White House back door to get away from the admiring mob? Roosevelt couldn't seem to get enough of "the people." On New Year's Day in 1907, anyone who wanted to could go to the White House and shake their president's hand (anyone who was clean and not drunk). Roosevelt set a record that day: he shook 8,150 hands.

The people loved him; the press did, too. He was always doing things that made good stories. Like the time he went hunting for bear but refused to kill a helpless little bear. When that story got out, a candymaker in Brooklyn, New York, made a toy bear and called it a "Teddy bear." He sent it to the president and asked his per-

TR never stopped talking. He had a high voice that squeaked when he got excited.

mission to use the name on more bears. Theodore Roosevelt said yes, and soon people were calling him "Teddy" Roosevelt. He hated that nickname, but he was stuck with it. The candymaker became a toymaker and got rich. Everyone wanted those bears, and that's how teddy bears came to be. (That first teddy is now in the National Museum of American History, in Washington, D.C., where you can see it.)

Reporters found TR's children were worth writing about, too. Alice, the oldest and a teenager, sometimes kept a snake in her purse. Quentin, who was nine, stood on the second-floor White House balcony and dropped a huge snowball on a White House guard. It knocked the guard over. All six children roller-skated in the basement, slid down the banisters, and played hide and seek in the attic. Sometimes government business waited while the president played tag with them.

But Theodore Roosevelt wasn't just fun and games. He was a strong president. He brought his energy, his habit of working hard, and his intelligence to the job. He helped see that pure food and drug laws were passed. He found ways to control some of those corporations that were acting as if they were above the law. The biggest of them had turned into "trusts." Congress had passed the Sherman Antitrust Act, but no one had enforced it. TR went "trustbusting."

"We demand that big business give the people a square deal," said TR. "When anyone...in big business...endeavors to do right he shall himself be given a square deal."

One day in 1905 a struggling poet named Edward Arlington Robinson went to his mailbox and found a letter from the president. It offered him a job that would allow him time to keep writing poetry. Theodore

When King Edward VII of England died in 1910, Theodore Roosevelt represented the U.S. at the funeral. The students at Cambridge University arranged for a special official to greet him.

Coal Crisis

It was 1902. Coal miners were striking and winter was fast approaching. The strike had been long and bitter, and coal was needed for fuel. The price of coal rose from $5 to $25 a ton. Homes became cold. Some schools closed. John Mitchell, representing the mineworkers' union, was demanding an eight-hour day for coal miners, a 20 percent wage raise, and union recognition. George Baer, representing the mine owners, said that workers' rights were the responsibility of the owners, to whom "God has given control of the property and rights of the country."

No president had ever before interfered with a strike. The attorney general told the president he had no power to intervene. But TR called both sides together. See if you can do some research and find out what happened next.

A Roosevelt Family Album

The Bear Plays Dead

The Bear Sits Up

"I don't think any family has enjoyed the White House more than we have," Roosevelt said. Above, TR and Edith with (left to right): Quentin, 5, Ted, 15, Archie, 9, Alice, 19, Kermit, 14, and Ethel, 11. Below, Archie and Quentin stand reveille with the White House guards. Above, TR's drawing for Archie of the bear that played dead, sat up—and got away.

Senator John Sherman, for whom the Antitrust Act was named (he had little to do with it, really).

Roosevelt invited the great black educator Booker T. Washington to the White House for dinner. Some prejudiced people objected; that didn't stop TR.

President Roosevelt was responsible for the building of the Panama Canal. That created a water passageway from the Atlantic Ocean to the Pacific Ocean at the midsection of the American continents. Just think about that. It took most ships more than two months to make the trip from San Francisco to the East Coast by sailing through the Straits of Magellan at the tip of South America. Cutting through Panama was like unlocking a door between the oceans.

Look at the map on the next page. It should be a simple thing to take some steam shovels to Panama and dig out a canal, shouldn't it? Ha. Digging that canal was a nightmare. The map does not show thick jungle, but that was only one of the things the canal builders had to contend with. The worst problem may have been the tiny mosquitoes that carried malaria and yellow-fever germs. Nearly 6,000 men died, mostly from disease. There were also accidents and political hassles and enormous engineering problems. It is worth going to the library and finding a book about the building of the Panama Canal. It is some story. Without Theodore Roosevelt it would have been even more difficult.

He had a favorite saying: *Speak softly and carry a big stick.* It was an African proverb, and TR was always quoting it. He believed that if you show you are strong no one will pick on you. The big stick he wanted for the nation was a strong navy. He helped build one.

Roosevelt talked a lot about war and soldiering, but his presidency was a time of peace. He was a good diplomat and was able to deal well with other countries. After he helped settle a war between Japan and Russia he was given the Nobel Peace Prize. He gave the prize money to

Top, a man sprays ditches in Panama with oil. The oil made a film on top of the water where mosquito larvae were breeding that killed them when they came up to breathe. Below, a tugboat, the very first to pass through the completed Panama Canal.

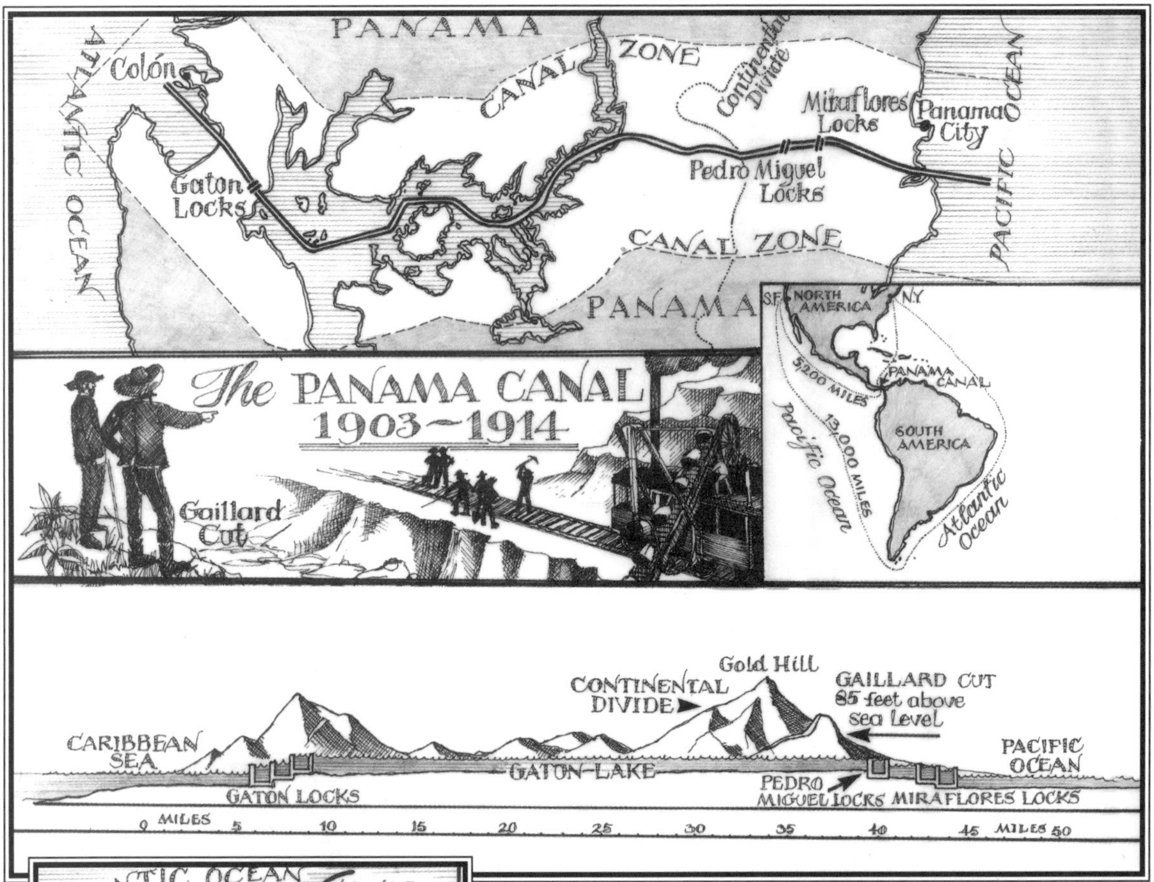

The PANAMA CANAL
1903–1914

Gaillard Cut

Colón

Gatun Locks

PANAMA CANAL ZONE

Continental Divide

Miraflores Locks

Pedro Miguel Locks

Panama City

CANAL ZONE

PANAMA

ATLANTIC OCEAN

PACIFIC OCEAN

SF NORTH AMERICA NY

8,200 MILES

PANAMA CANAL

13,000 MILES

Pacific Ocean

SOUTH AMERICA

Atlantic Ocean

CONTINENTAL DIVIDE ▶

Gold Hill

GAILLARD CUT 85 feet above sea level

CARIBBEAN SEA

PACIFIC OCEAN

GATUN LAKE

GATUN LOCKS

PEDRO MIGUEL LOCKS   MIRAFLORES LOCKS

0 MILES 5   10   15   20   25   30   35   40   45 MILES 50

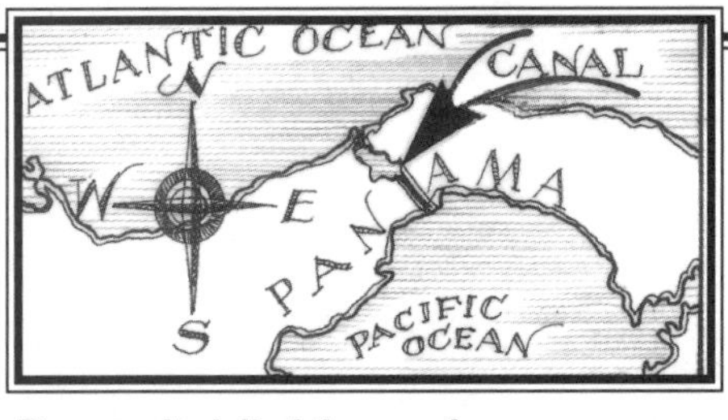

ATLANTIC OCEAN

CANAL

PANAMA

N W E S

PACIFIC OCEAN

Roosevelt visited the canal while it was being dug, in 1906. The canal cost $275 million and was a great engineering achievement, but the political dealings around its construction left bad feelings toward the U.S. among many Latin Americans.

the nation; he said it belonged to the American people (even though it came at a time when he could have used it himself).

Today we think that Roosevelt's most important contributions as president were in the field of conservation. We can thank him for saving many of the public lands that we enjoy today.

He did one thing he later regretted. When he was elected president on

PUCK

TR leaves his baby, "My Policies," with Taft, his successor in the White House.

his own in 1904 (remember, he first got the job because McKinley was killed), he said he would not run for a third term. When his second term was up he was only 50, and he loved being president. The American people loved having him as president. But he had given his word. So he didn't run for reelection. Instead, TR went off to Africa to hunt big game.

> **I have never known another person so vital nor another man so dear.**
> —WILLIAM ALLEN WHITE ON THEODORE ROOSEVELT

Shake and Bake

A news report from Jack London in Collier's Weekly, *May 5, 1906:*

The earthquake shook down in San Francisco hundreds of thousands of dollars' worth of walls and chimneys. But the conflagration [con-fluh-GRAY-shun—the fire] that followed burned up hundreds of millions of dollars' worth of property....Not in history has a modern imperial city been so completely destroyed. San Francisco is gone!

The earthquake started the damage, but the fires that resulted were much more devastating—and there was no water available to put them out. Here is a report by Will Irwin from the New York Sun, *April 21, 1906:*

The old San Francisco is dead. The gayest, lightest-hearted, most pleasure-loving city of this continent, and in many ways the most interesting and romantic, is a horde of huddled refugees living among ruins. It may rebuild; it probably will; but those who have known that peculiar city by the Golden Gate and caught its flavor of the Arabian Nights feel it can never be the same. It is as though a pretty, frivolous woman had passed through a great tragedy. She survives, but she is sobered and different....The city lay on a series of hills and lowlands between. These hills are really the end of the Coast Range of mountains which lie between the interior valleys and the ocean to the south. ...the greater water always tinged with gold from the great washings of the mountain, overhung with a haze, and of magnificent color changes....[the mountain across the bay] brought the real forest closer to San Francisco than any other American city....men have killed deer on the slopes of [Mount] Tamalpais and looked down to see the cable cars crawling up the hills of San Francisco to the north.

30 Jane Addams, Reformer

At Hull House, Jane Addams learned of "the struggle for existence which is so much harsher among people near the edge of pauperism." She said that private charity was "totally inadequate" to deal with the problems of the city's poor.

"The city is a granite garden," says landscape architect Anne Spirn. Do you agree?

What is a polygon? *What is a* glossary? *See if you can find other* poly *and* glossa *words.*

"No sensible and responsible woman wants to vote," said former president Grover Cleveland in an interview published in the *Ladies' Home Journal* in 1905.

There is a dandy word to describe America's cities in the 19th century. The word is *polyglot,* and it comes from two Greek roots: *poly,* meaning "more than one," and *glossa,* meaning "tongue." A polyglot city is one where many tongues (languages) are heard.

America's cities were polyglot because they were filled with immigrants—people from around the world. If all those diverse peoples, with their different languages and customs, could live together in a crowded city, perhaps they would find a way to teach the diverse peoples of the world to get along.

But they weren't having an easy time of it. To begin, they didn't understand American democracy. Many of the immigrants had come to America to escape oppressive rulers. They thought of government as the enemy. They didn't realize that in America the government is supposed to be the people. That was why they often let city bosses control their lives. The boss answered their questions, helped them find jobs, or did other things to ease their adjustment to the new country. Bosses did do many worthwhile things.

But most of them paid themselves for those worthwhile things by stealing from the people. In Chicago a boss named Johnny Powers passed out free chickens and turkeys on holidays, so everyone loved him. Hardly anyone knew that he bought those turkeys with city money that was in-

Harper's Weekly made the gulf between America's rich and poor very clear with this 1915 collage of newspaper articles.

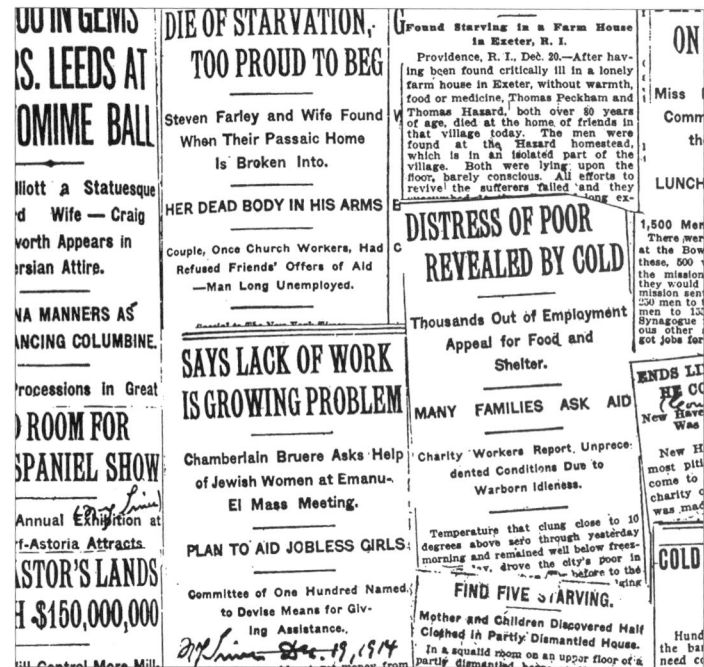

tended for schools. Powers also used city money to buy a house for himself and diamonds for his fingers. Since many of Chicago's citizens couldn't read English, it was difficult for them to know what was happening.

So when reformers tried to improve life in the cities, they had a fight on their hands. The bosses were popular. Many reformers were wealthy people who wouldn't live in the inner cities. They didn't know its polyglot population the way the boss did.

Jane Addams was the best-known reformer of her day. She became the most admired woman in America. A visitor called her "the only saint the United States has produced." Well, she wasn't a saint, but she was an intelligent, determined, college-educated woman who got things done.

Addams's ancestors had come to Pennsylvania in the days of William Penn. By the time she was born the family had moved west, to Illinois. Her father, an Illinois state senator and friend of Abraham Lincoln, was a wealthy man. But that didn't mean she had an easy childhood. Jane's mother died when she was two. Then Jane got tuberculosis, a common disease in those days. It left her with a crooked spine. That handicap helped her understand people who had problems.

Still, Jane Addams could have had a life of parties and ease. She chose not to. She chose to do something

Chicago, Chicago

Chicago stood in the borderland between the western prairies and eastern oak-hickory forests, and the lake gave it access to the white pines and other coniferous trees of the north woods. Grasslands and hardwood and softwood forests were all within reach," wrote William Cronon in a book called *Nature's Metropolis*.

Carl Sandburg described the windy city differently in a famous poem called "Chicago." Here is part of it:

Hog Butcher for the World,
Tool Maker, Stacker of Wheat,
Player with Railroads and the Nation's
    Freight Handler;
Stormy, husky, brawling,
City of the Big Shoulders.

Muckraker Lincoln Steffens wrote: "First in violence, deepest in dirt, lawless, unlovely, ill-smelling, irreverent, new; an overgrown gawk of a—village, the "tough" among cities, a spectacle for the nation....Chicago likes audacity and is always willing to have anybody try anything once; no matter who you are, where you come from, or what you set out to do, Chicago will give you a chance. The sporting spirit is the spirit of Chicago."

These nursery-school children lined up for a race were lucky to be at Hull House. Most of Chicago's poor children weren't as fortunate. What kind of child care is available in your community today?

Settling Down

Some Smith College graduates met in New York in 1887. They wanted "to do something concrete to solve social problems." They established the College Settlement in a New York tenement district. (They didn't yet know about Jane Addams in Chicago.)

Stanton Coit, an Amherst graduate who earned a Ph.D. at the University of Berlin, decided to use his training to help others. He came home and opened the Neighborhood Guild on New York's Lower East Side, and later, with Lillian Wald, founded the Henry Street Settlement in New York. By 1910, there were about 400 settlement houses in cities across the country.

important with her life. She chose to help others.

She bought a red-brick house, with white columns on the porch, in Chicago, right in the middle of the slums. Then Jane and her friend Ellen Starr got to work with paintbrushes and rags and cleaned up the house. It had been built by a Mr. Hull, so they named it Hull House. All the neighbors were curious. Why would anyone live in the slums if they didn't have to? Chicago's slums were dirty and full of crime. But Addams didn't want to be an outsider. If she was to help people she needed to know them; she needed to be a neighbor.

Jane Addams turned Hull House into a place where people could learn to speak English, get care for their children, take painting lessons, go to a concert, exercise in a gym, or act on a stage. It was a place where they could get together with friends and take pride in their heritage. There were German nights at Hull House when German newcomers sang and danced and put on costumes from the old country. There were Polish nights, and Italian nights, and Russian nights.

Hull House was so successful that it grew until there were 13 buildings and a staff of 65. About 50 people lived there. Some of them were writers or artists. Some were homeless. At dinnertime, the dining room might be filled with neighbors and political leaders and renowned philosophers.

Addams started clubs so that working boys and girls could have fun and learn, too. She worked to get child-labor laws passed to make it illegal for children to work long days. Chicago built its first public playground because of her efforts. She served on the Chicago school board and got new schools built.

When children committed crimes in the 19th century, they were treated like adults. Few people understood that children's problems are different from grownups'. Jane Addams understood. She helped establish the first juvenile court in the United States.

The Hull House neighborhood was full of garbage. Garbage stinks and brings rats. What did Addams do about it? She got herself appointed a city garbage inspector. Then she got up every morning at 6 A.M. and rode on a garbage truck, making sure the streets were clean. Most Gilded Age women wore long dresses and were expected to stay at home. The things Addams did took courage and energy. She had plenty of both. Because of that she attracted some of the most interesting people of the day to Hull House. A historian has written that "the Hull House community was perhaps the most formidable group of intellectuals and social activists gathered in this country since Jefferson's dinners at the White House."

There was one battle that Addams didn't win. Hull House was in Chicago's 19th ward, and the 19th ward was run by popular Johnny Powers. Powers was an alderman with a salary of three dollars a week. He grew rich, which meant that he must have been stealing from the city. Jane Addams tried to replace him with an honest alderman. She couldn't. Powers tried to close down Hull House. He couldn't. They battled, and

Do you wish you could have had dinner at Hull House? What would you have talked about? Suppose Jane Addams were here now— what problems do you think she would attack? How can you set about improving life in your community today? How can people on our polyglot planet learn to live together in harmony?

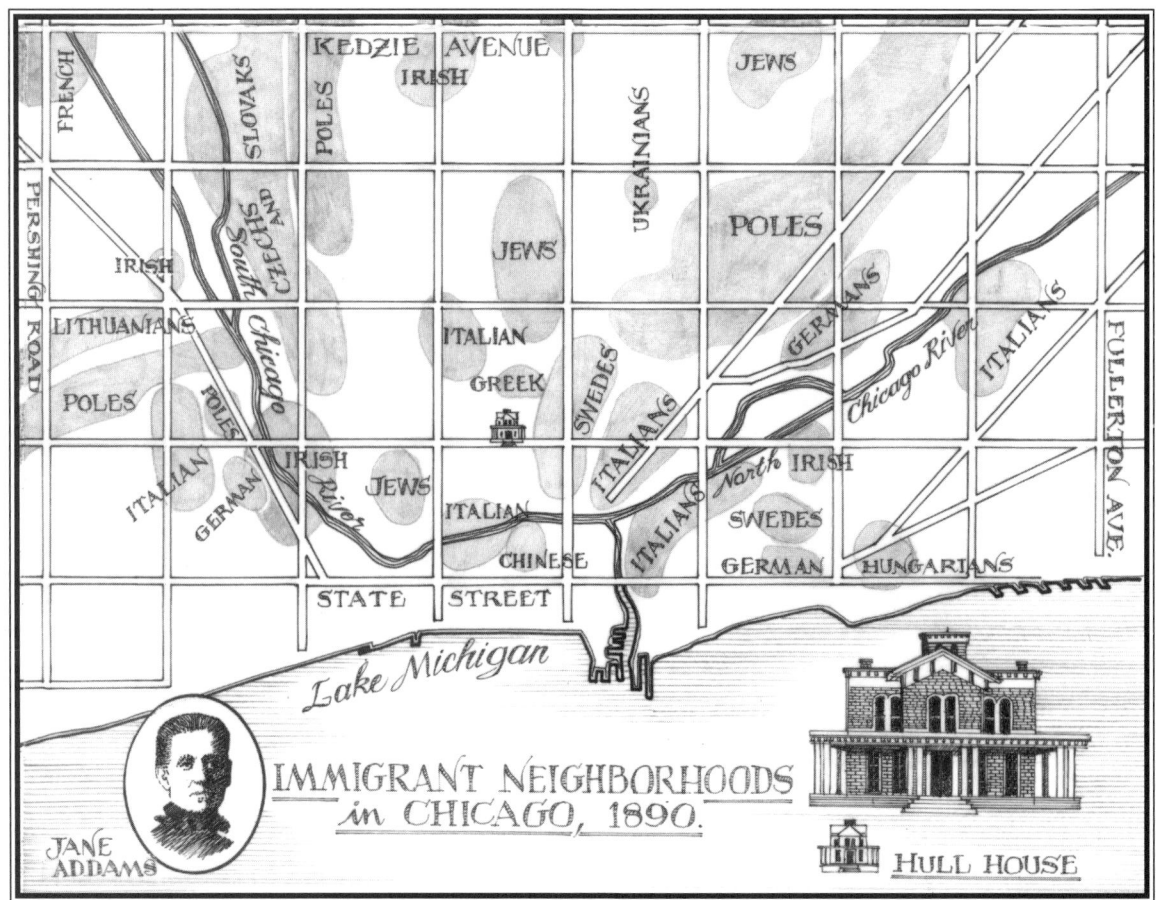

IMMIGRANT NEIGHBORHOODS in CHICAGO, 1890.

JANE ADDAMS

HULL HOUSE

Children in a makeshift playground in a neighborhood known as "Poverty Gap" on New York City's West Side.

Prairie Town Boy

Most Americans didn't live in cities; they lived on farms or in small towns. Carl Sandburg was born in 1878 in Galesburg, Illinois. Here is part of his autobiography, Prairie-Town Boy.

Carl Sandburg

Walking between rows of houses, many of them set widely apart—wider lots than at a later time—I came to know yards and trees—trees that I had seen in sun and rain in summer, and cloud and snow in winter, branches bending down with ice on them. Here and there in a backyard would be a tomato patch and carrots asking to be pulled out of the ground. Some yards had apple trees, and I helped myself to the windfalls.

For the little building in every backyard some said "backhouse," some said "privy." Carrying newspapers and later slinging milk I saw all the different styles of backhouses—the clean, roomy, elegant ones with latticework in front, those with leaky roofs and loose boards where the cold rain and wind came through, a few with soft paper that had no printing, but mostly it was newspapers neatly cut, or catalogues. When you had to go to the backhouse you stepped out into the weather—in rain or sleet. If the thermometer said zero you left your warm spot near the stove and the minute you were out the back door the cold put a crimp and shiver in you.

learned from each other. Powers was forced to be more honest: voters began watching him. Addams learned that reformers need to get involved in politics. She did. That wasn't easy; after all, women couldn't vote or hold office. Still, she became active in presidential campaigns and in a world peace movement. In 1931, when she was 71, Jane Addams was awarded the Nobel Peace Prize—the first American woman to be so honored.

The settlement houses sometimes ignored poor people's ability to help themselves; this son is teaching his father English.

160

31 Henry Ford

Ford's parents were Michigan pioneer farmers; he called his first farm vehicle an automobile plow.

Not many people get to change the world they live in. Henry Ford did. He did it because he had an idea he believed in, and he never gave up, even when people laughed at him.

Henry Ford's idea was this: to build an automobile so cheap that almost everyone could own one. A car that would cost about the same as a horse and buggy. Ford said that store clerks, schoolteachers, carpenters, farmers, librarians—ordinary people—would be able to buy his car.

Now, to any reasonable person at the turn of the century, the idea of an inexpensive car seemed nonsense. Henry Ford went to J. P. Morgan's bank and asked for a loan to get started. The House of Morgan was the biggest bank in the nation; the sensible bankers turned him down. Automobiles, they told him, were for rich people.

Back then, if you were wealthy and liked new gadgets, you might own a Stanley Steamer—an awesome car powered by a steam engine—or you might have an electric car, powered by a battery. Cars, by the way, were called *horseless carriages*. The

Driving a car did take some learning. Before there were licenses and driving tests, you read the instruction manual and hoped for the best. Here is the tale of a new car owner:

There was a young driver named Jake,
Who made the most stupid mistake,
He drove through a wall
And into the hall,
When he mixed up the gas and the brake.

The Stanley twins in their first Steamer (1897). Steam-driven cars were soon eclipsed by gasoline engines.

When Ford was a boy he took apart—and put together again—every watch he could find. As a grownup, he could explain a watch's workings even to little kids. One of his colleagues said, "They were living things to him, those machines."

You can visit the Henry Ford Museum in Dearborn, Michigan, to see this model of the place where it all started: the shop where Ford built his first car, in 1896—and here he is (right) driving it. Three years later, he left his job to run the Detroit Automobile Co.

trouble with the steam engine was that it sometimes blew up; the trouble with the battery car was that it often needed recharging.

Henry Ford was a tinkerer—he loved to design and make things. He believed he could design an inexpensive car powered by a liquid fuel.

Ford was a farmer's son with a thin, angular body and a head filled with ideas. He ran every day, long before running was a popular thing to do, and he had his own ideas about food: sometimes he ate grass sandwiches. Someone described him as having "a twenty-five-track mind with trains going out and coming in on all tracks at the same time." Even though he was full of energy, he had a casual manner. And he wasn't stuck up or fancy-acting. But he could be stubborn: he usually insisted on doing things his way. And he believed in the value of hard work. "Chop your own wood," he said, "and it will warm you twice."

When he was a boy, Ford became an apprentice in a machine shop.

The first taxis in New York and Chicago took people anywhere in town for a "jitney"—a slang word for a nickel. Today taxis, even buses, are sometimes called jitneys.

Then he got a job with Thomas Edison's company. He told Edison his idea about an inexpensive automobile powered by liquid fuel. Edison liked it. He encouraged Ford. "Young man, keep at it," he said.

Ford went to work. He tinkered away and designed several cars. Then he designed a car he called the Model T. It was just what he was aiming for: a car that worked well and was easy to build. Henry Ford needed to find a way to build it so the cost would be very low. He found that way.

Ford took Eli Whitney's idea of interchangeable parts and adapted it to cars. All the Model Ts were exactly alike. The parts of one Model T could be used on any other Model T. Then Ford took the factory system and make it work better than it had ever worked before. An architect named Albert Kahn supplied many of the ideas for Ford's factory.

In the old days, before modern factories, skilled workers, called artisans, built products by hand from beginning to end. In the new factories, workers made only one part of a product—the same part every day.

"The man who puts in a bolt does not put on the nut; the man who puts on the nut does not tighten it," was the way Ford described his factory system. Workers hated it. It made work boring, but it made car building very efficient. In Henry Ford's factory a wide, moving belt, called a *conveyor belt*, brought the car parts to the worker. He didn't even have to move. With this system—called the *mass-production assembly line*—cars could be built quickly by relatively unskilled workers.

The first Model T, which came out in 1908, cost $850. Many Americans could afford that. In 1915, Henry Ford drove his millionth car off the assembly line. Some friends who had lent him money to get started became rich. J. P. Morgan must have been writhing in his grave (he died in 1913).

By 1916, the price of the Model T had dropped to $360. Now there was no question about it: Henry Ford had made a democratic car! You didn't have to be rich to own one. People who had never been farther than they could walk now got in their cars and went traveling. Imagine not having a car and then suddenly getting wheels. It changes your world.

Putting the world on wheels was important enough, but Henry Ford did more than that. He showed that making products for average people was much more profitable than making products for rich people. There are only a few rich people, but there are many, many average folks. Ford's idea led to the building of American factories that were soon turning out washing machines, refrigerators, and other appliances, at prices ordinary people could afford. Those ordinary people

Jokes about rattling "flivvers" and Tin Lizzies were endless. "The jokes about my car sure helped popularize it," said Ford. "I hope they never end."

Regardless of earlier uses of some of these principles [interchangeable parts, conveyor belts, etc.]...mass production and its intensification into automation stems directly from what we worked out at Ford...between 1908 and 1913.

—CHARLES E. SORENSON, WHO WORKED WITH HENRY FORD

People bought gasoline for their cars in a store, usually where they bought kerosene for their lamps. Then, in 1913, a drive-in gas station opened in Pittsburgh. The owner thought the first day's business was terrific: he sold 30 gallons of gas!

FORD MOTOR CARS

Illustrating Four Positions of the Model T Touring Car with Top

Serviceable and of very pleasing appearance from every

Four Model T views: "Serviceable and of very pleasing appearance."

driving around in their cars would eventually need motels and want supermarkets. Automobiles created industries that no one had foreseen.

Henry Ford understood that if ordinary people were going to buy the new products they needed to earn reasonable wages. So, in 1914, when the average American worker earned $2.40 a day for a nine-hour day, Henry Ford announced that he would pay his workers $5 for an eight-hour day. That was an astonishing decision. It was also smart. That $5 an hour meant that workers at the Ford Motor Company could afford to buy Ford cars. Henry Ford was creating his own customers. Soon other manufacturers and businessmen followed his thinking. America became a nation of consumers. Ford, who always enjoyed simple living, helped bring about our complex modern way of life.

Henry Ford created a revolution. He wanted to build a car "for the multitude." He did that—and more, too. He helped bring democracy into the marketplace.

Below, the perfect daydream for the Model T owner: a family jaunt into the countryside. Left, the frequent reality on roads that were usually unpaved. The final humiliation was being pulled out of a ditch—by a horse.

32 The Birdmen

The first machines the Wright brothers tested at Kitty Hawk were gliders. They experimented on these before trying a powered plane.

Suppose, tomorrow, you open your front door and there before you is a flying saucer. A spaceman steps out and smiles.

The next day you go to school and tell your friends what you saw. Do you think they will believe you?

Today, it is hard for us to understand what people thought when they first heard that men had flown. Mostly, if they hadn't seen it themselves, they didn't believe it. Why, if people were foolish enough to say men could fly, the next thing they might say was that someday men would walk on the moon!

But on December 17, 1903, two men flew. They were brothers from Dayton, Ohio, and they owned a bicycle shop. Neither had graduated from high school. Their names were Wilbur and Orville Wright. It was not luck that made them the first persons in all of history to build and fly an airplane that lifted off the ground with its own power. It was hard work and determination. Before they built that plane they studied all that was known about flying. They thought, argued, and experimented. They built a wind tunnel and tested 200 differently shaped wings. Then they drew plans and built carefully.

When they flew, it was from Kill Devil Hill at Kitty Hawk, on North Carolina's Outer Banks. The Outer Banks are islands that run like a row of beads along the Carolina coast. Back in the 17th century, Sir Walter Raleigh planted a colony there, the Lost Colony. In the 18th century, the Outer Banks were home base to Blackbeard the pirate.

Today the islands are filled with tourists and hotels and cottages. But

"From the time we were little children my brother Orville and myself lived together, played together, worked together, and, in fact, thought together," wrote Wilbur. "We usually owned all of our toys in common, talked over our thoughts and aspirations so that nearly everything that was done in our lives has been the result of conversations, suggestions, and discussions between us."

X marks the spot where Wilbur and Orville set up camp in 1902. "I chose Kitty Hawk," Wilbur wrote his father in 1900, "because...there are neither hills nor trees, so that it offers a safe place for practice. Also the wind there is stronger than any place near home and is almost constant."

[The balloon] appears, as you observe, to be a discovery of great importance, and what may possibly give a new turn to human affairs. Convincing sovereigns of the folly of wars may perhaps be one effect of it; since it will be impracticable for the most potent of them to guard his dominions. Five thousand balloons, capable of raising two men each, could not cost more than five ships of the line; and where is the prince who can afford so to cover his country with troops for its defence, as that ten thousand men descending from the clouds might not in many places do an infinite deal of mischief, before a force could be brought together to repel them?

—Benjamin Franklin, in a letter to Jan Ingenhousz, 1784

in 1903, Kitty Hawk was empty sandy beach, with a few fishermen and a lifeboat station where men stood by to aid shipwrecks. Kill Devil Hill, which is just a big sand dune, was a good place to test an airplane.

On that windy December day, Orville won the toss of a coin. He got to fly first, lying flat on his stomach on the wing of the kitelike biplane. Wilbur ran beside him; the plane lifted a few feet above the sand and stayed in the air for 17 seconds. The brothers took turns and flew four flights that day. The longest lasted 59 seconds. It was enough. They had flown. The men from the lifeboat station had seen them and taken a picture.

The headlines in the morning newspaper in nearby Norfolk, Virginia —the *Virginian Pilot*—told of the flight, although most of the details in the story were wrong. The brothers were upset about the poor reporting, but it didn't much matter: no one paid attention, and other newspapers didn't carry the story. No one understood that birds now had competition: people would soon be flying.

Orville and Wilbur went home to Dayton and set to work. They knew they could fly, but they also knew their plane needed improving. Besides, they needed to learn to be pilots; they needed time in the air.

So they flew around a big pasture in Ohio. Neighbors saw them and talked about the flights. But only a few other people believed that men were actually flying. In 1904 a group of newspaper reporters came to see for themselves.

Now, the Wright brothers were not daredevils. They were very methodical and precise. They did everything as well as they could. They checked and tested and checked and tested again, each time they flew. That made sense. They didn't want to get killed.

When the reporters arrived, the brothers were having mechanical problems with the plane. The reporters stayed two days. The Wright brothers wouldn't fly on those days; the plane wasn't ready. The reporters left. Some wrote that the Wright brothers were fakes.

One writer did stay and see them fly. He was the editor of an apiary journal. An *apiary* (AY-pee-ary) is a place where bees are raised for their honey. Yes, you read that right: the first long article about the Wright brothers' flight was in a beekeepers' magazine!

Finally, in August 1908, Wilbur went off to Europe and flew his plane at a racetrack in France. This time he sat on the wing (instead of lying on his stomach.) There were 24 witnesses. They went wild—hugging and kissing him and throwing their hats in the air. They begged Wilbur to fly again the next day. But it was Sunday, his sabbath, and he wouldn't do it. On Monday, 4,000 people were at the racetrack to watch him fly. "*Il vole, il vole*" ("He flies, he flies"), they cried—and that soon became the title of a popular French song.

A month later, in Virginia, Orville showed Americans that people could fly. He lifted his plane into the air and swung around an army

The Wrights stayed with Kitty Hawk's postmaster, William Tate. They took a picture of his nephew Tom with the glider and a drum fish. "He can tell more big yarns than any kid his size I ever saw," Orville wrote.

Working with the glider, "we laid it down on the ground to change some of the adjustments of the ropes, when without a sixteenth of a second's notice, the wind caught under one corner, and quicker than thought, it landed 20 feet away. We dragged the pieces back to camp and began to consider getting home."

Wilbur in the workshop of the Wright Cycle Co. Later on the brothers used bicycle chains and sprockets to link their airplane's motor and propellers.

A **biplane** has two wings, one above the other, a bit like a box kite.

For a simple explanation of flight, look at **The Way Things Work,** *by David Macaulay (Houghton Mifflin, 1988).*

field one and a half times before he landed. The crowd of watchers rushed forward "screaming as loudly as they could, overwhelmed by the miracle that had taken place before their eyes."

Try to imagine that scene in 1908. For thousands and thousands of years, men and women looked at birds and dreamed that they too could lift themselves into the air. Some tried. Mythical Icarus, back in ancient days, took birds' feathers and a frame and made something like a hang glider. But when he soared into the air the sun melted the wax that held the feathers and Icarus fell into the sea. Others, who we know were real, had built gliders, or hot-air balloons that floated on the wind. What the Wrights did was different. They didn't depend on the wind. They used their intelligence to build a machine that conquered the skies. They solved the problem of flight.

Suddenly the two shy brothers were celebrities. They were carried in parades and toasted at banquets. Kings and presidents invited them for visits. Stores sold Orville and Wilbur caps. Now everyone believed it—people could fly!

Who were these brothers who had made it happen?

In Dayton they were known as the minister's sons. Wilbur had planned to be a minister himself, but in his senior year in high school he was hit in the mouth by a fast-moving hockey puck. Besides knocking out teeth, it hurt him seriously. It seemed a terrible tragedy—he gave up his hope of being a minister—but it turned out to be a lucky break for the rest of the world.

Wilbur was the older and more serious of the boys. Orville had a mischievous side. Both were slim and tightly built. Both were quiet and modest. Their father had given them hardworking habits. It was their mother who taught them mathematics and how to make things. When the boys wanted a sled—one that would win races—she taught them about wind resistance and streamlined design. Then she helped them make a plan—on paper first—and taught them to build a model.

On December 17, 1903,

If ever there lived a Yankee lad,
Wise or otherwise, good or bad,
Who, seeing the birds fly, didn't jump
With flapping arms from stake or stump,
Or, spreading the tail
Of his coat for a sail,
Take a soaring leap from post or rail,

And wonder why
He couldn't fly,
And flap and flutter and wish and try—
If ever you knew a country dunce
Who didn't try that as often as once,
All I can say is, that's a sign
He never would do for a hero of mine.

—JOHN TOWNSEND TROWBRIDGE,
"DARIUS GREEN AND HIS FLYING MACHINE"

John Daniels of the Kill Devil lifesaving station snapped this historic shot of Orville and the Flyer as they left the ground.

When my brother and I built and flew the first man-carrying flying machine, we thought that we were introducing into the world an invention which would make further wars practically impossible. That we were not alone in this thought is evidenced by the fact that the French Peace Society presented us with medals on account of our invention. We thought governments would realize the impossibility of winning by surprise attacks, and that no country would enter into war with another when it knew it would have to win by simply wearing out the enemy.

—ORVILLE WRIGHT, 1917

They were different from each other, but their personalities balanced. They loved to argue back and forth, and out of those arguments came good ideas. One good idea, when they were boys, was to start a weekly newspaper. They built their own printing press, wrote articles, and sold advertisements. But what they really enjoyed doing was making and fixing things. So they went into the bicycle business. Bikes, back at the end of the 19th century, were high-tech items. The brothers built their own bikes and made them faster and better than their competitors'. Still, they weren't satisfied. They wanted to do something special; they wanted to be famous, like the great inventors of their day.

On September 3, 1900, Wilbur Wright wrote this to his father:

It is my belief that flight is possible and while I am taking up the investigation for pleasure rather than profit, I think there is a slight chance of achieving fame and fortune from it. It is almost the only great problem which has not been pursued by a multitude of investigators, and therefore carried to a point where further progress is very difficult. I am certain I can reach a point much in advance of any previous workers in this field.

Three problems needed solving in order for people to fly. Scientists call them *lift, propulsion*, and *control*. The Wright brothers needed to find a way to *lift* a plane into the air and keep it there; they needed to *propel* the plane forward; and they needed to *control* the flight—to turn, to climb, to land. Those problems had baffled some of the greatest scientific minds of all time. The Wright brothers solved them.

It was just three years after Wilbur wrote that letter to his father that he and Orville flew. Five years after that (in 1908), people believed it had happened.

If men and women could fly, anything might be possible.

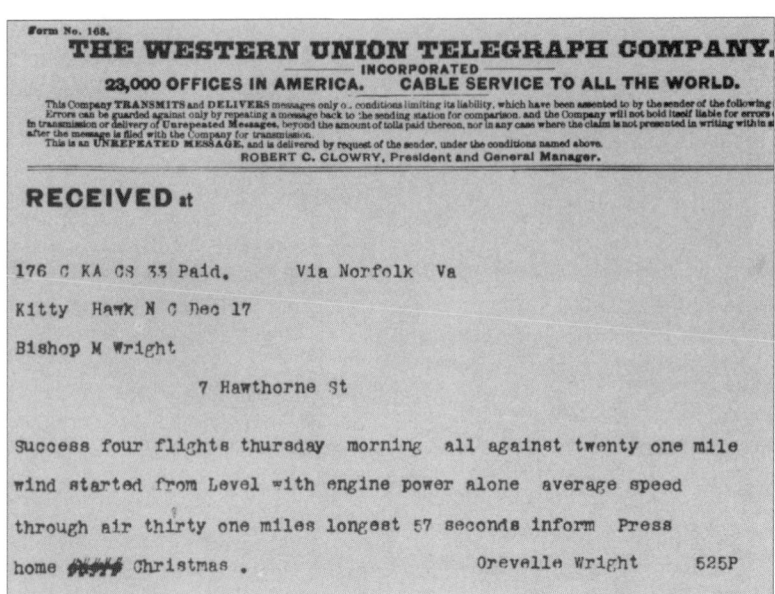

Orville's telegram announcing the news. They misspelled his name.

33 William Howard Taft

Taft campaigning for the presidency in 1908. He joked about his size: when Yale University offered him a professorship of law, which is called a "chair," he said a chair wouldn't do but a "sofa of law" might be all right.

William Howard Taft didn't want to be president. Theodore Roosevelt picked him for the job. And Taft's wife was determined that he have it. When she was 17 she said that the man she married would be president.

Taft was a huge man: he weighed more than 300 pounds. He was also sweet-natured and capable. After college he became a lawyer, and then the first American governor of the Philippine Islands.

He was a good governor, who gave the Filipinos much control of their own affairs. Theodore Roosevelt named him secretary of war. What he really wanted was to be chief justice of the Supreme Court, and one day he would have that job and handle it well. But his wife wanted to be first lady, so he ran for president.

As president, Taft did more trustbusting than TR, and he helped get some good laws passed. But after Teddy Roosevelt, people found him dull. His presidency seemed boring. Besides, as time went on, Taft turned control of the Republican Party over to the conservative party leaders. They were called the "Old Guard." They didn't want change or reform, although most Americans did. Many people wanted progressive leadership.

Some of Roosevelt's friends were alarmed. They wrote the ex-president and told him he was needed at home. They wanted to see him become president again. Teddy didn't need much urging.

Mrs. Taft was the first president's wife to ride with her husband to his inauguration.

When Juliette Low visited England (in 1912), she met Colonel Robert Baden-Powell, the founder of the Boy Scouts. Low thought girls should have the same kind of organization. So she went home to Savannah, Georgia, and started a troop with 18 girls. Today, millions of girls belong to Scout troops.

The news reaches Africa that Teddy is on his way.

On his hunting trip to Africa after he declined to run for the presidency in 1908, Teddy Roosevelt killed 296 lions, elephants, water buffaloes, and other animals. Do you think there is any contradiction in the idea of a conservation-minded president who is also crazy about hunting?

Now the politicians and financial leaders who headed the Republican Party were alarmed. They didn't want TR as president again. No one could control that man! They'd been happy when he went off to Africa. J. P. Morgan had said he hoped that "the first lion he meets does his duty."

The Republicans nominated William Howard Taft for a second term. (It was 1912.)

Theodore Roosevelt started his own party. It was called the Progressive Party. (Sometimes it was called the Bull Moose Party because Roosevelt once said he felt "like a bull moose.")

People who usually voted Republican were confused. Some voted for Taft; more voted for Roosevelt. But the Republican vote was divided. For the first time since Grover Cleveland—and for only the second time since before the

Some Political Theory:

This is not a free country. Hold on—what am I saying? Of course this is a free country.

No, it isn't. No country is completely free.

Are you free to kill your neighbor?

Are you free to steal?

Are you free to destroy property?

When people get together and form a government, they make rules—laws—that limit freedom. Usually those limits help protect other people's freedom. In this country we try to have as few limits as possible. It is a trick finding a comfortable balance between freedom and restraint.

It isn't as easy as you might think even to agree on what freedom means. "The world has never had a good definition of the word liberty," said Abraham Lincoln.

We all declare for liberty, but using the same word we do not mean the same thing. With some, the word liberty may mean for each man to do as he pleases with himself and the product of his labor; while with others the same word may mean for some men to do as they please with other men and the product of other men's labor....The shepherd drives the wolf from the sheep's throat, for which the sheep thanks the shepherd as his liberator, while the wolf denounces him for the same act....plainly the sheep and the wolf are not agreed upon a definition of liberty.

The problem of defining freedom is one that concerns every generation. People in the Gilded Age were suddenly confronted

A Discussion

with a need for new laws and regulations to control new industries and handle the great numbers of people living in cities. They worried about losing their freedom.

We have many more laws today than Americans had in 1900. Does that mean we have less freedom? Possibly. But that is not necessarily a bad thing. Conditions are different today from what they were 100 years ago.

Besides, we have found that some people abuse freedom. They harm other people. In the past, some enslaved others. We need laws to protect some citizens from others.

We have found that without laws, some businesspeople act dishonestly or unfairly. We need to protect the consumer. We need laws to ensure fair business practices.

Should people be free to cut down forest trees or pollute the atmosphere? Are we taking away a person's freedom if we don't allow him to litter?

Today some people say that American citizens should not be allowed to have handguns. Others say that would be a terrible loss of individual freedom. What do you think? Can you think of ways laws protect you from yourself? (How about speeding laws, drug laws, antismoking laws?)

James Madison said, "If men were angels, no government would be necessary." But people aren't angels and government is necessary. The idea is to make laws as fair as possible. Madison said that the great difficulty was this: "You must first enable the government to control the governed; and in the next place

A rather vivid and creepy cartoon about the country's need for pure-food laws.

oblige it to control itself." Most Americans worry about government that is too big and too active. It is something to worry about.

During the Gilded Age, the government began to do something besides protecting people and their rights. Government began actively to help people—children, army veterans, the poor, the working class, consumers, farmers, small businessmen. That was a new role for government. How active should the government be in helping citizens? That became an important question for citizens.

The government had often helped businesses and farmers with tariffs and money policies. Now the government was *regulat-*

ing business. It broke up trusts that were unfair to their competitors. Do you think the government should do that?

Today we have laws that make child labor illegal. Other laws say that an employer must pay at least a certain minimum for an hour's work. Another law says that employers may not make most people work more than eight hours without extra pay. With those laws the government has changed the way we live. Do you think that is the proper role of government?

Questions about the role of the government caused much discussion and disagreement during the Gilded Age. They still do.

173

The Progressive hope: the Bull Moose chases the Republican elephant and the Democratic donkey into the hills.

Civil War—a Democrat was elected.

He was Woodrow Wilson, and he wasn't at all like TR or Taft, although he was a progressive in his thinking. Wilson was a scholarly, serious man. He had been president of Princeton University. People didn't love him as they had Theodore Roosevelt, but they did respect and admire him. They believed in him, and were right to do so. He became one of the nation's great presidents.

Back in the States he fought his last fight when he came out for the Republican nomination in 1912 a Progressive, champion of the Square Deal, crusader for the Plain People; the Bull Moose bolted out from under the Taft steamroller and formed the Progressive Party for righteousness' sake at the Chicago Colosseum while the delegates who were going to restore democratic government rocked with tears in their eyes.... Perhaps the River of Doubt had been too much for a man of his age; perhaps things weren't so bully any more; TR lost his voice during the triangular campaign. In Duluth a maniac shot him in the chest, his life was saved only by the thick bundle of manuscript of the speech he was going to deliver. TR delivered the speech with the bullet still in him, heard the scared applause, felt the plain people praying for his recovery, but the spell was broken somehow.

—John Dos Passos, *The Happy Warrior*

Problems of Progress

The early labor movement—the union movement—came out of working people's longing for a just society. The industrial revolution and the new capitalism had created a new kind of world—a wonderful world of new products and new opportunities. But no one was prepared for the misery and imbalance it also created. Before the 19th century, no country had faced problems quite like those of the machine world. It was a world of extremes: of great riches and opulent living for a few, and of hard work, long hours, and despair for legions of workers (who were sometimes called "wage slaves").

Most Americans weren't at either extreme. Most weren't very rich or very poor. They were part of a middle class of small businesspeople, farmers, and professionals. But the extremes affected them more than they realized. They didn't understand that poverty is enormously costly to society. It breeds crime and waste, besides guilt and unhappiness.

The Progressives tried, but on the whole the middle class didn't face the challenge of creating a fair society. And the rich industrialists, financiers, and merchants didn't usually want to do anything that would lead to major changes (they were generally rich because of the way things were—which is called the *status quo*).

So the problems of poverty and injustice didn't get solved. Those problems especially affected women, immigrants, and minority groups; they would haunt the 20th century.

34 A Schoolteacher President

Wilson in his senior year at Princeton. He used to go off to the woods by himself to practice making speeches.

When Thomas Woodrow Wilson was nine he was still having trouble learning his abc's. When he was 10 he could read—but not well. Some of the people who knew him thought he was not very smart. Did they turn out to be wrong!

Woodrow Wilson's parents had faith in their son, but what was even more important, he seems to have had faith in himself. Today we believe he had a learning disability—probably dyslexia—which made it difficult for him to learn to read. In those days no one understood about learning disabilities. Wilson had to solve his own problem. He did.

Sometimes problems can become strengths. If Theodore Roosevelt had not had severe asthma when he was a boy, perhaps he would not have turned into a powerful man who loved "the strenuous life." If Woodrow Wilson had been able to read easily, perhaps he would have been less determined to study and learn.

Wilson was never able to read quickly, but that didn't stop him from becoming a college professor, president of Princeton University, governor of New Jersey, and president of the United States.

"My best training came from my father," he said when he was grown up. His father was a Presbyterian minister who read aloud to his son and taught him to think clearly and write exactly. He assigned the boy subjects for speeches

As a schoolboy, Tommy Wilson loved trains and made pictures of them all the time. This drawing survived.

Wilson (holding the hat) with co-members of Princeton's Alligator Club. He was handsome, determined, stubborn, and serious.

When cartoonists drew Wilson's picture they often showed him as a stern schoolteacher with a ruler in his hand. And he was a bit like that. He was a serious man; he didn't know how to be jolly (except with his three daughters). But people trusted him: they knew he was honest and honorable; they knew he was doing the best job he could do.

and essays and gave him suggestions to improve them. Woodrow Wilson became a brilliant speaker and a distinguished writer. But the most important thing the Reverend Wilson gave his son was a sure sense of what is right and what is wrong, which guided Woodrow Wilson all his life.

He was born in Virginia, four years before the Civil War began. The family soon moved to Georgia. His earliest memories were of war and grown-up discussions of politics, battles, and democracy. He was the son, grandson, and nephew of ministers. It was expected that Tommy (his childhood name) would become a minister, too. But from an early age it was politics that interested him.

When he went to college at Princeton, he signed his letters *Woodrow Wilson, Senator from Virginia*. It was supposed to be a joke—even though it was what he really wished to become.

He wasn't a great student at Princeton, although his writing ability did attract attention. A paper that he wrote in his senior year was published by an important magazine. Then he went to law school at the University of Virginia, with the hope of entering politics. But he wasn't successful as a lawyer. He was too shy; he had a hard time making friends or finding clients.

He was now a grown man—lanky, long-faced, and serious—and he didn't seem to be going anywhere. Politics was no career for a shy man.

So he went back to school—this time to Johns Hopkins in Baltimore—to study government and history. He had decided to become a college professor. Finally he had found something he could do well. He became an extraordinary professor. His specialty was government and politics. He thought, wrote, and taught

Princeton's president was a brilliant lecturer. Students lined up for his classes and often clapped.

about how the United States government should be run. He believed in a strong executive branch. (Later he had a chance to put his ideas into practice.) He was such a popular professor that it wasn't long before he was asked to be president of Princeton University.

Princeton was a fine old school when Wilson became its president, but a sleepy kind of place. (It had been called the College of New Jersey when James Madison was a student there.) Woodrow Wilson was determined to make it one of the best universities in the world. He did just that.

He had good ideas, and he got things done. Soon people began talking about Princeton's unusual president. And that got him into politics, where he had always wanted to be.

In New Jersey the state government was a mess. The citizens were disgusted with its corruption. Naturally, the political bosses didn't want to change things. But they wanted people to think things were changing. The bosses wanted a governor who would look good but whom they could control. Woodrow Wilson seemed perfect. He was well known, and his fine manners made him seem meek. The bosses were sure a college president wouldn't know much about the real world of politics. They thought he would be easy to push around. Were they fooled! Woodrow Wilson had steel in his bones and brains in his head. When he believed he was right he wouldn't bend or budge.

Wilson promised to clean up politics in New Jersey. Then he proceeded to do it. He became a reforming governor. The bosses tried to stop some of his reforms; Wilson spoke out and explained the issues to New Jersey's citizens. Remember, he was a great speaker. He asked the people to back him. They did. It was democracy at work. The bosses couldn't believe what was happening. Most were forced to retire. For a while, New Jersey became a model state.

In 1912 Woodrow Wilson was elected president of the United States. He knew just what he wanted to do as president—after all, he had been teaching about the presidency. He thought the president should be a strong leader. He believed in progressive goals. He wanted to improve working conditions, help the farmers with their problems, change the banking system, control monopolies, and lower tariffs.

Other leaders had wanted to do those things, too, but Congress and the special interests had stopped them. Wilson did exactly what he had done in New Jersey. He explained the issues to the American people. He told them to write their congressmen.

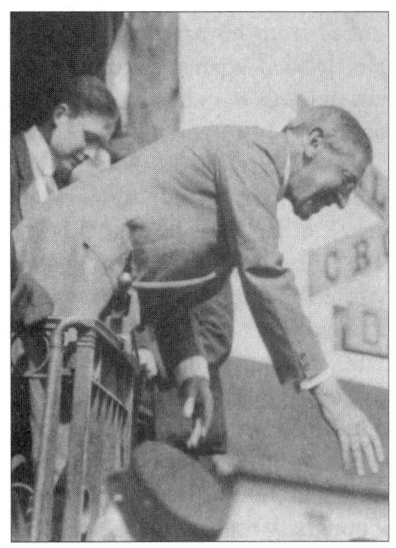

Wilson's training as a university lecturer stood him in good stead when he campaigned for the presidency. His speeches thrilled listeners. Below, Republican votes divided by TR's Bull Moose Progressives equal—a Democratic victory.

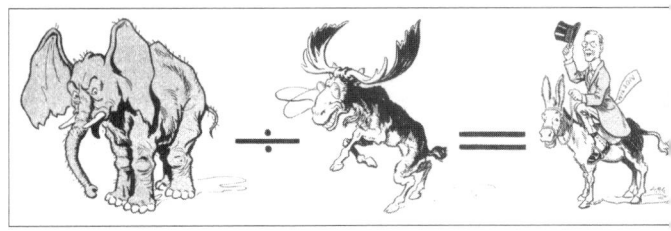

Great leaders have the ability to inspire people; they can make people do what they wish them to do. Woodrow Wilson was a great leader.

Wilson married Edith Galt (above) after his first wife died of kidney disease. Later, near the end of his presidency, Wilson had a stroke and Edith became a *de facto* president (she was—in fact—making a lot of the president's decisions).

Mr. and Mrs. Wilson on opening day, 1916, at Griffith Stadium, home of the Washington Senators baseball club ("first in war, first in peace, and last in the American League").

Democracy doesn't work well when citizens are uninformed or lazy. But when the people speak out, Congress listens. When President Wilson explained the issues, America's citizens understood and responded. Soon there were new and lower tariffs, a new banking system, and controls on the giant trusts. Wilson did what he had promised. He began to deal with the problem of the differences between rich and poor. He made our democracy reflect the wishes of the people, which was what Thomas Jefferson and James Madison had intended.

But Wilson wasn't perfect. He did nothing about the racism that was a poison in American life. He did not (until late in his life) believe in giving women the vote. Sometimes he was a little too sure of himself, and he wasn't very good at understanding the other side's view of a problem.

Wilson's ideas on foreign affairs were different from those of the presidents who came just before him. He was not concerned with making America powerful. He was not interested in treaties that gave unfair advantages to American business. He was not an imperialist. He thought that nations, like people, should not be selfish. He believed the United States should help other nations become democratic. Mostly, he hoped to stay out of foreign affairs.

Woodrow Wilson wanted America to fulfill the vision of the Founders. He wanted the United States to be great because it stood for the right things. He was getting things done in the nation when something happened that he hadn't expected. An archduke was assassinated in Europe, which started a war. A war that changed the whole world.

35 War

On June 5, 1917, conscription began: every American male between 21 and 30 had to register to be drafted into the armed forces.

It was called the "Great War." (Later it became the First World War.) It began in Europe in 1914. At first, the Central Powers (Germany, Austria, and Turkey) fought the Allies (England, France, and Russia). Before it was finished, many other nations were involved. It was unnecessary—as most wars are—and came about because of national pride and the struggles of huge empires for power and territory and economic gain.

Like the Civil War in America, it became ugly and hateful. Nine million men died—more than the whole population of New York City today. It left scars and wounds that refused to heal. It changed the fate of the world. But no one knew that when it started.

In England, young men hurried to enlist—afraid the war would be over before they got a chance to fight. No one believed it would last long. Wilson called the war "a distant event." He, too, thought it would soon be over.

That was a big miscalculation. World War I

Goodbye to the troops. The day war was declared, George M. Cohan wrote the song "Over There." "Send the word," it said. "The Yanks are coming."

1915: A luxury British ship, the *Lusitania*, is sunk by a German submarine. Among the passengers killed are 198 Americans. Innocent travelers have become victims of war. (The German embassy in the U.S. had issued warnings that travelers crossing the Atlantic did so at their own risk. No one believed that they meant what they said.)

A crew from the 23rd Infantry in the 2nd Division firing a 37 mm gun during an advance in June 1918 at Belleau Wood in France. "The 2nd Division has been moving, marching, entrenching, and fighting since May 30," a general said. "There are no troops to relieve them."

At home, boys played soldier.

The Germans called submarines "U-boats," short for *Unterseeboot*, or "under-sea-boat."

was worse than anyone could have dreamed. Many of those 19th-century inventions, which people thought would prevent war, were turned to killing. Airplanes shot at each other overhead, machine guns cracked their deadly staccato, submarines ejected killer torpedoes, and poison gas turned men blind or unable to breathe.

But the killing machines didn't seem to make much difference. It was men—huge armies of men—that determined the outcome. Armies of men who dug themselves into trenches and shot at enemies in other trenches. Both sides fought on, stuck in bloody mud, for four years. They wasted a generation of young men.

The United States had the vast Atlantic Ocean as a moat to keep it isolated from Europe's troubles. Washington and Jefferson had warned the nation to stay away from the Old World and its problems. Most Americans had no interest in Europe's fight. But America was now a world power. It became harder and harder not to be involved.

Woodrow Wilson wanted to be a peacemaker. He tried talking to leaders on both sides; he tried to end the war. But Germany insisted on being given French and Polish land before it would stop fighting. France and Russia (which ruled most of Poland) wouldn't agree to that.

Woodrow Wilson believed America should stay out of the battle. He wanted the nation not to take sides—to remain neutral. He remembered the Civil War from his southern childhood. He knew how awful the effects of war could be. But when German troops marched on peaceful Belgium, many Americans became angry.

Then, when German submarines began sinking ships—even passenger ships—Americans were horrified. In past wars there had been rules of fair play: ships were given warning and passengers allowed time to get into lifeboats. The submarines gave no warnings.

More and more people in the United States began to side with the Allies. Americans sold war supplies to the Allies. The Germans began sinking American ships. American lives were being lost. In 1917, Germany declared war on all ships that went near England or France. Eight U.S. ships were sunk. Then the nation learned of a German plot to make Mexico fight against the United States. Germany was said to have promised to give Texas and New Mexico to Mexico as a prize for entering the war.

On the night of March 31, 1917, Woodrow Wilson got out of bed and took his portable typewriter to the south veranda of the White House. Mrs. Wilson brought him a bowl of milk and crackers from the kitchen. Then, in the quiet of early morning, the president typed out a message that was to become famous.

In wartime, boys could "do their bit" by knitting clothes and blankets for the troops.

Women did men's jobs everywhere—from making weapons to hauling ice. One woman who made gas masks said, "It has been one of the richest experiences of my life—meeting all the wonderful women...there, not only the professionals but the little seamstresses and factory girls who have given up their old work to do their bit." Their masks came too late for these soldiers (left), already blinded by gas at the front, some of them permanently.

More than 260,000 black men volunteered or were drafted. They were often given menial jobs but many served with distinction in spite of it. Below, the war is over: Armistice Day, November 11, 1918.

It was a declaration of war. Wilson said our nation had no selfish aims, and it didn't. America wanted no territory—no gain for itself.

> *The present German submarine warfare against commerce is a war-fare against mankind. It is a war against all nations....We are accepting the challenge....The world must be made safe for democracy.*

On April 2, Wilson went before Congress and spoke his message. It was a fearful thing to lead this great, peaceful people into war, he said:

> *...into the most terrible and disastrous of all wars, civilization itself seeming to be in the balance. But the right is more precious than peace, and we shall fight for the things which we have always car-ried nearest our hearts—for democracy, for the right of those who submit to authority to have a voice in their own governments, for the rights and liberties of small nations, for a universal dominion of right by such a concert of free peoples as shall bring peace and safe-ty to all nations, and make the world itself at last free.*

The congressmen cheered and cheered.

Woodrow Wilson went back to his office. He looked at his aide. "Isn't it strange that men should cheer for war," he said. Then he put his head on his desk and wept.

182

Chronology of Events

1854: Elisha Otis demonstrates safety-equipped elevator at New York's Crystal Palace

1858: Edwin Drake discovers oil in Pennsylvania

1858: Frederick Law Olmsted appointed chief architect of New York City's Central Park

1859: silver discovered in Nevada's Comstock Lode

1865: Andrew Johnson becomes 17th president when Abraham Lincoln is assassinated

1867: John Muir sets out on his 1,000-mile walk

1869: Ulysses S. Grant becomes 18th president

1870: Standard Oil Co. sells its stock to the public

1871: much of Chicago destroyed in the Great Fire

1872: Montgomery Ward puts out his first mail-order catalogue

1873: wartime monetary policies end; nation returns to gold standard

1874: James Eads builds the first steel bridge in the U.S. over the Mississippi River at St. Louis

1875: Civil Rights Act guarantees blacks equal rights in theaters, hotels, buses, parks, and on juries

1876: Rutherford B. Hayes becomes 19th president after a disputed election

1879: Frank W. Woolworth opens the first 5-and-10-cent store in Utica, New York

1879: The first skyscraper, the Leitner Building, with 16 stories, is erected in Chicago

1880: George Eastman patents the first practical roll film for cameras

1880: the Kampfe brothers invent the safety razor

1881: James Garfield becomes the 20th president but is shot and fatally wounded by an assassin. Vice President Chester Arthur becomes 21st president

1883: Civil Service reformed; employees chosen by examination instead of political appointments

1883: the Brooklyn Bridge over New York's East River, the longest suspension bridge of its time, completed

1883: the Supreme Court rules the 1875 Civil Rights Act unconstitutional

1883: the Chinese Exclusion Act aims to keep Chinese immigrants out of the U.S. for 10 years

1883: Joseph Pulitzer buys the *New York World*

1884: Lewis Waterman invents the fountain pen

1885: Grover Cleveland becomes 22nd president

1886: the Statue of Liberty dedicated (finally)

1886: four labor activists are hanged after Chicago's Haymarket riot

1886: the American Federation of Labor (A.F. of L.) founded, with Samuel Gompers as president

1886: Don Vincente Martinez Ybor opens a cigar factory in Tampa, Florida

1886: Apache leader Geronimo surrenders to U.S. troops in Arizona Territory

1887: President Cleveland establishes Interstate Commerce Commission to regulate railroads

1887: the Dawes Act attempts to compensate Native Americans by dividing up reservation lands

1888: Louisville, Kentucky, introduces the secret ballot; voters go into a private booth

1889: Benjamin Harrison becomes 23rd president

1889: Two million acres of Indian land in Oklahoma opened to white settlers

1889: Electric light installed in the White House. Staff members have to turn them on because President Harrison is afraid to touch the switches

1889: Jane Addams founds Hull House in Chicago

1889: Montana, North Dakota, South Dakota, and Washington 39th, 40th, 41st, and 42nd states

1889: More than 2,000 die in the Johnstown Flood, one of worst disasters in American history

1890: Jacob Riis's *How the Other Half Lives* reveals the plight of poor urban immigrants

1890: Yosemite Valley and other areas become federally protected national parks

1890: Idaho and Wyoming the 43rd and 44th states

1890: in a last effort of Native American resistance, a group of Sioux massacred at Wounded Knee, South Dakota

1890: Sherman Antitrust Act passed in attempt to curb monopolies

1890: Sherman Silver Purchase Act allows partial backing of Treasury bonds by silver

1891: Populist Party organized in Cincinnati, Ohio

1892: S. S. McClure founds *McClure's* magazine

1892: steelworkers attacked in Homestead strike

1893: Grover Cleveland again elected president; a five-year-long depression begins

1893: George Ferris's huge revolving steel wheel, with cars holding more than 1,000 people, is the hit of the World's Columbian Exposition in Chicago

1893: Hawaii's native government toppled; U.S. eventually annexes islands (1898)

1893: Cleveland restores country to gold standard

1894: federal troops break up Pullman strike

1895: Frederick Douglass, the great abolitionist and ambassador to Haiti, dies in Washington, D.C.

1895: first professional football game played by two Pennsylvania teams. Latrobe beats Jeannette, 12–0

1896: gold discovered in the Yukon. Prospectors rush to Alaska and northwestern Canada

1896: Utah becomes the 45th state

1896: Republican William McKinley elected 25th president despite William Jennings Bryan's pro-silver, populist Democratic candidacy

1898: after explosion of warship *Maine* in Havana, U.S. declares war on Spain. Cuba independent, U.S. annexes Philippines and Puerto Rico

1900: L. Frank Baum publishes *Wonderful Wizard of Oz*

1900: army doctor Walter Reed discovers that mosquitoes spread yellow fever

1901: President McKinley shot and fatally wounded soon after reelection; Vice President Theodore Roosevelt becomes 26th president

1901: oil found at Spindletop, Texas

1903: *McClure's* publishes muckraker Ida Tarbell's exposé of Standard Oil

1903: Orville and Wilbur Wright make the first successful airplane flight at Kitty Hawk, N.C.

1904: Theodore Roosevelt elected by large majority

1905: Industrial Workers of the World (Wobblies) founded by Bill Haywood and Eugene Debs, Chicago

1906: over 700 die in an earthquake and fire that destroys much of San Francisco, California

1906: Oklahoma becomes the 46th state

1906: Theodore Roosevelt visits Panama Canal during construction; becomes first president to make a trip outside the U.S. while in office

1908: Henry Ford introduces the Model T, the world's first mass-produced and affordable car

1908: Attorney General Charles Bonaparte (great-nephew of France's Emperor Napoleon Bonaparte) founds Federal Bureau of Investigation (FBI)

1908: William Howard Taft becomes 27th president

1910: African-American leader W. E. B. DuBois founds the National Association for the Advancement of Colored People (NAACP)

1911: one hundred and forty-six women die in Triangle Shirtwaist Company fire in New York City

1912: Lawrence, Massachusetts, millhands' strike brings workers' hardships national attention

1912: in a four-way presidential race, the Democratic candidate, Woodrow Wilson, defeats Taft, Progressive candidate Teddy Roosevelt, and Socialist Eugene V. Debs to become 28th president

1912: New Mexico and Arizona enter Union as 47th and 48th states, the last admitted for almost 50 years

1913: national income tax permitted by 16th Amendment to Constitution

1913: Federal Reserve Act changes banking system

1914: Panama Canal opens

1914: war in Europe (later known as First World War). President Wilson says U.S. will stay out of war

1915: Margaret Sanger taken to court for writing and distributing a pamphlet on birth control

1916: National Park Service established

1917: 17th Amendment to Constitution permits direct election of senators

1917: U.S. declares war on Germany

More Books to Read

These books are truthful, interesting, and, most important, exciting and fun to read.

Willa Cather, *One of Ours,* Vintage, 1971 (first pub. 1922). Not many people know that Willa Cather, the author of *My Antonia* and *O Pioneers!,* wrote a story about a Nebraska farm boy who goes to fight in the Great War in France. This book is for adults, but it is not hard to read. You can also read **Erich Maria Remarque**'s *All Quiet on the Western Front* (first pub. 1929). Some books you never forget. This book is like that. It was written by a German, and it tells the story from our war enemy's point of view, but when you read it you will understand that people all over the world are much alike.

Susan Coolidge, *What Katy Did,* Octopus (first pub. 1872). You should be able to find this book in a good library even though it is out of print. At the turn of the century, Katy and her unruly brothers and sisters have been out of control since their mother's death. Katy is the oldest and the worst of the lot. Then there is an accident, and Katy has to learn how to be brave and how to look after her family.

Dorothy Canfield Fisher, *Understood Betsy,* Dell, 1987. Sickly, overprotected Elizabeth Ann is sent to live with her "horrible Putney cousins" in Vermont. Suddenly, Betsy has to do things without being told—washing dishes, walking alone to school (in one room!), exploring, thinking for herself. A funny, affectionate story of country life at the turn of the century.

Jack London, *The Call of the Wild* and *White Fang.* Many eds. Thrilling books about men and dogs in the Alaskan wilderness. London was a sailor, a Klondike adventurer, and one of *McClure's* best-known writers.

Susan Lowell, *I Am Lavina Cumming,* Milkweed, 1993. In 1905 Lavina Cumming lives with her father and brothers on a ranch in Arizona Territory. Her father fears she will grow up wild without a mother; Lavina must go to Santa Cruz to live with her aunt, her Cousin Maude, and Maude's spoiled daughter, Aggie. Lavina goes to a big city school, misses her family, and lives through the San Francisco earthquake.

John Muir, *Stickeen,* Heyday (first pub. 1909). On a chilly Alaskan morning in 1888, wilderness lover John Muir wakes up to find a howling flood storm in the glaciers. He sets off to explore with Stickeen, his mongrel dog companion, and their adventures that day—leaping precipices, sliding over ice bridges—bind them as friends forever.

Carl Sandburg, *Prairie-Town Boy,* HBJ, 1963 (first pub. 1953). Sandburg was a poet, writer, and ballad singer who fought in the Spanish–American War, supported workers' causes, and won a Pulitzer prize for his biography of Lincoln. *Prairie-Town Boy* is about his boyhood in 19th-century Illinois.

Ruth Sawyer, *Roller Skates,* Viking Penguin, 1936. Ten-year-old Lucinda Wyman lives comfortably in New York City in the 1890s. Her parents leave her to stay with a teacher for a year, and she is free to roller-skate to school, to have adventures, and to make friends with all kinds of people. Tomboy Lucinda has a great sense of fun and a kind heart.

Vicky Shiefman, *Goodbye to the Trees,* Atheneum, 1993. Fagel Fratrizsky leaves her mother, brothers, and sisters in Russia and boards a ship for Boston. In Chelsea, Massachusetts, she lives with her aunt and uncle and works as a dressmaker. She has adventures: shopping, a trip to the beach, going dancing and to a vaudeville show. But will she find a way for her family to come and join her?

Laura Ingalls Wilder and Rose Wilder Lane, *On the Way Home,* Harper & Row, 1962. This is Laura Ingalls Wilder's own story, made from a diary into a book by her daughter, who was seven in 1894 when the pioneer family left drought-stricken South Dakota for a new farm and a new life in Missouri.

Lawrence Yep, *Dragonwings,* Harper & Row, 1975. Moon Shadow Lee's father works in a San Francisco laundry in 1903. But what he and Moon Shadow really love to do is to make kites and flying machines. They write to the Wright brothers for advice—and get it, too. This is a wonderful book about many things—prejudice, kindness, creativity, hope, persistence—and flying machines.

A Note From the Author

Isaac Ginsburg lived with his father in Ivia, a *shtetl* (village) in Poland. Isaac had no mother; she had died when he was a baby. One day a troop of Russian cossacks (soldiers on horseback) raced through Ivia. Right away the people in the village knew it was a *pogrom*, which meant that the soldiers could be expected to steal, destroy, rape, and murder.

Isaac and his father ran for the woods. They ran as fast and as far as they could. Then they huddled under a tree to sleep and wait for the soldiers to leave. It was winter and cold. In the morning, when the boy shook his father, the man didn't move. He was dead.

Isaac was now an orphan, a very poor orphan. He went to live with his uncle, a candlestick maker. His uncle was an artist (at heart), and he taught the boy to love beautiful things and to understand craftsmanship; but, since he had children of his own, there was no extra money to send Isaac to school, so he never went.

Isaac was smart and energetic, had a sense of humor, and was a whiz with numbers. But it was clear he had no future in Ivia. He began to dream of the land of freedom and opportunity. It was called a golden land, and it was far away. First you had to take a long land journey; then you crossed the broad ocean. Isaac didn't know anyone who had been there, but he wanted to go anyway. Besides, if he stayed in Ivia, he could be drafted into the Russian army—no one knew for

Isaac Ginsburg

how long, but some conscripts had been held for 25 years. In the army he wouldn't be allowed to practice his religion (Isaac was Jewish). He wouldn't be treated well. He wouldn't be free.

So he worked and saved, and, finally, in 1884, set out for America. He was 19, and he already had a wife—her name was Rachel—and a baby on the way. He told Rachel that as soon as he had money for her ticket he would send for her.

When he landed in New York, someone was looking for a man with muscles. Isaac was wiry and strong. He showed his muscles. Then he got a job shoveling coal on a barge that took him up the Hudson River. At Troy he got off the barge. He couldn't speak much English, but he had a big grin and he was eager to work, so he got jobs.

At Glens Falls he persuaded a storekeeper to trust him with some goods. He put them in a pack, strapped it to his back, and went off walking from farm to farm. He headed north—to Warrensburg to Wevertown and on. The farmers were happy to see the young peddler—especially when he unrolled his pack and they found useful and pretty things. They usually gave him dinner and a bed for the night. If they wanted something but had no money, he would trust them to pay on his next trip, just as the merchant had trusted him.

He was soon known as "Honest Ike," and was proud of that name and what it meant.

Before long he had enough money to send a

ticket to Rachel and baby Abraham. Unlike Isaac, Rachel was not an orphan; her parents wept and wailed—they knew they would not see their daughter again.

The trip across the ocean had been exciting for adventurous Isaac. It was terrifying for shy Rachel. But the voyage didn't last long, and then she was in the land of promise and Isaac was there. They soon had more children (seven in all). By now Isaac had stopped walking. He had a horse (named "Million Dollars") and a wagon that he loaded with goods.

One day Isaac came home and said they were moving into a big house. It was next to a swift-running river at Hudson Falls. Rachel worried: would the children fall in? (None did.) Another family shared the house. They flipped a coin to see who would live upstairs and who down. The rent was $2 a month downstairs and $1.50 up. Much later, when the children were grown, and Rachel and Isaac gone, no one remembered if they'd won the toss or not. They just knew they'd lived upstairs.

By that time they were all proud to be known as Honest Ike's children. In a story about Glens Falls, a national magazine called him a leading citizen. Isaac never did go to school, and he never learned to read or write, but his grandchildren and great-grandchildren include professors, business-people, doctors, lawyers, film makers, artists, and writers. An American family. My family.

Looking upriver in Glens Falls, New York, in 1884, the year Isaac Ginsburg arrived. The covered bridge is gone now.

187

Picture Credits

Cover (left): George Wesley Bellows, *Cliff Dwellers*, 1913, Los Angeles County Museum of Art; **cover (right)**: Fernand Lungren, *Washington Square North*, c. 1890, Hirschl & Adler Galleries, New York, private collection; **5**: Arnold Arboretum, Harvard University, photo by Sheila Connor; **6 (top)**: Lewis W. Hine Collection, George Eastman House; **6-7**: Library of Congress; **7 (top)**: National Women's Christian Temperance Union, Washington Court House, Ohio; **8**: Brown Brothers; **9 (top)**: Library of Congress; **9 (bottom)**: Long Island Historical Society; **10**: International Center of Photography, George Eastman House; **11 (top)**: Yale University Art Gallery; **11 (bottom)**: New-York Historical Society; **12 (top)**: Museum of the City of New York; **12 (bottom)**: Smith College Museum of Art, Charles B. Hoyt Fund; **13 (bottom left and right)**: Carnegie Company of New York; **14 (top)**: Library of Congress; **14 (bottom)**: Library of Congress; **15 (top)**: Thomas Anshutz, *The Ironworkers' Noontime*, 1880, Fine Arts Museum of San Francisco, gift of Mr. and Mrs. John D. Rockefeller 3rd., 1979.7.4; **16 (right)**: *Harper's Weekly*, April 10, 1886; **17**: *Harper's Weekly*, July 16, 1892; **18 (bottom)**: *Punch*, May 29, 1901, New York Public Library; **19 (right)**: American Petroleum Institute; **20 (top)**: Library of Congress; **20 (bottom)**: Long Island Picture Collection; **21 (left)**: *The Verdict*, January 22, 1900; **21 (right)**: Spindletop File, Center for American History, University of Texas, Austin; **22 (top)**: Carey Orr, *Chicago Tribune*; **23 (top)**: drawing by John R. Neill; **23 (bottom)**: collection of Mrs. Robert Baum; **24**: drawing by John R. Neill; **25**: Museum of American Folk Art, New York City; **26 (top left, bottom left)**: *Baum Bugle*; **26 (right)**: drawing by John R. Neill; **28**: Museum of Modern Art, New York (CK); **29 (bottom)**: New York Public Library; **30**: Hayes Memorial Library; **31 (bottom)**: *Puck*, May 7, 1890; **32**: *Puck*, January 23, 1889; **33**: *The Verdict*, 1879; **34**: Culver Pictures; **35 (left)**: National Portrait Gallery, Smithsonian Institution; **35 (right)**: Bancroft Library, University of California, Berkeley; **36 (top)**: Library of Congress; **36 (bottom)**: Museum of the City of New York; **37**: Norman Thomas and W. W. Rock; **38**: New York Public Library Picture Collection; **39**: Missouri Historical Society; **40 (top left, bottom left)**: Rutgers University; **40 (bottom right)**: *Harper's New Monthly Magazine*; **40 (top right)**: *Scientific American*; **40 (top center)**: New York *Illustrated Weekly*; **41**: *Harper's Weekly*, June 2, 1883; **43 (top)**: collection of Andrew Spano; **43 (bottom)**: National Park Service, Ellis Island Collection; **44**: Library of Congress; **45**: collection of the Société Miége et Buhler, Paris; **46 (top)**: Bartholdi Museum, Paris; **46 (bottom left)**: Brown Brothers; **46 (bottom right)**: New York Public Library; **47**: Mariner's Museum, Newport News, Virginia; **48 (top)**: Library of Congress; **48 (bottom left)**: Museum of the City of New York; **48 (bottom right)**: Library of Congress; **49**: *Le Journal Illustré*, October 10, 1875, Bibliothèque du Conservatoire National des Artes et Métiers, Paris ; **50 (bottom)**: *Harper's Weekly*, 1872; **51**: painting by W.R. Leigh, courtesy Charles Scribners & Sons; **52 (top)**: Library of Congress; **52 (bottom)**: Hayes Memorial Library; **53 (top)**: Smithsonian Institution, Division of Political History; **53 (bottom)**: *Puck*, 1884; **54 (top)**: Brown Brothers; **54 (bottom)**: Library of Congress; **54 (top)**: National Museum of Natural History/National Anthropological Archives #3200-B-2; **55 (bottom)**: National Portrait Gallery, Smithsonian Institution; **56**: Library of Congress; **57 (top)**: New York Public Library Picture Collection; **57 (bottom)**: Culver Pictures; **60**: Kansas State Historical Society; **62 (top)**: Georgia Department of Archives and History; **62 (bottom)**: George Eastman House; **63 (right)**: *Harper's Weekly*, 1875; **64**: *Harper's Weekly*, February 16, 1878; **65 (top)**: *Puck*, 1892; **66 (bottom)**: *Puck*, December 7, 1887; **67 (top)**: Jacob A. Riis Collection, Museum of the City of New York; **67 (bottom)**: Museum of the City of New York; **68**: Library of Congress; **69**: Culver Pictures; **70(top)**: New-York Historical Society ; **70 (bottom)**: Brown Brothers; **71 (top)**: Library of Congress; **71 (bottom)**: Frederic Remington, *Harper's Weekly*, July 21, 1894, General Research Division, New York Public Library; **74 (bottom)**: collection of J. T. Yarnall; **76 (top)**: Library of Congress; **78 (right)**: New York Public Library Picture Collection; **79**: *Puck*, September 16, 1896, Culver Pictures; **80 (bottom right)**: *New York Journal*, 1896; **81**: New York Public Library; **82**: Brown Brothers; **83**: Museum of the City of New York; **84**: New York Public Library; **85 (top)**: Sears, Roebuck & Co.; **86 (left)**: David R. Phillips; **86 (right)**: State Historical Society of Wisconsin; **87**: Culver Pictures; **88 (left)**: National Portrait Gallery, Smithsonian Institution; **88 (right)**: New-York Historical Society, Robert Crandall; **89 (left)**: *Puck*, October 4, 1893; **89 (right)**: National Archives ; **90**: Library of Congress; **91 (bottom)**: *Leslie's Illustrated Weekly*; **92**: Chicago Historical Society; **95 (top)**:

National Portrait Gallery, Smithsonian Institution; **95 (bottom)**: International Center of Photography, George Eastman House; **96**: New York Public Library Picture Collection; **97 (left)**: Museum of the City of New York, Jacob Riis Collection; **97 (right)**: International Museum of Photography, George Eastman House; **98 (top)**: National Archives; **100 (top)**: New-York Historical Society, Bella C. Landauer Collection; **101**: gift of Mrs. and Mrs. James E. Shields, El Kiosko Gallery, Key West, Florida; **102**: Burgert Brothers, No. R310, Tampa Public Library; **103 (top)**: International Center of Photography, George Eastman House; **103 (bottom)**: New York Public Library Picture Collection; **105 (top)**: Edward L. Bafford Photography Collection, University of Maryland, College Park Libraries; **105 (bottom)**: Bettmann Archives; **106**: Edward L. Bafford Photography Collection, University of Maryland, College Park Libraries; **107 (bottom)**: Library of Congress; **109 (top)**: *Harper's Weekly*, October 28, 1871; **109 (bottom)**: Chicago Historical Society; **110 (top)**: Wayne State Archives of Labor and Urban Affairs; **111 (left)**: William A. Rogers, *Harper's Weekly*, July 14, 1894, Scott Molloy Labor Archives; **111 (right)**: Charles H. Kerr Publishing Corporation; **112 (top)**: National Archives; **112 (bottom)**: Library of Congress; **114, 115 (top)**: UPI; **115 (bottom)**: Wayne State University, Archives of Labor and Urban Affairs; **116**: National Portrait Gallery, Smithsonian Institution; **117, 118**: Bettmann Archives; **119**: Reis Library, Allegheny College; **120 (top, inset)**: Bettmann Archives; **120 (bottom)**: New York Public Library Picture Collection; **122 (top)**: *New York Telegram*, May 5, 1906, Tarbell Collection, Drake Well Museum; **123 (bottom)**: *Judge*, 1904, Culver Pictures; **124 (top)**: John T. McCutcheon, *Chicago Tribune*, April 8, 1905; **124 (bottom)**: UPI/Bettmann Archives; **125 (top)**: John Sloan, *The Masses*, June 1914, Library of Congress; **125 (bottom)**: Library of Congress; **126 (top)**: Meserve Collection; **126 (bottom)**: National Park Service; **128**: University Archives, Bancroft Library; **130**: Berkshire Museum, Pittsfield, Massachusetts; **131**: Library of Congress; **132 (left)**: Minnesota Historical Society; **132 (right)**, **133 (top)**: Library of Congress; **133 (bottom left)**: Culver Pictures; **133 (bottom right)**: Staten Island Historical Society; **134 (top)**: State Historical Society of Wisconsin; **135 (top)**: Samuel D. Ehrhart, *Puck*, January 2, 1889, New York Historical Society; **136-138**: Theodore Roosevelt Collection, Harvard College Library; **139 (left)**: Roosevelt Memorial Association; **139 (right)**: Library of Congress; **140**: Mary Evans Picture Library, London; **141**: Library of Congress; **142**: Theodore Roosevelt Collection, Houghton Library, Harvard University; **143**: Library of Congress; **144**: Culver Pictures; **145 (top)**: New York Public Library; **145 (bottom, 146 top)**: Library of Congress; **146 (bottom)**: Chicago Historical Society; **147 (top)**: Culver Pictures; **147 (bottom)**: Library of Congress; **148**: New York Public Library; **149 (top)**: Brown Brothers; **149 (bottom)**: Culver Pictures; **150 (top)**: New York Public Library; **150 (bottom)**: Brown Brothers; **151 (top)**: New York Public Library; **151 (bottom)**: Library of Congress; **152 (top left)**: Bettmann Archives; **152 (bottom)**: Library of Congress; **153 (top left)**: Brown Brothers; **153 (top right, bottom)**: National Archives; **155 (bottom)**: California Palace Legion of Honor; **156 (top)**: University Library, University of Illinois, Chicago; **158 (top)**: University of Illinois at Columbus Circle, Jane Addams Memorial Collection, photo by Wallace Kirkland; **160 (top)**: Museum of the City of New York; **160 (bottom left)**: New York Public Library Picture Collection; **160 (bottom right)**: Museum of the City of New York, Jacob Riis Collection; **161 (bottom)**: Smithsonian Institution; **162 (top)**: Ford Motor Company; **162 (middle)**: Ford Archives, Henry Ford Museum, Dearborn, Michigan; **162 (bottom)**: Free Library of Philadelphia; **163 (top)**: Culver Pictures; **164 (top left)**: Free Library of Philadelphia; **164 (middle left)**: National Air and Space Museum,

Smithsonian Institution; **164 (bottom left)**: Automobile Manufacturing Corporation; **164 (right)**: Brown Brothers; **165 (top)**: Wright State University; **165 (bottom)**: National Air and Space Museum, U.S. Air Force; **166**: Wright State University; **167-170**: Library of Congress; **171 (left, right), 172 (top)**: Library of Congress; **172 (bottom)**: Brown Brothers; **175, 176 (top)**: Library of Congress; **176 (bottom)**: Underwood & Underwood; **177 (bottom)**: *Puck*, 1912; **178**: Library of Congress; **179 (top)**: National Archives; **179 (bottom)**: National Archives; **180 (top)**: UPI; **180 (bottom)**: National Archives; **181 (top)**: New-York State Historical Association, Cooperstown; **181 (bottom left, right)**: National Archives; **182 (top)**: UPI; **182 (bottom)**: *New York Times*; **187**: Chapman Historical Museum/Queensbury Historical Association, Glens Falls, NY; **188**: Images From the Past, Bennington, VT

Index